TODDLER SURVIVAL GUIDE

Child behaviour secrets from a professional nanny

LAURA AMIES

(Channel 5's Toddler Tamer)

WATKINS
1893

The Toddler Survival Guide
Laura Amies

First published in the UK and USA in 2025 by
Watkins, an imprint of Watkins Media Limited
Unit 11, Shepperton House, 83–89 Shepperton Road
London N1 3DF

enquiries@watkinspublishing.com

Commissioning Editor: Lucy Carroll
Managing Editor: Sophie Blackman
Project Editor: Brittany Willis
Head of Design: Karen Smith
Production: Uzma Taj

A CIP record for this book is available from the British Library

ISBN: 978-1-78678-901-3 (Paperback)
ISBN: 978-1-78678-919-8 (eBook)

10 9 8 7 6 5 4 3 2 1

Typeset by Lapiz
Printed and bound by CPI Group (UK) Ltd, Croydon, CR0 4YY

www.watkinspublishing.com

MIX
Paper | Supporting
responsible forestry
FSC® C171272

To my parents, thank you for your never-ending
support and for raising me to be resilient,
grateful and understanding of others.

To every parent who has ever allowed me to
care for or work alongside your child – thank
you from the bottom of my heart.

To my husband, the man I chose to be a parent
with, thank you for your love, support and for
embarking on the journey of parenting with me.

CONTENTS

Author's note   1

1. **Parenting styles**
"You don't have to follow the rules!"   2
2. **Dealing with tantrums**
"Where's Bob?!"   19
3. **Aggressive behaviours**
When toddlers attack   39
4. **Potty training**
The most challenging milestone of all   60
5. **Days out with toddlers**
All eyes on you   80
6. **Social skills**
"They won't play with me!"   94
7. **Screen time**
The good, the bad and the ugly   113
8. **Sleep success**
Bedtime battles   134
9. **Dummy dependency**
The dummy fairy has their work cut out here   156
10. **Eating habits**
"They won't eat that!"   178
11. **Emotional development**
"Here, have some chocolate!"   200
12. **Speech and language**
"C c c cat"   220
13. **Illness and trauma**
"Caller, what's your emergency?"   240

Appendix   257
Extra resources   267
About me   275
Acknowledgements   276
Index   277

AUTHOR'S NOTE

My entire career has been fuelled by a desire to help families. No matter my role, I've always gone out of my way to try to make things a little bit easier for them. As I entered my third decade of childcare, I decided to collate all (well, almost all) I've learned and witnessed into this book with the hope of supporting more families from afar.

I wanted to create something that was ultimately very helpful, but also that made parents smile and feel less alone in their struggles. I've shared stories of some of the best and worst times of my career to shed light on typical toddler behaviours and, in turn, how our behaviours also count.

During my 24 years of caring for children, I have witnessed a huge array of behaviours that commonly cause stress within family homes. Viewing these behaviours and scenarios objectively, I have determined why toddlers do what they do. Within these chapters, I share that experience, alongside tips, advice and information that will aid you on your journey as a toddler parent.

I haven't sugar-coated anything! You don't make it through all these years of working with children without relying on both humour and a no-nonsense approach. So, buckle up, pour yourself a cuppa and use the information provided to your advantage.

Oh, and thank you! Thank you so much for spending your precious spare time with the upcoming pages.

Laura

CHAPTER 1
PARENTING STYLES

"You don't have to follow the rules!"

The first chapter of any book could be compared to the first sounds and utterings that a baby makes, all offering a glimpse into their tone of voice, thoughts and perhaps even a hint of their personality. And in the same way that a baby will watch and wait for their parents' reactions, I write these words hoping you'll smile (and possibly even coo) at the appropriate junctures, and maybe more importantly, feel a genuine connection with them as you read.

In this chapter I focus on you, the parent, because your approach to parenting has a huge influence on your child's development and their behaviours. While a child's life experiences, temperament traits and the relationships they have with extended family and teachers will have an impact on their development, your influence is the most powerful.

Nature provides each of us with innate characteristics that affect how we respond to our environment. In turn, our environment also goes on to shape and nurture the behaviours that we display. The nature vs nurture debate is long-running because it's impossible to draw an exact science about which of these two aspects has the biggest impact. I have spent the past two decades working with an array of families, settings and circumstances and I truly believe it's *how* a parent nurtures their child's innate nature that holds the key that allows them to flourish.

As a basic example, we may witness a child knock over a tower of bricks in protest of one brick not sitting quite as they hoped. If the child has a role model who demonstrates a calm and patient response, in time, the child is more likely to develop a higher level of tolerance. However, if their frustration is met by adult behaviour of a similar ilk (which, may I add, is understandable in busy homes with long to-do lists), they are much more likely to form a pattern of behaviour that stems from impatience. This is why delving into the topic of parenting styles is of the utmost importance.

Depending on your upbringing, culture and personal circumstance, you will approach parenting in a way that is specific to you. As unique as each family unit is, we can identify four main parenting styles. While it's common for parents to slip between styles depending on energy levels and mood, the style you predominantly sit in will hold the biggest insight into your child's development.

> **Nanny Amies' Top Tip:** You, your emotional and physical health, alongside your presence, are far more important to your child than they can express. You matter! So, looking after your own wellbeing will also benefit your child. Drink water, rest when you can and stop scrolling the internet at silly o'clock to allow yourself some proper rest and sleep.

Parenting styles

There are so many things that impact and shape a child's behaviour, some of which we have no control over and many of which are governed by your parenting style. In the box on the next page, I have listed some key physical, individual, experience and environmental factors. It's these factors that offer up a beautifully diverse human race full of different characters, interests, beliefs and ways of life. For ease, I have split them into two main categories: nature and nurture. I invite you to think about which ones you think that you, as a parent, can influence.

Nature	Nurture
Physical • Hunger/nutrition • Tiredness • Health • Routines • Exercise • Time spent outdoors • Hormones	**Environmental** • Your parenting style • Relationships • Teachers/nursery nurses • Resources/family income • Free play • Opportunities to learn • Screen time • Atmosphere at home
Individual • Age • Ability • Temperament traits • Development • Neurodiversity • Extra needs	**Experiences** • Culture • Community • Time spent with role models • Time spent with peers • Holidays/travel • Toddler classes • Extracurricular activities

Although factors vary for every family and every child, ultimately everything from bedtime to who children spend their time with outside of the family home is in your hands. A little like the hands on a clock face, it always comes back around to the same place in the end: your parenting style.

And so, at this stage, I'm asking you to consider which of the upcoming parenting styles you feel you predominantly sit in (or perhaps slip into on particularly busy days or after a terrible night's sleep). The incredible thing about this reflection is that it allows you to peer into your child's future – to consider how varying styles impact a pre-schooler's behaviours, not only in the here and now, but also for their adult self too. (I know, I'm sorry! As if you needed another thing to worry about.)

In the 1960s, Clinical psychologist Diana Baumrind identified three main parenting styles: authoritarian, authoritative and permissive. Twenty years later, Eleanor Maccoby and John Martin identified a fourth: neglectful. The 1980s saw a huge boost in studies surrounding child development, marking a turning point and setting many parents on a different trajectory from the mindset of "a child should be seen and not heard".

This new awareness of child psychology and parenting brought huge benefits, such as adults giving more focus to a child's emotional needs and not just their physical ones. However, in some cases, we might have gone a little too far, particularly today with social media holding parenting skills under a microscope and offering up a wide array of opinions, parenting trends, hacks and memes! Some of which are wonderful, and some, in my opinion, quite damaging.

> **Important note:** If you are currently in what feels like parenting hell, with raised stress levels and exhaustion, thinking about "long-term development" or "behavioural goals" might be something that gets little headspace. This does not mean you are a "bad parent" and therefore currently positioned in a parenting style that leaves a little to be desired. It means you are human. Any parent who takes the time to read this parenting advice book is a wonderful one ... so hold on to that thought, especially throughout this chapter!

The four parenting styles

So, how do these parenting styles play out? Let's look at the earlier example of a child knocking over a tower of bricks in response to feeling frustrated.

Authoritarian	Authoritative
• Adult-led/controlling • Strict rules • Harsh punishments • High expectations • Child's emotions aren't considered • "Child should be seen and not heard" mentality	• Adult- and child-led scenarios • Age-appropriate boundaries • Natural or logical consequences • Age-appropriate expectations • Emotional development is prioritized • Child is heard and validated (alongside predictable parental boundaries)
Neglectful	**Permissive**
• No lead • No rules • No involvement • No consequences • No expectation or guidance • Not aware of child's emotions • Provides bare minimum in terms of care, food and interaction	• Child-led • Inconsistent or no boundaries • Overindulgence via physical items and a lack of age-appropriate responsibility • Emotional distress is prevented at all costs and children are rescued from scenarios which may create frustration, boredom or disappointment • Child's feelings trump an adult's awareness of right from wrong

An authoritarian parent may stand above the child, shouting and criticizing their behaviour, and perhaps proceeding to ban the bricks from play for the next day or two.

A neglectful parent may not have noticed the outburst due to being so uninvolved or showing little to no interest in their child's play.

A permissive parent may dash to pick up the bricks, restacking them quickly in a bid to soothe their child's frustration, assuring them they are okay and that they can fix the tower without any repercussion or consequence to the unleashing of their anger.

An authoritative parent would be calm and purposeful, noting both the action and cause while also offering support. For example, an authoritative parent may kneel beside their child and say, "You were upset with your brick and pushed over your tower; it's hard when our toys topple over!" They might pause to allow their child the chance to connect to the emotion and their response to what they felt before offering them an opportunity to try again with help. For example, "Would you like any help to restack them?" An authoritative parent would model the behaviours they hope to see and encourage their child to work on the solution with them to build up their resilience and emotional understanding.

Can you relate to any of these responses? Your approach to your child's outbursts can, and likely does, differ on any given day depending on tiredness, stress and many other factors, and that is entirely normal and human. However, your child requires consistency, predictability and repetition as much as possible to enable their ability to process and understand rules, boundaries and the development of new skills.

Authoritative parenting gets my vote because it sets children up to become well-rounded, resilient and effective members of society. It's also the style of parenting that has recently taken social media by storm under the title of "gentle parenting". Those of you who have seen any of my social media content with regard to gentle parenting will know that I really (and I mean REALLY) dislike this term! I find it to be so misleading and often confused with permissive parenting. In my experience, there's a huge number of parents who are desperate to break generational cycles, who are doing their best and who proudly state they are of the gentle kind ... but, often without having fully researched the ethos behind it.

While the *act* of gentle parenting is something I promote (it also sounds lovely and is certainly popular, even having its very own hashtag), we now have millions of parents aiming for gentle but instead adopting permissive parenting.

I believe this is because the word "gentle" has many parents convinced that anything that remotely resembles tears in response to a boundary can't possibly be "gentle". Tears are a key method of communication for young children, so tears alone do not equate to trauma. When tears hugely influence your parenting approach, it can mean that the captain of the ship is not yet old enough to drive.

This is why I'm on a one-woman mission to replace the term "gentle parenting" with "logical parenting". I feel that, when we can use it, logic trumps fear, doubt and emotionally fuelled reactions. Essentially, logic can block out all the noise made by social media and ties up the overall ethos behind authoritative parenting in a nice little bow!

Not only is the word authoritative a bit of a mouthful, it sounds a lot like authoritarian, and that's not something we want to confuse. Maybe this book will inspire you to join me in a rally where we all hold up signs as we march that say "End the confusion! Logical Parenting gets our vote!" while chanting "Give me an L, give me an O, give me a G ... "

When parenting goes wrong!

There's no better way for me to try to convince you of the power that parenting styles hold than to share a real-life instance of parenting that left me utterly flabbergasted. I was charged with the task of accompanying a toddler and their parent for a walk around their local village. The village was peaceful, very picturesque and the type of place that had me taking purposeful gulps of gratitude! I love the outdoors and believe that gifting children with a love of nature is as vital as teaching them how to walk and talk.

However, no amount of gratitude could have sheltered me from the feelings of concern and upset that came my way. The parent who walked beside me ran a powerful business and were a force to be reckoned with. Like a tiger who stalked their next meal, this parent was fierce ... until they were in a room with their own toddler! Then they were in helpless, fluffy kitten territory as opposed to the king of the jungle (and if truth be told, I've never really been a cat person!).

As we walked, the toddler waddled this way and that, inquisitive by nature. I took the role of trying to encourage their curiosity while also trying to maintain safe boundaries near the road and with passing dogs (whose nature was unknown to us). We reached a house with a large stretch of garden and gorgeous, manicured flower beds. The homeowner clearly cared a great deal about their garden and had placed a white sign at the front of the lawn that read, "Please keep off the grass!"

Now, the toddler in question couldn't read, and something deep within their soul must have flicked an internal switch that told them to run toward the beautiful garden the way we would run toward a water fountain in the middle of the desert! I gently took their hand, guided them back to the path, crouched down, pointed to the path and said, "We'll stay on the path; that's not our grass". (A logical parenting style means making a statement about what your child can do, as opposed to what not to do.)

However, the parent grabbed their hand from mine and started marching over the grass saying, "You don't have to follow the rules! You can do whatever you want in this life! No one tells you where you can walk or what you can do. You're a [insert family surname] and never forget it!"

As I watched the toddler now allowed to trample over someone's prized garden, all I could see in that moment was the adult version of that child. Does this type of behaviour even require a psychologist and years of research to suggest the damage that adult behaviour like this can do?

If we, as adults, teach the message that a child is above other people's boundaries, they will likely suffer from an overinflated ego, leading to arrogance, entitlement and a lack of respect for other members of society. If truth be told, I felt sorry for the toddler. No amount of temporary excitement can save someone from growing up to be self-entitled, and sadly, the narrative being channelled their way offered this toddler a one-way ticket on the "I have a superiority complex" train.

As a professional nanny, under no circumstances was I permitted to tell a parent I thought they had made a damaging decision. My role is to simply care for a child to the best of my ability and not to advise the parent unless I'm asked to do so. However, from both a personal and professional stance, I couldn't stand by and watch. I hung my head and walked away in the hope that the toddler would follow suit. I took some deep breaths while silently considering if there was any chance at all that this child would grow up to become a nice person.

> **Nanny Amies' Top Tip:** As difficult as it can be, wherever possible, maintain a united front between you and your parenting partner when around your children. Despite the irritation that comes from seeing another adult behave in a way that you feel is against your own parenting style (or undermines you), in that moment, your child will benefit from you taking some deep breaths and holding your tongue. I advise this for consistency; children feel safer and more able to make good decisions when both parents/caregivers sing from the same hymn sheet. You could choose a code word or sign that lets each other know that you'd really like to discuss this at the next possible chance.

Now, had I have been asked to critique this moment of parenting, it would have gone something along the lines of: While I was trying to calmly instil an appropriate boundary that falls in line with societal expectations, respecting other people's property and just generally being a nice person, the parent offered up a contrasting notion (a blend of permissive and neglectful parenting). It's typical toddler behaviour to be driven toward a new and exciting sight, so it is our job as adults to decide what are appropriate playgrounds and what are not. The parent undermined my position within the family unit, putting me at a disadvantage for any future instances where an assertive approach was required.

The delivery and maintenance of appropriate boundaries is essential because toddlers need multiple opportunities to process the information available to them. Before the age of around three years, children are physically unable to use impulse control. They simply see, feel and do. For example, the toddler saw the beautiful garden, felt the urge to run toward it and therefore ran.

For me, this example highlights why parenting styles that not only trample over people's lawns but generally trample over boundaries and the respect of others are sadly very harmful to a developing child's behaviour and their outlook on the world around them.

Boundaries

While reading about the lawn trampling, I wonder if some of you may have had an opposing view to that of mine. Some may have decided to place blame on the homeowner, who chose not to erect a fence. While this would have certainly prevented this story from ever being told, I could have chosen many other stories because in this family boundaries lacked in all areas of life. This story may offer insight into where you might sit on the parenting style chart. Physical barriers may prevent some behaviours; however, they do not remove urges or the need to develop impulse control and respect for others. The question we have to ask is, is prevention really better than the cure? Boundaries are what teach your child how to behave appropriately, and if parents persistently place blame on others or expect strangers to accommodate for their child's behaviour, this can unfortunately lead to a disrespectful or an expectant attitude from the child.

Some parents claim valid reasons for being unable to maintain predictable boundaries, such as a stressful job that impacts their energy levels. However, this does not negate the need for boundaries. In my mind (and in my practice with families) the best way to do this is by considering the factors that impact a child's behaviour. If their behaviours are somewhat predictable, yours as the parent or caregiver will be more so too. For example:

Physicality: Pick an age-appropriate bedtime in line with your child's recommended sleep needs. Work toward getting them into bed at that time every night. A lack of sleep has such a negative impact on a child's overall behaviour that this is the first priority I work toward within a family home. (See Chapter 8 if you and your toddler are currently struggling with bedtimes and sleep patterns.)

Environmental: At the risk of inducing a nervous twitch in my readers, I must mention another huge force at play in toddler wellbeing and behaviour: screens. For example, by having a "no screens in bedrooms" policy for young children, you can prevent stimulating content from impacting melatonin production (melatonin being the sleep hormone that is tempered by artificial light). We will look at this in more detail in Chapter 7 (because screen time isn't all bad!).

Individuality: For me, the most obvious contributor to focus on when setting boundaries is your child's age. Knowing what a child is and isn't physically capable of will ensure your expectations are appropriate.

For example, expecting your toddler to oversee their own dental hygiene is setting yourself up for a whole world of frustration. A young child doesn't have the full dexterity to brush their teeth effectively, and they also lack the foresight required to understand why cleaning teeth effectively is so important. Therefore, to make teeth brushing a less chaotic chore, I introduce an age-appropriate motivation such as:

- **One year old:** I sit them on my knee, give them the toothpaste to hold (ensuring the lid is on tight) and sing a fun song while I help them to brush.
- **Two years old:** I ask them to stand "So high!" on the big step at the sink while I tell them a story.
- **Three years old:** I offer them a choice between standing on the step or sitting down on it while they brush, appealing to the independent nature of this age group.

Experiences: No matter your household budget, location, health, etc., there's one thing you can always provide for your child: daily love, affection and support. Over time, this will boost your child's self-esteem. Children with healthy self-esteem display more predictable behaviours, which naturally makes home life run more smoothly.

A quick and easy way to promote self-esteem is to start every single day telling them: "I love you!" and hugging, if you can. No matter what's going on that day or how rough your night was, declare love, even before reaching for that bucket of coffee!

Nanny Amies' Top Tip: Give your child the gift of knowing that love doesn't have to be earned. No matter what they do or how they behave, your love isn't something they'll ever lose. This goes for you too. Saying "no" and offering rules that your child doesn't like will not mean they love you less. They may not love your rules and that's okay, but love for immediate family members is not fragile or dependent on being made to feel happy all the time.

It pains me to say that with regard to the unruly toddler and their rebellious parent, consistency wasn't something they cared for, and so behaviours worsened. Back then, I was still relatively new to the prospect of looking into the hows and whys of childhood behaviours, but even so, I'm sure that the parenting style was a huge contributor toward the tantrums and challenging scenarios I witnessed. Over a decade later, I can now confidently say that, had the parent wanted to work with me, as a team, to create a loving environment that ultimately taught their child right from wrong, irrespective of the toddler's temperament, traits and nature, their behaviour would have been much more manageable. For that, I would bet my bottom dollar.

The logical parenting award goes to ...

Despite knowing that all children are unique and never to be compared, I do have a contrasting, real-life example to share with you. In this family, the parents made predictable, logical decisions that benefited their children, showing what a huge impact parenting styles can have.

I was charged with caring for a toddler who not only had a strong will and confident manner, and who certainly kept me on my toes, but they also had older siblings. As some of you will know, this can add extra stress and time pressures to day-to-day life. Luckily for me, the older siblings were polite, dare I say, charming and very well-behaved. Sadly, I have found this to be a rarity over the years, so this was definitely a "let's acknowledge the gratitude I have for this" moment!

Nanny Amies' Top Tip: By purposefully expressing gratitude, whether it be silently or out loud, we program our brains to notice the good stuff and to expect it too. This can go on to help manage negativity and improve your own overall wellbeing. You can do this with your toddler too – share with them things you are grateful for. This can have a wonderful impact on their overall behaviours and self-esteem. For example, "I love how high you've built your Lego! That shows me how hard you tried!"

Just a month into my contract with this family, we attended an evening family party. As the older children mingled happily, I stuck with the tiny tot to ensure their safety (and mood) were kept in check. After an hour or so, one parent approached me and said, "Wow! The youngest is really having a blast, thank you for being here with us". I was shocked! The parent had practised a moment of gratitude out loud on me, and it felt wonderful!

After a short conversation about how lovely their extended family was, they then said, "Let's leave with the little one on a high now, get them home to bed and I'll come back for the big guys later". It was at this point I had to discreetly pick my jaw up off the floor. It was the norm for me to be the one saying, "Erm ... I'm ever so sorry to interrupt, but would it be okay if I got the little one off to bed as they are starting to get a little fractious?" and for parents to then respond with, "No, give them another hour; they might sleep in tomorrow then". (PS. Never did they ever wake up later the next day!)

The little one, the parent and I successfully manoeuvred out of the party without any upset. At home, we worked as a team to get them bathed, into their PJs and tucked up in bed at their usual bedtime. I felt so respected and part of a team when that parent backed up my ethos on routines, sleep and the importance of appropriate boundaries. The toddler had the best of both worlds – they'd had fun at the party, socialized and cuddled with family, all before having a lovely bedtime routine and, in turn, a wonderful night's sleep.

Upon waking the next day, the parent greeted their youngest with, "You had such a great time at the party! You saw grandma ... had some cake ... and made me so proud!" The toddler beamed back at their kind-hearted parent as they seemingly took it all on board. They might not have understood the whole meaning behind all the words being spoken, but the tone of voice, eye contact and the connection made were invaluable tools in helping the little one to feel safe and loved.

Part of logical parenting is to promote the behaviours we hope to see more of. We do this by connecting with a child via descriptive praise and positive interactions, alongside role modelling. While boundaries will still be needed, connecting with a child in the way described above is an incredibly effective strategy because it builds a child's self-esteem. Sadly, low self-esteem can create more dysregulated behaviours.

Please don't misunderstand my admiration of this family for being completely detached from reality – I am so aware of how much easier it can be for parents to be calmer when they have a live-in, professional nanny. Being able to leave a trusted adult with your youngest child so you can go and focus on your older ones makes an unbelievable difference to the practicalities of parenting, as well as the style. However, this doesn't guarantee a stress-free life.

Some parents I've worked for have had incredibly high-pressured roles and have had to work hard on not bringing that stress to the breakfast table. Either way, if we pop me to one side for a moment, I don't think it's a coincidence that the toddler who enjoyed restorative sleep patterns and parents who delivered appropriate boundaries went on to behave in a calmer manner. Dare I say, they were also much nicer to be around, and in my eyes, were being set up for life outside of their comforting family home.

The dos and don'ts of logical parenting

See the table on the next page for some key examples of things to do and things not to do if you're striving toward a logical style of parenting.

Do	Do not
• Establish a routine • Allow child-led play and scenarios • Offer descriptive praise • Set appropriate boundaries • Offer appropriate consequences • Have age-appropriate expectations • Encourage problem-solving • Validate emotions	• Forget the importance of an appropriate bedtime • Allow a child to lead the household • Over-inflate a child's ego • Expect your child to adhere to boundaries without your support • Offer harsh punishments • Expect more than a child is capable of • "Rescue" a child or fix things before trying to help them work through it • Allow tears to change a "No" to a "Yes"

The impact of parenting styles

I feel it's important to finish this chapter by highlighting the potential long-term impacts of each of the four parenting styles. While some of them may appear extreme, I can't be the only person to have met people similar to each of the four descriptions (see page 18). I hope it helps you determine the style in which you'd like to parent.

Ultimately, the child who gets frustrated with their blocks and knocks them over in protest will grow up to become an adult who will experience frustration in the big, wide world. Being able to deal with what life throws our way confidently while having faith in our own ability will result in problem-solving and determination, both things that this modern world of ours needs in abundance. Without determination and the ability to problem-solve, a child's chance of reaching their full potential is hampered.

Authoritarian upbringing	Authoritative upbringing
• People pleasers • Feels that obedience equals love • Lack of self-esteem • Lack of self-discipline • Highly reactive to emotional stress • May be more susceptible to feelings of guilt, depression and social withdrawal • Can also become rebellious	• Confident • Feels worthy of love and lovable • Healthy self-esteem • Self-disciplined • Leans on coping skills and resilience during times of stress • Enjoys healthy relationships • More likely to be academically successful
Neglectful upbringing	**Permissive upbringing**
• No confidence • No self-love • No self-esteem • No internal motivation • No coping skills • Limited academic or work prospects • Lack of confidence can be masked by bullying and bravado	• Expectant • Potentially arrogant • Not very self-reliant • Lack of motivation • Higher risk of depression due to the amount of instant gratification experienced throughout childhood. • Strong adverse reaction to leadership, boundaries or directions

No one is a perfect parent at all times (if at any), and I can assure you that I've been unable to offer up perfect nannying skills every day! I think Mary Poppins was telling porkies. "Practically perfect" in every way? I don't think so! Perfect doesn't exist, and at no point in this book will I suggest it does. However, authoritative – or logical – parenting with practice is certainly attainable.

CHAPTER 2
DEALING WITH TANTRUMS

"Where's Bob?!"

Like a rite of passage, tantrums go hand-in-hand with toddlerhood and leave so many parents feeling a cocktail of emotions, ranging from helplessness to anger. Tantrums can immediately increase stress levels within the home or cause huge embarrassment when they occur in public places, and if they happen regularly enough, they can even impact a parent's mental health. I believe this to be the reason why thousands of parents have reached out to me over the years seeking advice on this troublesome topic and, luckily, I have lots of advice to give.

Placing the emotional impact to one side, tantrums are a normal, developmental behaviour for children under four years old. A little like the weather, tantrums vary from a light sprinkling of tears to a full-on, gale-force storm. And just as the climate and atmospheric pressure impacts the weather, there are certain factors that increase the likelihood and strength of tantrums. Understanding these factors will help make your child's tantrums much easier to navigate.

I respond to the tantrums today very differently to how I reacted to them in my early career. The contrast in my approach makes an undeniable difference to a youngster's behaviour and so I want to impart this gift of understanding tantrums to as many parents as possible. My aim is to ease your stress levels, but also to advocate for your child who, to be frank, has got no idea how difficult their tantrums can be to experience, which, as it happens, is one of the reasons why tantrums are commonplace throughout toddlerhood.

So, why do tantrums happen?

When a child is young, particularly under the age of three, tantrums are subconscious – an automatic response to the emotion they feel. They react the way they do not only due to a lack of life experience (which essentially lets us know that not being allowed an ice cream for breakfast is not life-threatening), but also because they have a developmental lack of impulse control. Impulse control only becomes possible from around the fourth year, and even then, it is intermittent. In fact, the frontal lobe (the part of the brain responsible for impulse control) isn't fully formed until around 25 years of age! There are many factors that impact how a child goes on to develop their impulse control and, in turn, how regularly tantrums occur after the toddler phase. However, for now, the main reason why young children have tantrums is because they become overwhelmed by an emotion that they are not yet equipped to cope with calmly.

The cause of the increase in emotion is known as the "trigger". The trigger is the first of five stages throughout the course of a tantrum. The level of agitation that's displayed will depend on a child's temperament, developmental phase, environmental factors and, importantly, the previous outcomes to past tantrums.

The best way to visualize a tantrum is by considering a rise and fall in emotions, like going over a hill (see diagram opposite). Like a stretch of flat land that lays just in front of a hill, a child's emotional state is regulated and calm until they experience a trigger that sends them over the hill.

The other four stages are bargaining, escalation, acceptance and detachment.

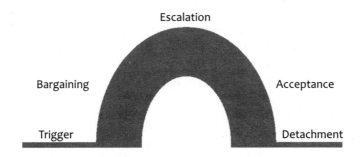

Bargaining: In this stage of a tantrum, you may be met by complaints, a raised volume and an obvious unease in your toddler's demeanour. If the trigger remains, just as the incline of the slope steepens, so does their behaviour, until it peaks at the crest of the hill and enters into the escalation stage.

Escalation: Within this stage, volume levels also peak, screaming likely occurs and a child is now fully dysregulated. This is the most difficult and stressful stage of the tantrum. The length of the escalation stage will depend on environmental factors and the physicality of a child's situation. For example, if a child is hungry or tired, the escalation stage will likely be tougher than that of a child who is well-rested. The same goes for if the child is met by a dysregulated adult.

> **Nanny Amies' Top Tip:** Staying calm during a tantrum can be difficult. Instinctively, screaming means distress and we are hardwired to act quickly in response to distress signals. Today's children rarely need to rely on their survival instincts – the hard truth is that the majority of tantrums stem from a perceived inconvenience or frustration. So, parents usually have time to "think first and act later".

Acceptance: Irrespective of the reasons behind the tantrum, if enough time passes, a child will emerge from the escalation stage, and their emotional responses will reduce enough for them to enter the acceptance stage. Here, there may still be a little crying, but their volume has now decreased and your toddler will be more susceptible to the notion of calming and moving past the trigger.

Detachment: The detachment stage can be a little bittersweet because it's where a child will put the past behind them, often moving on from their upset as if nothing happened, while parents can be left reeling. A parent might still have a raised heart rate and even potential resentment toward their post-tantrum offspring.

What does a tantrum look like?

Tantrums are as varied as each child themselves, which is why they can be so hard to deal with. For example:

Trigger	Emotion	Contributing factor	Behaviour
Sibling snatches toy from them	Frustration	Limited language skills	Screaming
Tower of wooden blocks falls over	Stress	Hunger	Shouting
Wants ice cream for breakfast	Anger	Appropriate boundary	Crying
Doesn't want to go to the dentist	Fear	Toothache	Throwing and crying
Doesn't want to go to bed before an older sibling	Jealousy	Tiredness	Hitting and crying
Doesn't want to get dressed	Annoyance	Craving autonomy	Throwing and screaming

Nanny Amies' Top Tip: Where possible, during a tantrum, try to avoid changing your rules or boundaries. As stressful as it can be, it's preferable for your child to be able to express their emotions while experiencing calm and predictable responses from the adults around them.

Things to avoid during a tantrum

While tantrums are a natural behaviour, there are things we can do as parents and carers that can lead to tantrums becoming a much-used coping strategy for frustrated tots. For example, if a child asks for a biscuit as dinner is being served and the parent declines their request, it's reasonable to imagine this could result in a tantrum. If the toddler reaches the escalation stage and the tired, and somewhat defeated, parent gets them a biscuit, the toddler's brain can learn to recognize that the tantrum worked. When tantrums are "successful", they can build an association between a feeling and an action.

Nanny Amies' Top Tip: There will, of course, be times when you are struggling to remain calm and/or hold a boundary – you are an emotional being! So, choose your battles. If you are having a bad day, consider saying "yes" before a tantrum turns your "no" into a yes.

Parent dysregulation

Your child's behaviour can be classed as your own trigger, one that then sends you into some form of emotional dysregulation. It's at this point that I would love for you to consider if there was ever a time in your childhood when you were taught how to manage and cope with stress. If, like me and most other adults on the planet, you weren't, I will delve into this further in Chapter 11. For now, consider how you'd cope with today's pressures if you had been. Faced with your toddler's tantrum, you might find yourself on your own hill of emotions! With or without an intensive childhood course on emotional development, there are valid reasons why it is hard for adults to move on from a child's tantrum. I truly believe that learning about a child's behaviour from a developmental perspective can really help us to get to the detachment phase too.

It's incredibly common for parents to be triggered during the initial stages of their child's tantrum, especially if they are a regular occurrence. This will usually result in one of two responses: as the noise and stress levels peak during the escalation stage, parents may turn to permissive parenting and give in – or avoid – boundaries to appease their child. Or a parent might take a more authoritarian approach, where parental voices rise and body language can become aggressive. An authoritarian approach will likely push the already dysregulated child into their "fight or flight" mode.

Fight or flight mode is a stress response triggered from the brain in response to danger, whether real or perceived. The amygdala, a small almond-shaped part of the brain, lets us know that we are going to either need to fight for our survival or run away from the threat. In response, the body is flooded with stress hormones, breathing shallows, the heart pounds, muscles can feel like coiled springs and we lean on reflexes and instinct as opposed to logical thoughts. Bear in mind that before any perceived or real threats occur, toddlers are already naturally lacking in the ability to lean on logic, so either parental response, whether permissive or authoritarian, adds fuel to the fire. I call this tantrum fuel.

Tantrum fuel

Tantrum fuel is exactly what it says on the tin: inflammatory, yet understandable, behaviours from adults, which not only increase the length of time a child takes to pass through each stage of a tantrum, but also increase the likelihood of tantrums occurring in the future.

There are six things that parents and carers can so easily do or say without even realizing that act as tantrum fuel. We can inadvertently reinforce the very behaviours we are hoping to see decrease. Here's what we get wrong:

1 **Asking questions:** I have learned that it's preferable to avoid asking a child questions while they are at a heightened level of emotion. Questions can increase their frustration due to the extra environmental stimuli in the form of noise. They can offer the behaviour more attention than necessary and confuse or frustrate the child. Also, an often-overlooked issue is that we offer them an opportunity to tell an untruth. For example, if you ask your toddler, "Did you just hit your brother?" when they are dysregulated, you are unlikely to get a truthful answer!

2 **Increasing our volume:** Shouting at a child can spark their fight or flight reaction. This can take a tantrum from a light spot of rain to a full-blown monsoon.

3 **Threatening body language:** For example, standing over a child while wagging fingers or shouting at them can be perceived as a physical threat. Imagine if someone twice your height stood over you while being obviously upset with your behaviour. Threatening body language can tap into a child's survival instincts.

4 **Offering a bribe:** Offering a privilege in response to negative behaviours or refusals to do perfectly acceptable tasks (such as popping shoes on) can send a clear message that certain behaviours reap rewards. In the heat of the moment, offering a bribe can be very successful,

so it's commonly used. This results in the ball being in the toddler's court for future requests.

5 **Using complicated sentences**: Adults have an innate desire to explain themselves or the apparent reason for a child's upset. I used to feel huge pressure to explain to anyone in earshot why the child in my care was crying ... via the child in my care! For example, "You are crying because you wouldn't put your shoes on and now we can't go to the park. You threw a shoe at my head; that was unkind". However, without impulse control and a full understanding of emotions and social awareness, this isn't a conversation to be had during an outburst, as it only fans the flames of upset. The same goes for debating a rule or boundary – if a child is offered a lot of sway in that moment, they may also think there is wiggle room. If there isn't, it will lead to further frustration.

6 **Using threats**: When a child isn't doing what you ask, things can feel out of control, so using motivation to get the job done becomes a reliable tool. Yet, fear-based language results in a child doing something for the wrong reasons; this also removes a chance for your toddler to develop an internal motivation to do the right thing. Or some toddlers will see it as an opportunity to seek an impact on their environment and look you square in the eye as they partake in the very thing you've just told them not to.

When tantrums go wrong ...

Before I learned about the stages of a tantrum, I had no idea that I was pouring tantrum fuel over stressful moments, the way we'd throw confetti over the happy bride and groom at a wedding! So, let me tell you about when I made a situation much worse than it needed to be. Reflection is a tool I've used my entire adult life and I believe that constantly asking myself, "Could I have done that better?" has been an incredible aid throughout my career. I urge anyone reading this book to try reflection as a tool at some stage too.

> **Nanny Amies' Top Tip:** In a bid to use reflection effectively, you need to send your inner critic packing. This is not about allowing your negative thoughts to take centre stage – it's more along the lines of reviewing a recent purchase you've made! Would you buy it again, and if not, why?

On the day of the mishandled tantrum, I had only a few years of experience under my belt. I was caring for a youngster who was highly intelligent and, if truth be told, it didn't seem to matter what I suggested or planned, they were compelled to argue, debate or just outright refuse to comply! I would find myself feeling quite helpless because it didn't matter how positive and upbeat I delivered enthusiastic ideas, there was constant resistance as I tried to cajole the toddler toward the various elements of our daily routine. I must say at this point that I went on to develop a very strong bond with this child and cared for them a great deal (even though they did outfox me on a regular basis!).

The day in question had been particularly tough with lots of shouting, throwing and challenging behaviours, so I decided it was time to try to save what remaining sanity I had left by getting our shoes on and heading outside to enjoy some fresh air. Even with a lack of experience, I knew that offering the youngster a chance to run off a bit of steam would help both of us! Sadly, my little charge had other ideas and did everything in their power to prevent us from leaving the house (or so I felt at the time)!

While I gathered water bottles and snacks, my charge had somewhat settled and began to build with Lego. The few moments I'd taken to prepare for our outing were nice and peaceful; a real treat, if truth be told. I approached my charge and made several polite requests and attempts to put their shoes on. The best they could muster was to pick up one shoe and pretend to be unable to get it on their foot. You may have witnessed this type of behaviour? When they go all floppy and claim complete inability? Grrr!

As they mimicked dropping the shoe, I could feel my pulse rate quickening. The toddler was physically capable of putting their shoes on independently and really enjoyed going to the park, so I could not wrap my head around why they were seemingly doing all in their power to prevent us from getting out of the house.

With my patience wavering, I offered a firm, "Please put your shoes on!", which resulted in them huffing and throwing one of the shoes across the room. Sadly, I saw red. I grabbed the shoe, sat down beside them and attempted to put it on their foot. As I was wrestling with their uncooperative toes, they picked up the unattended shoe, drew their arm back, stared me dead in the face and aimed it at my head. As they were milliseconds from throwing it at me, a phrase rolled off the tongue, something that I now know was a classic dose of tantrum fuel: "If you throw that shoe at me, I'll take Bob!"

Before I continue, let me tell you a little bit about Bob. He was a much-loved, highly dependable cuddly toy. You know the kind – missing eye, bald patches where fluffy fur used to reside, next to no stuffing left in his arms and a constant companion to the shoe-flinging toddler.

As the beloved Bob lay on a heap on the floor, his once shiny eyes seemed to glare at me. If Bob could talk, I'm certain he'd have protested, "Don't bring me into this!"

Sadly, no sooner had I uttered those words (and apparently read Bob's mind), the shoe in question was hitting me in the face – with force, may I add! Well, that was it. Annoyance turned to rage. I was too far gone for logic and, not content with my first round of tantrum fuel, I added another shot in the form of, "That's it! We aren't going to the park and Bob is not happy with you for throwing shoes, so he's going away!"

At this point my charge was triggered and as I walked away with Bob, they began bargaining, "No! I don't want Bob to go away! I want to take Bob to the park! Give me Bob, NOW!"

Bearing in mind that not only was my face still smarting from the shoe, I was also unaware of the psychology behind the emotional hill that the youngster was quickly climbing. I made a snap decision. I hid Bob in the microwave with the sole thought of, "Out of sight, out of mind". At this point I must state that:

1 The youngster didn't know that's where I'd put Bob.
2 There were no threats of "Behave or Bob gets it!"
3 There was certainly no cooking of the much-loved toy.

Eventually, the youngster calmed down and allowed me to put the offending articles on their feet, and we hurried off to the park where, surprisingly, we went on to have a really lovely time!

Later that night, I got home, showered, ate and, just as I was beginning to unwind, was caught completely off-guard by an 8pm phone call from my boss.

"Hello?" I answered.

"Hello Laura, I'm so sorry to bother you at this time of night. I'm just putting the little one to bed and wondered if you had any idea where Bob could be? I've looked all over the house! They can't sleep without Bob, Laura. Any ideas?"

My heart plummeted and I think I stopped breathing.

"I can explain ... "

Why did my reaction make things worse? I panicked, in all honesty. In my bid to gain some semblance of control, I resorted to a firm authoritarian approach. So, how could I have handled it better?

1   I could have avoided this whole scenario altogether by connecting with my charge over the Lego. For example, "Wow, I love how hard you are working on your Lego!" Children learn via play so connecting with them in a playful manner, even when you have an important task to complete, can be incredibly beneficial.

2   I could have also highlighted the type of behaviours I hoped to see more of in the future. For example, "When we pop our shoes on, we can go outside and have so much fun at the park".

3   I thought that Bob was so well-loved that the threat of removing him would have that shoe put back on the floor quickly. I now know that threatening a child who is too young to have developed impulse control is not only pointless, but if you are also caring for a strong-willed child who is desperately seeking autonomy, threats actually set them up to do the very thing you are trying to stop them from doing. Ultimately, doing something that someone is telling you not to can feel empowering!

4   Finally, I could have appeared less bothered by their refusal. Had I shrugged my shoulders and offered a calm, "No problem. If you'd like to head to the park, pop your shoes on", before taking some deep breaths, the situation wouldn't have escalated as it did.

Nanny Amies' Top Tip: Try to create opportunities that allow your child age-appropriate control. This can satisfy their developmental need for control, while getting tasks done. For example, "Shall we sit by the door and pop shoes on or sit here on the step? You choose".

As the saying goes, we live and we learn. While my reaction lacked a few vital ingredients that I simply hadn't considered at that time, I'm ever so grateful that despite my inexperience in those early days, I was able to keep a lid on my volume levels and body language. I never wanted a child to feel scared in my presence, and of course, I was in their home as a professional, so I had standards of care to uphold that were always very important to me.

Luckily, the ingredients I lacked then are now available in abundance in the form of tantrum tamers and for that, I am also very grateful!

Tantrum tamers

In contrast to tantrum fuel, tantrum tamers are things that can help prevent, reduce or redirect escalated emotions. Every parent needs to know these lifesavers.

Touch and hugs: Offering emotional support through a hug or a gentle touch is a wonderful way to maintain a boundary while also showing that we can do this with love. Touch activates the skin receptors, which send a message to our toddler's brain to let them know that they are safe and loved. This is the reverse of fight or flight. As opposed to being flooded with adrenaline, your toddler (and you) receive a dose of oxytocin, which increases feelings of positivity.

Give space: Some children don't want a hug or any contact, so offering them space is preferable. In these instances, it's vital to know that you don't have to "fix" their difficult emotions, and in some cases, it's preferable if you don't. Your toddler might simply need space to calm down.

Role model: If you feel your patience is wearing thin, model how to cope. For example, "I'm feeling cross, so I'm going to take some deep breaths".

Do nothing: In some cases, the less you do and say the better. I try to stop, look and assess the situation before responding.

Allow time: Where possible, being allowed time to work through the wave of emotion can be very helpful for your toddler and you. While you may not have this luxury outside of the home, when you do have the chance, allowing time to pass through all the stages of a tantrum helps a child to build resilience and emotional awareness.

Keep it short and sweet: Keep your language use to a minimum. Too many words can confuse your toddler.

Whisper: If you lower your voice to a whisper, your child will have to quieten in order to hear you. This role models that staying calm is possible with practice. It also prevents this behaviour from reaping unnecessary attention.

Be the life raft: Let your child know that you are there if they need you. The raft you offer will be dependent on the scenario, while you maintain boundaries or carry on with what needs doing. For example:

- Hold your hand out and say, "Let's go tidy up together".
- Begin doing the task at hand while suggesting, "Would you like to hear a story while we tidy up?"
- If it's mid-tantrum, try sitting down with a book or toy and become engaged with it in the hope that your toddler becomes interested and chooses to sit beside you.
- You could walk over to a window and talk about the huge bird that just flew by, or something similar.

The benefits of using tantrum tamers

Leading with calm, consistent and logical responses during your toddler's heightened emotional reactions prevents them from further escalation. Like a domino effect, the more predictable your response is, the more quickly a child gets to the detachment stage and the tantrum will pass. Each time, your toddler will gain the skills they require to move away from tantrums altogether.

Sadly, if tantrum fuels are regularly offered, tantrums will go on to outlive toddlerhood. While it is important to teach a person that all emotions are valid, children need to learn that it is not acceptable to express heightened emotions wherever we go, whenever we feel.

A great many years on from hiding a much-loved toy in the microwave, I can share with you how I am now able to confidently defuse situations while maintaining a predictable boundary. It's these two things that reduce the overall number of tantrums.

I recently found myself in the company of a toddler who was enjoying role-play with their toy kitchen. As they stood beside the wooden kitchen unit, I sat on the floor pretending to mix ingredients and make cups of tea. After five minutes, at the ripe old age of 40, my knees could take no more of the tiled floor. Knowing this may be a bit of a blow for the toddler, I furrowed my brow, rubbed my knees and said, "Ouch, my knees hurt". I then patted a chair and explained, "I will sit on here while we mix our food".

The toddler wasn't ready for this, and shouted, "No Wara! Sit here!" and patted the unforgiving floor.

I calmly offered a choice. "I can sit here, or we can choose another toy?" (All other toys were in a carpeted room.) Offering a change of scenery during the bargaining stage of a tantrum can be a great life raft.

However, the toddler chose to stick a pin in that life raft by screaming, "Nooo! Wara, you sit here, now!"

At this stage, I felt it was important to gently offer a boundary around the tone and volume in which they were communicating. I calmly placed my hands over my ears to offer a visual aid that backed up my words and said, "Shouting hurts my ears".

I then dropped my hands and picked up the bowl and spoon to enable me to get back to my imaginary cake mix. While tapping the chair, I repeated, "I can sit here and play, or we can choose another toy?"

Not happy with their options, the toddler entered the escalation stage, picked up a basket brimming with play food, cups, saucers and cutlery, and threw it over the floor.

Side note: At no point in this book will I pretend that this type of behaviour doesn't affect me. It does! I don't like mess in general, so seeing a child make a mess on purpose is when I really have to lean on my frontal lobe for logical thoughts and impulse control!

Giving in and sitting where – or doing what – a toddler demands in times like this can seem like the only option. However, permissive responses limit the chance for toddlers to work through their big emotions. This reduces the chance for them to build a tolerance toward events that don't quite go as they planned and to understand that they cannot control others. These lessons are vital for a child's personal, social and emotional development.

By now, the toddler was crying at the sight of the mess they had created. I chose to let them have a little time to process what had occurred. Before standing up I said, "Let me know if you'd like help to clean up". I walked over to the kettle to show that type of behaviour wasn't going to reap a big reaction, and to keep a lid on any potential tantrum fuel that could have snuck out had I stayed. Even now, I can still feel my pulse rate sharpen in these moments!

As I walked away, they upped it one last notch and shouted, "No! You pick it up!" (You have to admire their nerve!)

Nanny Amies' Top Tip: When your child is displaying an emotional outburst, stop, look and assess the scene before responding. By doing this, you can convince your nervous system that you and your child are physically safe and prevent your own fight or flight kicking in. This means you are more likely to respond with tantrum tamers as opposed to tantrum fuel.

After a few seconds, I calmly walked back over to the angry chef and offered them an opportunity to connect to what had happened and what could happen next. It went something like this:

> **Me:** "You were really cross I couldn't sit on the floor."
> **Toddler:** [Watching me intently while sniffling their way through the acceptance stage.]
> **Me:** [While placing a hand on their arm.] "Let me know if you'd like some help to clean up, so that we can play again."
> **Toddler:** [More sniffling.]
> **Me:** [Calmly walked back over to the kettle (a cup of Yorkshire Tea helps me remain grounded).]
> **Toddler:** "Help please, Wara." [While reaching out a saucer they had retrieved from the floor.]
> **Me:** [Fighting back the "Wow! They are AMAZING!" tears, I calmly approached the toddler who's now firmly in the detachment stage.] "What a great choice. Let's get cleaned up." [I join them to pick up the toys.]

While it was the toddler who'd tipped the toys all over the floor, they did that while in a fit of rage when they could not physically control their actions. So, for me, offering to help tidy shows I'm there for support, but my calm behaviour during their escalation stage shows that I'm not going to entertain any nonsense either.

Once we had tidied, I gently led the toddler toward another favoured toy that was kept in a carpeted room. The toddler had fun with me next to them, and my old knees were happier!

Being the calm in the storm

Your toddler does not wake up every morning determined to drive you round the bend. Inconveniently, it's something they have a natural flair for! You are their safe place, so they feel comfortable expressing themselves freely, and they do so with gusto! No matter how they behave, they love you dearly, so don't take their behaviour personally.

To help you practise the art of *responding* to a tantrum, as opposed to *reacting*, I will detail a method I rely on again and again: Listen, Validate and Move on.

By following these three steps, each time your child experiences a trigger, they will be offered multiple chances to develop resilience while being supported through this difficult lesson. Let's take a look.

Listen: No matter how silly you feel their complaint is, try to listen to your child. When your toddler feels heard, there's less need for them to shout. To them, what they are shouting about is very important, and their priorities are entirely different to yours. As a fellow adult, I know that toddler requests and complaints are often unimportant, but to a child they are not.

Validate: Use a phrase that confirms the fact that you heard your child's protest. For example, "I can see you are upset about having to go home. I wish we could stay longer too". All feelings are valid and we can't change how we feel about something. However, feelings are not facts or orders to follow, which leads us to ...

Move on: Once you have validated your child's feelings, it's time to confidently move on. There is no need to convince your toddler that your boundary is a good idea or that there is nothing to be upset about – just try to offer them a new focus that's relevant to your circumstance. This will look very different for each family or scenario. For example, when trying to leave the park you could say, "Shall we listen to a story in the car, or music?"

> **Nanny Amies' Top Tip:** Practise being their calm in the storm at home, away from prying eyes. The more this happens, the easier it becomes for toddlers to learn how to deal with their big emotions. This, alongside choosing your battles, makes maintaining boundaries at home or in public much more manageable.

At what age do tantrums stop?

While tantrums are a developmentally normal behaviour for young children, and for many who have extra needs, how adults respond to them plays a vital role in how long they last. For a neurotypical child where tantrums are dealt with effectively, tantrums usually begin to cease throughout the fourth year of a child's life.

If tantrums typically result in more tantrum fuel than tantrum tamers, a child may not have the chance to develop the skill of staying calm, even when impulse control becomes a possibility from a developmental perspective.

If your child isn't showing any signs of leaving their tantrum days behind them and you are wondering if they require a bit of extra support, I ask you to consider the following.

1 Are they over the age of five?
2 Are tantrums happening multiple times a day?
3 Are tantrums lasting more than a few minutes?
4 Are tantrums having a negative impact on day-to-day life?
5 Could your child be sleep-deprived?
6 Is your daily routine unpredictable?
7 Are tantrums met with tantrum fuel?

If you've answered yes to any or most of these questions, choose one to focus on and try to implement a positive change in either your routines or approach. Keep going until you feel that environmental factors can be crossed off the list of potential causes. With confident and consistent responses from you, your child will learn how to manage their emotions in the same way that you can too.

If you feel that your child may need extra support, reach out to your doctor, paediatrician or health visitor. The questions above will prepare you for the types of information they will require in order to consider best strategies moving forward.

Finally, please remember ...

- You are important too! Ask for help if you need it. If you've had a tough day, have an early night and be kind to yourself.
- Remain calm whenever facing a tantrum. If you need to step away for a breather, do so if it's safe.
- Avoid responding to anger with anger.
- Talking things over with your child when they have calmed down is more effective than during the escalation stage.
- Offering logical consequences for behaviours (and not emotions) will allow a child to process why we need rules.
- Avoid placing much-loved toys into kitchen appliances!

CHAPTER 3
AGGRESSIVE BEHAVIOURS

When toddlers attack!

Parents can be really caught off-guard when one minute they are cradling their innocent bundle of joy and seemingly the next minute, their toddler suddenly swings for them or someone else. Now what? The term "aggressive behaviours" conjures up images of hostility and violence, perhaps with intent to cause or inflict harm. But fear not! While aggressive behaviours should certainly be taken seriously, if your little one is physically lashing out, it doesn't mean that they are destined for a life of crime or combat.

If your child has not yet displayed aggression (and they may never do so), I suggest you read this chapter anyway. If that day does come or if you are ever faced with aggression from another child, you'll be equipped to respond in an effective and mutually beneficial way that will limit the chances of aggression happening again.

There are varying levels and different types of aggressive behaviours that, generally speaking, run parallel to a child's age. For example, a 12-month-old child may pull your hair, and while this is painful, it's more about the exploration of their environment than purposeful aggression. Whereas a three-year-old child may scrunch up their face and purposefully hit you (or another child) on the arm out of frustration.

It is important to note that children under the age of five do not lash out to cause pain. Their actions are simply an extension of their feelings. There's no denying that aggressive behaviour can be challenging to deal with, but I do find that knowing that they are not trying to hurt you or other children helps.

For reasons we'll get to, it's incredibly common for toddlers to behave aggressively. This is one of the reasons I describe my early career as "being in the trenches!" I've experienced the full house of injuries, from being hit, scratched, bitten and kicked to having objects thrown at me. I've been there, done that and got the "Please don't hurt me!" T-shirt! Despite the injustice I may feel as a toddler lashes out, I try hard not to take it personally. I strongly urge parents to take this on board – your youngster isn't behaving aggressively because they don't like you.

As living creatures, we naturally feel defensive if aggression is aimed in our direction. In fact, our survival instincts perceive any form of aggression as a threat, so it's natural to react strongly when fists, teeth or feet head in our direction. The same can be said for when we witness aggression toward others, particularly so if you see your own child being hurt. Naturally, your parental instinct to protect will kick in, and quickly. However, if we want our children to develop into a well-rounded member of society, it's worth trying to curb your own fight or flight response (see page 24) and exchange it for a more disciplined and logical one. Save the adrenaline rush for when (or if) you truly require it.

Recipe for a perfect storm

Behaviours become aggressive when certain ingredients mix together to create a perfect storm. First, a child's gross motor skills will have developed as well as their hand-eye control, so they can choose to make purposeful movements.

This comes at a time when they still have a lack of impulse control in how they respond to emotional stimuli (see page 20). Add in a limited vocabulary and they cannot verbally express their frustrations and emotions. Youngsters are also oblivious to any build-up of anger that can result in outbursts. They have a naturally egocentric nature, so it's easy to see how aggressive behaviours can peak so quickly.

RECIPE FOR A PERFECT STORM

1 A good helping of gross motor development.

2 A heap of hand-eye coordination.

3 Combine with a lack of impulse control.

4 Stir in a portion of limited vocabulary.

5 Introduce a source of frustration.

6 Finally, heat up a dash of anger, before mixing.

"It's just a phase!"

Children do not begin to experience remorse until around the age of six so this phase can take a while. When your toddler grows out of aggressive behaviours depends on their innate character, their role models and the experienced outcomes of their behaviour. Alongside the development of remorse comes a greater understanding of – and the ability to control – their actions. Until then, toddlers aim their feelings in the direction of those closest to them, whether that be emotionally or physically close, because they haven't yet developed coping strategies to manage themselves.

Toddlerhood is full of dramatic, developmental changes. Yet, while their physical and language skills seem to improve day by day, emotional development can be much slower off the mark. Before a youngster can experience frustration, anger or any other negative feeling without some form of outburst in response, they must first learn how to acknowledge their own emotions. Having emotional awareness is the first rung on the ladder toward being able to communicate their feelings both calmly and effectively. However, emotional awareness takes time to develop, alongside input from the adults within a child's environment (see Chapter 11).

Aggression can certainly be a passing phase that many, if not most, children under five go through, but where environmental factors provide the right ingredients, phases can easily become habits. In my experience, parents all over the world, irrespective of parenting styles, simply want their child to grow up to be a nice person, but wanting that and knowing how to achieve that are two very different things. It is common when toddler aggression starts emerging for parents to have reactive responses, designed to "nip it in the bud" as opposed to preventative responses. So, let's look at the difference.

Why is aggressive behaviour happening?

Let's look in more detail about why a toddler might use aggression to express themselves.

Natural temperament
One factor is a child's natural temperament – there are certain innate characteristics that make it much harder for some children (and even adults) to keep a lid on their emotions. For example:

- **Low-adaptability:** We all vary on how much time we need to adjust to a change of plan or current activity. Children low in adaptability can become frustrated more easily and may rebel against change.
- **High-intensity:** Children who are high in intensity can display strong, emotional reactions to things. This doesn't necessarily mean they are in more emotional distress then those who sit at the lower end of this trait – it's more a case of natural volume levels being loud and their behaviours full of gusto! When children are high in this trait, they may even seem confrontational in the face of an event that displeases them.
- **High-sensitivity:** Children who are higher on this trait react strongly to environmental cues such as sounds, sensations and lights. Pain and emotional stress are expressed strongly and they can be labelled as dramatic or even attention-seeking.

There is no right or wrong position to sit on any temperament trait. I share these with you to help you identify how a child is innately programmed to respond to their environment, to give you an insight into their individual behaviour.

Physical wellbeing

Next up, we have tiredness, illness, hunger and other physical factors. You will know from your own life experiences that you have much less tolerance in those times when you aren't feeling 100 per cent. Whether it be hormonal changes, a drop in blood sugar levels or sleep deprivation, toddlers are much more likely to display irritability in times when their physical state is somewhat weakened.

Children with extra needs or developmental disorders can experience heightened sensitivities and may resort to aggressive behaviours if they become both emotionally and physically overwhelmed.

Nanny Amies' Top Tip: Consider anchoring meals, snacks and rest periods to certain times of the day for a week to see if it improves overall mood and behaviours. Eating every two to three hours, and resting midday, can have such a positive impact that further behavioural interventions aren't even necessary.

Environmental factors

Does your toddler only display aggression in one particular environment? For example, some children only hit their peers while at nursery, whereas other children only hit their parents at home. Frustration-based aggression will occur wherever a child feels most frustrated.

In addition to these factors, each individual child behaves the way they do for a specific set of reasons. While that list is long and varied, here's a few reasons to get the cogs turning.

1 Don't forget the tantrum fuel we looked at (see page 25). This can fan the flames of anger to the point where a child physically lashes out. I've witnessed parents crouched down, either trying to calm their child or reprimanding them and, as if by reflex, their child reaches out and physically hits them.

2 First-borns or only children have the freedom to play with any toy as they please. Parents can also offer a nurtured one-to-one approach to routines and activities. This can sometimes mean that opportunities to develop patience and tolerance are limited, so when they come up against another child of a similar age who wants the same toy, they may lash out as a result of their frustration.

3 If a previous aggressive outburst has resulted in boundaries being relinquished (for example, a child asks for a biscuit, parent says no, the child becomes aggressive and then gets the biscuit), when the toddler is met by that same

rule or emotion in the future, they may repeat the aggressive behaviour.

4   If aggressive behaviours from a child result in aggression from the parent (verbal or physical), this severely limits the learning opportunities of how to cope with big emotions. Therefore, each time emotions rise, aggression can become the go-to response.

> **Nanny Amies' Top Tip:** If you have one child at home, try to create opportunities where they must wait for a turn or share a toy. It's important that they are given the chance to build their patience and awareness of others. If you have multiple children, consider ways in which you can build their conflict resolution skills by supporting them to come to a compromise.

Whatever the reason for the aggression, the outcome and experiences a child has moving on from it will largely govern how long you witness this behaviour for. I have had multiple opportunities to discover this over the years, and the story I am about to share will offer you the chance to consider the importance of our responses in the heat of the moment.

One angry toddler …

The day had started with all the classic battles, from getting the toddler in my care dressed, teeth brushed to breakfast, etc. Everything was a battle with this toddler, who I would describe as being high in intensity, low in adaptability and highly persistent.

Most days, I was the sole-charge nanny. That's where parents don't partake in the day-to-day routines. Sometimes, when one or both of parents felt like spending more time with their child, I would take the role of a shared-care nanny.

Shared-care roles can be wonderful when you sing from the same hymn sheet as your boss, but when you approach child behaviour from opposing teams, it's a recipe for disaster.

Whenever this parent joined us, no matter what we were doing, they wanted everything to be fun. Anyone who offers 24/7 care to a child will know that, sadly, not everything can be fun. While I certainly advocate for adding in elements of fun whenever possible, I also think it's wise to know when to dial the "Lets party!" switch down a notch!

So, the toddler didn't want to get into their car seat. However, with the nursery bell beckoning, I had to act quickly. I picked them up and the wrestling began.

"Into the car seat. It's time for nursery", I chant.

Meanwhile, their parent hovered over me, trying to get their head into the car, in a bid to "help". It definitely felt more like hinder.

"Shhh, it's okay! Can you sit down, for me? Shhh!", they called through the car window.

"Would you like to have a try?" I smiled.

"Absolutely not! I HATE that car seat too!" the parent replied … loudly! Brilliant. Vent your disdain toward the car seat, right in front of your child. Professional Nanny rule 101 though – in those moments, never say what you are thinking!

The toddler was becoming increasingly aggravated, when the parent added: "It's okay darling, just sit down, we won't strap you in."

I daren't open my mouth for fear of saying something that would blacklist me from every nannying agency in the country. But I wasn't about to drive anywhere without the seat belt being fastened. I tried to dislodge the belt, which was tucked underneath them.

The toddler started shouting, "No! No! No!"

In popped the parent's head, again. "What's happening now Laura? Why are they upset?"

"I'm trying to get to the belt. They are sat on it."

"Oh for goodness sake Laura! Look at them, they don't want it on! Leave them!"

I stopped and looked at the parent, while very clearly stating, "The belt goes on or they get out of the car and we walk to nursery today ... Ouch!"

The overwhelmed toddler who, to be honest, had every right to be annoyed at this stage had sunk their teeth into my hand. Ooh, it didn't half sting! But before I could even think about how to react, the parent put in one last astonishing performance. They laughed.

They then reached their hand into the car, and said to the toddler, "Yes! High five! No means no, right?"

The parent then turned to me and said that, despite their toddlers' age, they knew exactly what they wanted, and how proud they were of them for standing up for themselves.

With utter disbelief (and while holding back the tears), I took the toddler out of the car and proceeded to get the buggy. I delivered the little one to nursery that morning, late and flustered, out of breath and with a really sore hand! However, I offered them a hug and wished them a nice morning (I think I needed that hug more than they did). I then walked back to my place of work, and my home too. That was a really bad day to be a live-in nanny.

Why did the toddler bite the nanny?
Just as the chicken crossed the road to get to the other side, it may be fairly obvious to see that the toddler bit the nanny to get through a surge of emotion. Yet, as this was such a unique circumstance and the fact that aggressive acts can happen in such a blur, I feel it's wise to unpick it.

First, let's look at what I got wrong. I was so focused on getting the toddler to nursery on time, I bypassed any connection with them. I picked them up swiftly in robot mode. Calm, yes, but devoid of anything that may have offered the toddler comfort in that moment, sadly.

Because their parent tended to be the "fun" one when we were all together (don't need to wear a seat belt level of fun), I often counteracted that with zero fun. I know this is true of so many parenting duos – it's common for one person to take on the majority of the responsibility.

The toddler, who was already struggling with the car seat, had to tackle other environmental factors, such as noise. I was chanting, "Into the car seat; it's time for nursery", while the parent was offering up shhh sounds and promises that I could never deliver. Over-stimulation will often result in flared tempers and this was no exception.

The conflicting messages between myself and the parent were a catalyst. Toddlers have no idea why we need to wear seat belts, and rightly so. While we can tell them they are to keep us safe, we can't tell them the heart-breaking and downright scary outcome of what not wearing them can mean.

The parent advertised their own disdain for the car seat. While I'm all for validating emotions, that was unnecessary. Toddlers require us adults to confidently lead the way, to offer up a solid role model for them to observe and hopefully mimic. If an adult can't keep a lid on their feelings toward something, it's wrong to expect a toddler to do so.

Had it not been for the interventions from the parent, I'd have likely come up with a distraction for the toddler to divert their focus. My brain was so focused on keeping my own emotions in check, I failed to think outside the box.

The parent high-fived their child for biting me. That one needs no other explanation beyond the fact they reinforced the act of biting via praise.

Nanny Amies' Top Tip: If your child bites you or someone else, first try a calm response and limited attention (see page 53). If they continue to bite, it can help to show them the power behind their teeth. Give them an apple and encourage them to try to squeeze it in their hands. You try too, demonstrating that hands have little impact on an apple. Next, encourage your toddler to take a bite and to notice the difference in what their teeth can do.

How you react to a toddler matters. There is a difference between being calm and being unresponsive. Calmness is soft, quiet and predictable, irrespective of the behaviours displayed, all while being present and still. Unresponsive is blank nothingness, unmoving and seemingly unaware of anything, which can be unnerving. In the example above, I entered into unresponsiveness. I've found that it's far better to aim for calm. In instances where it was just me and the toddler, I remained both unharmed and, unsurprisingly, very much responsive.

How do we prevent aggression?

Let's look at how we can prevent aggression in the first place. There are three strategies to have ready. The first is foresight, which is where you plan ahead to avoid potential triggers and schedules that may increase the chances of aggression occurring. The second is redirection, which you should use when negative emotions start emerging. The third focuses on our response when aggression does occur.

Here are some of the strategies you can use to help avoid aggression in your toddler in the first place.

Have a clear, calm routine

Plan the day to include ample rest times, regular meals and snacks, alongside opportunities to move freely. Sounds obvious? Never underestimate the impact that hunger, tiredness and restlessness can have on energy levels and mood! Getting this right will really help to prevent aggressive behaviour happening.

Have realistic expectations

Knowing what your child is emotionally and physically capable of is a major preventative. For example, if you arrange a play date for your two-year-old child without knowing that they are not yet capable of playing co-operatively for more than a few minutes, you might be heading for issues. Your toddler will need your close presence and help to build social skills to help them learn how to "play nicely" with another.

If your children partake in sibling rivalry, expect that you leaving the room (to prep a meal, for example) can increase the chances of aggression occurring. Can one child be given a puzzle at the table while the other is on the carpet? Can one child help you in the kitchen while the other stays to play? Sometimes a physical barrier is a necessary preventative measure.

Help your toddler develop emotional awareness

When you read to your child or watch TV together, note the mood change in characters to widen your toddler's understanding of emotions. For example, "Peppa looks really sad that she can't play outside". There are many wonderful books that aid a toddler's understanding of emotions (more information on this in Chapter 11).

Use descriptive praise

When your child behaves calmly, kindly or in a way that you'd love to see more of, tell them. For example, "I love how calmly you are sat with your Lego". Sounds a little cheesy

I know, but we so often tell children what not to do, therefore piling our attention toward the negative behaviours. Flip that and let positive attention work in your favour.

Give high-quality attention

Fill up your toddler's "love bucket" at least once a day with one-to-one attention. This could be with eye contact, a smile, kind words, etc. Choose moments without screens or distractions. In a busy home this may look like a hug first thing in the morning and an "I love you" or sitting down to eat dinner together. Positive connections are so important for a child's overall development and their behaviour.

> **Nanny Amies' Top Tip:** Play games that require impulse control, such as hide and seek or musical statues. These games offer multiple opportunities to practise resisting the urge to move. Learning how to control impulses during play can increase the chances of doing so during times of anger too.

Use redirection

This strategy involves you being aware of a rise in frustration and acting quickly yet calmly to help your toddler move on from the trigger. Redirection takes a great deal of effort and consistency, but gets easier with practice. The rewards redirection can reap mean that it gets a firm place on my list of preventatives. Here are two scenarios and some redirections you could try.

Trigger	Redirection
Two toddlers wanting the same toy.	1 Calmly approach and say what you see, offering an opportunity for them to problem-solve: "You both want this car. Hmmm, how can we solve this?" 2 You might want to place your hand on the toy to prevent it from becoming a weapon or one snatching it. 3 If they are unable to problem-solve independently, create options for them: "I can pop a timer on and Alexa will tell you when it's time to swap." 4 Over time, they'll be able to do this on their own initiative.
Toddler wants something they are unable to have at that time.	1 Validate the child's desire, before either physically removing the trigger or physically redirecting your child. 2 For example, if your toddler is asking for a snack as you are prepping dinner, use a simple sentence to explain that food will be available soon. 3 Take their hand and walk them toward their toys. Pick out a toy and ask, "Would you like to play with this here or in the kitchen?" 4 A simple choice can be enough to help the toddler to temporarily realign their focus.

Nanny Amies' Top Tip: If true hunger is at play, I will offer a wholefood to help stretch them until the main meal is ready. This may be some vegetable sticks or a piece of fruit that won't diminish their appetite for the meal.

How to respond to aggression

Where toddlers are concerned, we can't always avoid aggression, but we can certainly have a positive impact if it does occur, which in turn will lead to less aggression.

The key here is less is more! Your response needs to be simple to allow your toddler to connect the dots. A calm adult must have control of the scenario, no matter their own feelings in the moment. If two toddlers are involved, we certainly cannot expect the "victim" to remain calm and quiet as the "aggressor" chomps down on their hand, so it's preferable that you are calm. Here's how:

1 **Focus on the victim first:** Whether that be yourself or a child, calmly note the injury and assess the level of hurt. For example, "You've been bit, are you okay?" or "My arm hurts".

2 **Body language:** Use your body and facial expression to highlight your words in a way which offers visual emphasis to the overall message. For example, rubbing your arm, furrowing your brow or hugging the victim.

3 **Say what you see:** You do need to address the aggressor and not ignore them, as it's important they link their own actions to the situation. Where possible, avoid questions, accusations and any excess noise. Consider phrases such as, "Your sister is crying, biting hurts" or "Hitting hurts".

4 **Talk it over once you are both calm:** In the heat of the moment, damage limitation is the goal. Calming things down with the view to discuss the behaviour a little later will prove much more beneficial than offering lots of heightened attention in that moment.

5 **Apologies:** Children under the age of six do not fully understand the concept of apologies. Our adult brain might feel the need for some sign of remorse, but forcing a child to say "I'm sorry" isn't particularly effective. When calm, ask your toddler things like, "What could help Sarah

feel better?" This is a nice way for a child to think about using their own actions kindly. It might be that they offer a hug, give the victim a toy to play with or draw them a picture. A kind gesture is a great way for a child to connect to more positive interactions.

6 **Consequences:** In some cases, offering an appropriate consequence is necessary for a child to understand that their actions do have a ripple effect. Consequences do not have to be big or scary, they just need to link to the behaviour or circumstance at hand (see page 257).

Nanny Amies' Top Tip: Help your child consider what they could have done instead of hitting or biting. Show that we can use our words instead of lashing out. For example, "You felt really cross that Sarah had the train. What could we do next time Sarah has a toy you want?"

When these preventative strategies are used consistently, children are much more likely to develop a new skill set and, in turn, develop positive habits. Because children require multiple opportunities to create new habits, it's helpful to have all the adults in their environment tackling aggression with the same approach.

When children experience the same reactions every day, they take comfort in predictability, which in itself can create calmer behaviours. One of the greatest joys from my days of being a nanny was working as a team with an entire family toward a mutual goal, which leads me to tell the tale of a converted tiny tearaway.

Learning to get on with others

In this instance, the little one under the spotlight had two older siblings. The older siblings were impeccably behaved, and while this meant they set a wonderful example for their younger sibling, the toddler got used to being the centre of attention. If they wanted something, they got it. A drink, snack or toy would magically appear. Which is wonderful until you find yourself in playgroup where you are just one of many funny, gorgeous, egocentric rebels. This can lead to conflict, namely over toys!

The first time I ventured to a local group with the toddler in question, we were sitting playing with some sensory balls and as another toddler reached out for one, my little charge immediately opened their mouth, leaned over and grabbed their hand in a bid to sink their teeth in. Luckily, I was able to physically intervene. I realized this was a reflexive behaviour in response to my toddler feeling that their space, or belongings, were being intruded upon.

This toddler had zero capacity for sharing, and although it's developmentally normal for sharing to be a tricky lesson to learn, aggressive reactions coming so thick and fast meant that it was time to sort this out.

I spoke with the parents and explained that, without intervention, this behaviour could go on to impact social skills and coping mechanisms as they get older. So, with their permission, I was able to put a plan in place. Using a team-like mentality, I explained to the older children how it would help if they didn't immediately relinquish their toys to their younger sibling or dash to their rescue each time they witnessed an age-appropriate struggle, such as their sibling getting flustered with a puzzle piece. It became a group project. We'd all sit on the floor playing with toys while following a specific set of rules.

1 Keep hold of what they had long enough to model an appropriate sentence. For example, if an older sibling was playing with a car and their sibling tried to grab it, they'd hold on tight while saying, "Could I have the car please?"

2 Don't purposely aggravate the toddler. Knowing that this process would take time was important, and purposely goading the younger sibling with desired objects would have had the opposite impact.

3 I ensured that the older siblings didn't always relinquish the toy they were playing with. If they hadn't finished, it was okay to tell the toddler that using sentences such as, "I'll let you know when I'm finished".

4 Finally, I advised that when the older children had finished with a toy, they would place it down on the floor and announce, "Finished now".

> **Nanny Amies' Top Tip:** "Finished" is a word I use with toddlers to purposely signal that meals, teeth brushing or bath times, etc., are over. As obvious as this may sound, when spoken in an upbeat manner, "finished" can be something that little ones learn to wait for when they are doing something they don't necessarily love. You can also add in the baby sign for finished to create a visual aid. Start with both your hands open and palms facing you, then flick them outward to face baby or child.

Initially, these new rules resulted in raised conflict levels within the home, which sounds stressful, I know! But it meant that, from a behavioural perspective, the youngest member of the family was now experiencing opportunities within a safe and supportive environment. They were learning to wait and not always be given exactly what they wanted when they wanted it.

In turn, this gave me multiple opportunities to implement a response that encouraged them to develop new habits. For example, if the toddler lurched toward their older sibling in anger, I would calmly redirect them. This would sometimes leave them sat on the floor hitting the carpet in frustration.

Trust me, this was a step up from hitting unsuspecting toddlers at playgroup! If the toddler snatched a toy from their sibling, I would calmly give it back, saying, "Your brother hasn't finished yet". If the toddler looked or acted frustrated, I would calmly say, "You are angry; you want the train your brother has".

I dealt with any outbursts calmly, and within a relatively short space of time, I began seeing a difference. Fast-forward to playgroup a few weeks later: myself and the toddler were gathered around a table looking at mini figures when another toddler approached and joined in. The toddler in my care glared at them while remaining perfectly still. Were they happy to share? It certainly didn't look that way! But irrespective of mood, the toddler didn't lash out, shout or cry in any way. I offered a physical connection by placing my hand on their arm while noting, "It's nice to play together". Then we carried on playing without drawing any more attention to the new person at the table with us.

Over time, the toddler became more accepting of others in their space, near the toys they were playing with, and more tolerant when things didn't go immediately their way too. I was also more relaxed when other children approached us as that innate reaction to lash out seemed to dissipate.

Every day is a school day

It would have been much easier for me to forgo that playgroup, and I would be lying if I said I looked forward to Tuesday mornings in that role! However, when we avoid a task or activity for fear of a child's reaction, we severely limit the opportunities for them to adapt and develop new skills. Every day, there are ways to gently encourage better behaviours.

Thinking outside the box and having purposeful play sessions at home with their older siblings was a huge turning point for this toddler. I've done these types of play sessions with a single child too. You could regard aggressive behaviours as a phase, or developmentally normal, and wait. While that's necessary in some instances, it's rare to be in a situation where you cannot positively impact a child's behaviour. No matter their age, by adding in some purposeful behaviours from ourselves, we can make a difference.

There's an abundance of advice, suggestions, tips and tricks available now to help parents with day-to-day life with toddlers, but what I see all too frequently is a lack of honesty with regard to the effort and time these take to make a real difference. This can leave parents feeling increasingly exasperated or to think that the tips don't work because they didn't work after a day and a half! "Use your kind hands" is a perfect example of this. Telling parents to use this phrase with their aggressive child without any further information doesn't work with a naturally egocentric toddler who has limited language skills and life experience. You need to teach a child what "kind hands" are at home before you stand any chance of your child using "kind hands" at playgroup.

> **Nanny Amies' Top Tip:** A lot of social media trends, such as how to calm a tantrum, can leave parents feeling like their toddler is the only one not responding to certain interventions. It's rare for one tip to suit thousands of individual children. You will need to tailor the advice you read to suit your child and individual situation.

Tracking behaviour

If your toddler is going through a phase of aggressive outbursts, try to track their behaviour to pinpoint any patterns or triggers that will help you understand why. This can be done on a piece of paper or your phone and takes just a couple of minutes each day. The more days you track their behaviour, the more likely you are to notice a pattern. For example, you could use a similar table to the one below.

Day	Time	Who	Where	What	Cause	How it ended
Monday	11:50am	Mum and toddler	Kitchen	Hit and screaming	Wanted snack	Offered snack
Tuesday	4:55pm	Mum, Dad, toddler	Dining room	Bit and hit Dad	Unclear	Offered food and drink
Wednesday						
...						

In order for your data to be as true to life as possible, it's important that your toddler is unaware that you are tracking their behaviour so they act naturally. This is because understanding why your child behaves the way they do is the key to knowing how to help them develop the skills necessary to create new behaviours.

You are your toddler's "safe place" and the best teacher they'll ever have. Whether your child is still very young and investigating their environment via seemingly aggressive acts or is experiencing restraint collapse after nursery, offering them understanding and support alongside appropriate boundaries and guidance will teach them how to behave in ways that are socially acceptable. Avoiding the urge to cheer if your toddler lashes out will certainly help too!

CHAPTER 4
POTTY TRAINING

The most challenging milestone of all

BEFORE YOU FLICK PAST THIS CHAPTER

If you have read the title of this chapter with a sigh of relief, thinking "Thank goodness that's over!", hold your horses! You may not need these tips, but I'm sure you could use a good giggle! If so, skip to the story on page 70.

Potty training is the messiest, most challenging milestone of all! I feel no shame in saying that, even at this point in my career, I can still get a little bout of pre-match nerves if I'm tasked with helping a toddler to potty train. I know that no matter what, they will become fully potty trained, but I am so aware of all the stumbling blocks a family can endure if certain factors apply. Read on if you are thinking about starting, if you are already in the thick of it or have met a few bumps in the road.

If you are yet to embark on potty training and can take just one thing from this chapter, it's that **preparation is vital**. We are going to cover that in detail.

You will also need three Cs: Confidence, Calmness and Consistency. Toddlers require a great deal of support and guidance to learn how to use a potty and, in turn, the toilet, so when you approach it with the three Cs, it makes it much easier for them to follow your lead.

A typical potty-training journey will begin, on average, after two years of wearing nappies. That's two years of a child's life without thought of where, when or how they pass urine or faeces, and that's something adults can easily overlook. The leap between passing all urine and faeces without any thought to suddenly being expected to stop what you are doing, approach a potty and release a wee or poo is *huge*. And while it can only seem like one small step for parents, it's definitely one giant leap for a toddler!

When should you potty train a toddler?

Potty training is a time where lots of contradictory advice tends to surface. You will hear anything from, "They will train when they are good and ready!" to "You've got to get them out of nappies as soon as they hit two!" It can seem like every man and his dog has advice, but the tricky thing about receiving advice from many directions is that each family has their own unique journey, and what may work for one is not guaranteed to work for another.

Nanny Amies' Top Tip: If you hear phrases such as, "Well, I potty trained my little one in two days and never had an accident!", take it with a pinch of salt. Either their child is indeed a world record holder of potty-training prowess (I mean, it does happen) or they are sugar-coating things. Either way, every child develops at a different pace, and no one hands out medals at the end of a non-existent race!

Over the years, being privy to seeing how individual children can respond so differently to potty training has given me an amazing insight into how some approaches can be much more effective than others. This is why I always highlight the importance of the preparation phase. Planning the type of potty training you'll embark on, what props you'll need and when your journey will begin are the first decisions to make.

In my experience, waiting until the toddler is showing signs that they are ready will help you take positive strides moving forward, whereas starting due to societal pressures will not.

If you start before your child is physically capable, it's going to be messier than necessary, take longer than needed and be incredibly frustrating – for both you and your child. Having people expect a certain level of capability from you, which you are not equipped to deliver, is both physically and emotionally draining.

Also, if you start too early and it goes terribly wrong (sit tight if this sounds familiar), you run the risk of building negative associations with the bathroom and potty. This means that the next time you try, you are starting on the back foot.

The ten signs of readiness

There are ten signs of potty-training readiness, and if I'm tasked with the job, I won't start until the toddler is showing at least seven or eight of these, and ideally, all of them.

1 Tugging at soiled nappies.
2 Showing an interest in toileting habits.
3 Having a basic understanding of toileting habits.
4 Begins hiding while doing a bowel movement.
5 They pretend to use the potty or mimic your toileting behaviours.
6 Telling you that either they are – or they have done – a wee or a poo.
7 Longer gaps between wet nappies.
8 They may ask to wear underwear like you, friends at nursery or older siblings.

9 They can follow a two-part command. For example, "Pull your pants down and sit on the potty".
10 Not fearful of the potty.

Generally speaking, you will see some of these signs from around 18 months of age, and they'll continue to come through up until around the third year. Many toddlers will not display all these signs, and there is a fine line to tread between waiting for just the right time and leaving it until your child makes it past the age where every new lesson is fun. From the age of three, many toddlers develop a stronger sense of self, and for every incredible leap in their development comes a challenge that can make the potty-training journey just that little bit tougher.

There are valid reasons for some parents waiting for a child to be three or over, such as neurodivergence, extra needs, physical disabilities, speech delays, bladder infections and illness. There is no one-size-fits-all time for potty training. If you are holding off for that perfect moment to get started … well, there's no such thing as perfect!

As well as considering if your child is ready to begin this journey, it's important to ask yourself – are you? You will need to steer the potty-training ship, so make sure you have time and energy to do so. I very much hope that the rest of this chapter will help you to feel confident and ready when the time comes.

Getting ready to potty train

First things first, you need to introduce the concept of potty training – using you as the model! Start mentioning when you go to the toilet, using simple language such as, "I can feel a wee coming; I'm going to the toilet". You could also use an open-door policy, so your child can see you on the toilet. This will help your child connect to and understand the process.

Place a potty in the bathroom to introduce the new item. Perhaps your toddler can sit on it as you go to the toilet or you can model their favoured teddy taking a toilet break.

A holistic approach to potty training, where we use multiple opportunities to strengthen the learning, can shorten the length of time it takes for this skill to click. This also reduces the risk of toileting becoming a taboo or awkward topic.

Nanny Amies' Top Tip: Another great way to normalize the topic of going to the toilet is to talk about animals, whether it be a trip to the farm or zoo, your pets at home or a nature programme. You can point out the differences in animal droppings based on their diet (for example, some bird droppings are made purely of berries, whereas donkey droppings contain hay). When children begin to understand that what goes in must come out, they are more accepting of the process. Use your child's inquisitive nature to your advantage!

Next up, use a "Say what you see" approach toward their toileting habits. Using simple, matter-of-fact language can help your toddler to connect to their body, for example, "You did a poo, time to get clean".

Avoid any kind of language that can have a shaming effect. We've all pulled a nappy back and said, "Oh dear, what a stinky bum!" in a jovial manner, but when preparing for this journey, I've found matter-of-fact language more effective. Not only does it help children to process what's happening, but it helps them to accept that this is a normal part of life!

You will need

The following is a list of items that I wouldn't consider starting a potty-training journey without.

- **A potty**: It can help if your child gets to choose their own.
- **A toddler toilet seat**: This is to offer the toddler a choice between using the potty or toilet.
- **A step stool**: To help with more independent hand-washing and to ensure that their posture is appropriate if they choose to sit on the toilet. Place the step under the toilet seat, and check that the toddler can sit with their knees bent and slightly raised, while feet are flat on the step.
- **A potty-training basket**: I like to offer a couple of toys and books that are only used at potty time. This can help the toddler stay seated for longer and builds a positive association to visiting the potty. Books about potty training can be especially helpful, and you can use them before you start too.
- **Spare clothes**: Get stretchy, easy up and easy down clothes that you can throw in the wash and that do not require ironing. Stock up on lots of spare underwear too! (For your own sanity, a line must be drawn between the salvageable and non-salvageable pants!)
- **A travel potty**: This will help you get out and about.
- **A new water bottle or cup**: A new drinking vessel can help a child to consume more liquid than usual, which can encourage wees. Or some new straws can work too.

> **Nanny Amies' Top Tip:** Add a toy or musical instrument to the potty-training basket – something that involves taking a deep breath and blowing it out with purpose, such as a harmonica. This helps the child relax and encourages them to use the muscles necessary to help a bowel movement.

You've been shopping, so now what?

Once you feel that you and your little one are ready to start potty training, clear the diary! Housework, holidays, trips out

... most things, unfortunately, need to take a back seat to get this life skill off to a good start. Your child needs you to be vigilant, supportive and observant throughout. As exhausting as that sounds, you get out of this what you put in. There is no sugar-coating that, sorry.

Right before you begin, decide upon a specific day to get started. Show your toddler the number of nappies they have left. Use that matter-of-fact language to back up the visual aid, and say, "When all the nappies are gone, you'll do your wees and poos on the potty".

Finally, one of the most important decisions to make before getting started is which potty-training method you will use. And yes – there is more than one way to potty train a toddler. You will need to decide and be consistent. You, and any co-parents or carers, need to be on board with this.

Nanny Amies' Top Tip: The potty fairy can be a wonderful way to introduce your child to potty training. They can leave a personalized letter on the day you begin, with a little glitter to represent the fairy dust, and a present of new underwear from the fairy can get you off on a positive note. The fairy can even come back to visit for a progress report and extra support if needed!

Potty-training methods

Let's look at the six most well-known methods that people use for potty training. I include here what the method involves and the pros and cons of each. Having supported so many families *after* they've begun their potty-training journey, I've heard many cries of, "I wish I'd have known that sooner!", so I hope this helps you to decide the right method for your family.

Method	Child-led
How	1 Wait until the child announces a desire to sit on the potty. The child can stay in nappies in between requests to use the potty. 2 Back off at any sign the child is becoming upset, fearful or deterred. 3 Start slowly until the toddler recognizes the signs from their bladder and bowel. They'll then begin to increase the frequency of when they initiate their bathroom trips.
Pros	• There's low stress because nappies stay on until the toddler is ready to have them removed. • There are fewer battles. • It offers chances for toddlers to listen to their own bodies and learn to use the toilet in a relaxed manner.
Cons	• If a child is low in adaptability (see page 261) or fearful of the potty, they may never choose to initiate potty training. • This can get harder as a child gets older and can lead to an elongated training journey. • Lack of impulse control can result in limited progress.

Method	Elimination communication
How	Young children will naturally signal when they need to pass a bodily function, so once a baby can sit upright, parents can place them on the potty when they predict a bowel movement. Over time, they will develop an association between feeling the urge to go and sitting down on the potty.
Pros	• There are multiple opportunities for little ones to learn about toileting. • Due to the age of the child when parents tend to start, their approach is more gentle and supportive. • By the time a child is physically able to control their bladder and bowel, they have built an awareness of where and when to go. • There's limited pushback because it's a normal part of the routine.

Cons	• Placing a baby on the potty requires time, energy and thought that isn't always available. • Children aren't usually able to control their bodily functions until the age of two years and upward, so potty training can feel like a very long process if it begins from six months old.

Method	Three day
How	1 Stay at home for three days with the little one. 2 Offer them excess liquids throughout the three days. 3 Keep the child naked from the waist down, so they don't have an opportunity to go to the toilet in their nappy or pants. 4 Take them to the potty as and when necessary.
Pros	• Parents are heavily focused on their little one, so ample support is given and accidents are noticed quickly. • There are multiple opportunities for potty success and less clothing to clean.
Cons	• Carpets, sofas and soft furnishings get the brunt of any accidents in those first three days. • Children can experience a huge drop in support from the fourth day. • Children have to adjust to wearing pants after being bare-bottomed. • Parents can feel very frustrated when accidents occur as normality resumes from the fourth day onward.

Method	Timed
How	1 Track your toddler's bowel and bladder movements. 2 Take the little one to the potty at appropriate times throughout the day according to your estimated schedule. For example, if they previously urinated every 90 minutes, take them to the toilet every 90 minutes to give them an opportunity go on the potty. 3 Tell them "It's toilet time" or set an alarm so they know what to expect.

Pros	• This method limits the opportunity for both parent and child to forget about potty training, therefore limiting the risk of accidents. • It can help to create a rhythm or pattern when bowel movements are passed. • It can make the potty-training journey a little more predictable and offer up windows where leaving the home without a potty is safe to do so.
Cons	• If parents pressure their child to wee or poo at set intervals, it can create an unease and dislike toward the potty. • If the timed gaps are too short, it can also mean that a child empties their bladder before necessary, which isn't ideal for bladder strength and capacity. • If the timed windows are too short, children may miss out on the chance to listen to their own bodies.

Method	Routine
How	1 Implement predictable toilet trips at specific slots throughout the day, alongside your current routine. For example, wake up, go to the potty, have breakfast, then go to the potty. 2 Continue this until you feel that the little one can either hold their bladder for longer periods of time or begin to fully initiate all potty trips themselves.
Pros	• Generally, there are fewer accidents with this method as children are regularly encouraged to sit on the potty. • It can create healthy habits surrounding the understanding that, irrespective of whether we want to stop playing, etc. we do need to visit the bathroom a few times each day. • As the trips become aligned to a predictable routine, pushback from your toddler can lessen.
Cons	• Too much pressure can lead to power struggles and negative associations toward potty training. • If children attend day care, it can be hard to get the setting to establish the exact routine. • If children aren't encouraged to listen to their own bodies alongside this method, parents will have to remind them for many years to come.

Method	Combined
How	Parents combine methods to create a style of potty training that fits well with their family.
Pros	Potty training can be tailored to the child in question, while parents feel confident that they have chosen the right approach for their family.
Cons	If there's a lot of flexibility, it can lead to mixed signals, so it's important to have a clear plan that all adults in the home share.

So, what do I use? Rightly or wrongly, I'm happy to share that I usually aim for somewhere between the routine and timed methods. I find this to be a methodical and supportive way to potty train. Once a child has made progress and displayed bladder control, I will transition toward a more child-led approach.

However, I have been a little scarred from a fully child-led approach in the past. Here is a perfect example of why I developed a more assertive stance moving forward.

Potty training vs public transport

The toddler in question was some way into their child-led training by the time I came to offer them care. They were no longer in nappies; however, I soon came to realize that no nappies didn't mean no accidents.

My charge was going through a phase of selective eating, so I decided we'd go to the local market to choose some fresh fruit and vegetables in a bid to pique their interest in new ingredients and become more involved in the food prep. I felt it would be more of an adventure if we took the bus into town (mistake number one) and so off we went. As they were my oldest charge to date at that point, I honestly hadn't considered the need for a portable potty, wipes or spare clothing (mistake number two).

We had a 10-minute walk to the bus stop, a 10-minute wait for the bus and the bus ride was 20 minutes. Then the market was around a 10-minute walk from the station! So, before we'd so much as picked up a punnet of strawberries, we were almost an hour into whatever bladder capacity the toddler had.

At this stage in my career, I'm not sure I'd ever contemplated anyone's bladder capacity, let alone a child's (mistake number three).

Oblivious to this oversight, we gathered bags of fruit and veg while discussing the meals we could cook together. We also stopped at the fish market to eat a delicious pot of prawns while we sat looking at the fish, crabs and shrimp on ice! As far as days out go, it was up there with regard to educational benefits, but it did mean that time had somewhat escaped me (you guessed it, mistake number four).

Once I clocked the time, we set off for the bus station. It was before the days of digital travel schedules at our fingertips, and we had a 20-minute wait for the next bus (mistake number five).

Just as the bus was pulling in, I heard the words that anyone potty training a child longs to hear: "Wara, I need a poo."

Ah! I was pleased they could tell me they needed the toilet, but there was no bathroom at the bus station, and we were at least half an hour from home. We had no choice but to take our place on the packed bus.

"Thank you so much for letting me know, love! We'll be home soon", I smiled (through gritted teeth).

Even if I'd packed a travel potty, I honestly don't think a crowded bus is the place to sit a bare-bottomed child down to do their daily movement! The only solution I had was a rousing game of eye spy.

The toddler began to wiggle in their seat and their brows furrowed as they announced, "I think my poo is nearly here, Wara".

My cheeks burned as I could feel the glare of other passengers. Even if they couldn't hear what my expectant charge was saying, they could surely smell the excess gases that were now permeating through the bus.

"Just a few minutes longer, sweetie!" I lied.

In that moment, my charge stopped wiggling, a look of relief washed over their face as they said, "It's okay, Wara. I don't need a poo anymore".

My immediate thought was that they'd held it in and now they'd have constipation, which really is the enemy at any point in a human's life, but especially during potty training (mistake number six).

The rest of the bus ride was pretty quiet. It was when we arrived at our stop and stood up to get off the bus that my cheeks returned to a crimson red. As my young charge walked down the aisle as if they'd lost their horse, they spoke words that will forever be engraved in my mind ...

"I did *really* need a poo, Wara, but then I didn't ... now I just need clean pants."

Wow. Where's a sinkhole when you need one?!

My approach to potty training

That was the first and last time I made those mistakes while caring for a potty-training child. As my nanna used to say, "It's only a fool who doesn't learn from their mistakes lass!" I had allowed myself to get caught up in the excitement of fruit and veg shopping, and while it's now clear that I should have got out more, I didn't think to keep one eye firmly on the practicalities of daily life with a pre-schooler.

From that day forward, I have refined and tweaked my approach to potty training, culminating in effective language use, routines and techniques that have dramatically reduced the occasions where I've prayed for a sinkhole to open up and swallow me whole.

My approach covers ten basic rules that can act as both prevention and cure to many potty-training hiccups too.

1 **Routine:** No matter the home, family or scenario I have worked in, having a predictable routine to your day is always beneficial. It helps to keep things consistent and everyone knows where they stand.

2 **Low pressure:** I have found that offering support in a low-pressure manner was far more successful than my "Just do a wee!" days! Phrases such as, "No problem, we'll try again soon" can go a very long way.

3 **Adult-led:** A confident, adult-led approach is key. This isn't about an authoritarian approach; it is simply because adults are fully potty trained, have a fully formed brain, understand social norms and know how to get from A to Z in as few steps as possible. In the nicest possible way, your toddler ticks none of these four boxes.

4 **Teamwork:** Potty training is a group effort between all the adults who care for a child *and* the toddler. Working together toward the end goal will make this journey much easier than a "You vs Them" approach. This may include offering your toddler a choice between singing a song while they sit on the potty or reading a book, for example. Open communication between home and nursery – or parents and grandparents – is as vital as toilet paper in this equation.

5 **Clear language:** Ditch the optional questions. For example, "Do you need a wee?" is far less effective than "It's toilet time, let's go". Keep things short and sweet and say what you see.

6 **Positivity:** Children learn best through play. Adults can learn a great deal about how to teach a child something new from this perspective. For example, perhaps you could blow bubbles over your toddler as they sit on the potty or hide a tiny toy in the ball of your hand and have them guess which hand it's hiding in.

7 **Connection:** Eye contact, affection, attention and conversation are important tools in boosting your child's self-esteem. A child learns better when they have good self-esteem, so ensure you fill up their love bucket (see page 51) every day!

8 **Preparation:** Take a portable potty, spare clothes, wet wipes and nappy sacks (to hold soiled clothing) out with you. Don't be like me on that bus! Also, know how far to push them in those early days of training – there's no need to go on big adventures when you are all finding your feet with this developmental milestone.

9 **Consistency:** If one day you follow points one to nine and the next day you don't, your child's potty-training journey (and your sanity) will suffer. Be consistent and keep going. I know how hard this is, but let's not make it harder than it has to be by being inconsistent.

10 **Be ready for accidents:** Accept that accidents are going to happen – there's no escaping them! Have appropriate cleaning supplies at home, ready, so you can respond as quickly as possible to those "Clean up on aisle three!" situations. As frustrating as accidents are, getting angry, criticizing your child or offering a punishment will not help them to progress. I like to ask parents if they ever shouted at their little one if they took a tumble while learning how to walk? Inevitably, their answer is always a firm "No!", so let's do the same during potty training.

Potty-training "accidents"

Accidents are as much a part of the journey as the successes. In fact, in some instances, they actually help. Children can feel their wet or soiled clothes, or perhaps see their bodily functions on the floor instead of in the potty, so accidents can offer up great learning opportunities. As adults, we need to be able to push our annoyance of accidents to one side.

I have potty trained children where accidents have been limited to a couple at most, and that's because I have religiously followed my ten rules. Even then, it's rarely plain-sailing, and it would be wrong of me to imply as such.

Please do not be disheartened if your toddler is currently having multiple accidents a day. I would consider taking a break and starting at the beginning with the preparation phase. Going back into nappies, if necessary, is okay! But I do suggest you take that step just the once – if you flip-flop between no nappies and nappies, your child can become very confused and learn that when the going gets tough the tough gets a nappy!

> **Nanny Amies' Top Tip:** In a bid to prevent cabin fever from setting in during the early days of training, I introduce a new activity to keep myself and the toddler occupied. One of my favourites is to cover the floor with a roll of cheap wallpaper (blank side up) and offer pens, crayons, stickers and stencils for an art extravaganza. The best thing about this? It also acts as a protective layer against accidents!

Potty training and "Nooo!"

Potty training so often coincides with the developmental phase of power struggles and the word "Nooo!" This is one of the reasons why potty training can be challenging and why there must be a balance between encouragement and low pressure. During potty training, toddlers have the perfect opportunity to assert their desire for control, and just like the proverbial horse, we can lead a toddler to the potty but you can't make them poo!

With this in mind, I'm going to share a great story of a wonderfully spirited toddler who had well and truly entered their "No!" phase. But they were showing all the signs of potty-training readiness and we'd prepared for the task ahead, so we went for it.

The first couple of days passed smoothly – I led with confidence and the toddler seemed to be happy with the process. Until day three, when the novelty began wearing off and the toddler needed to poo. This can be the tipping point for many potty-training journeys. It's incredibly common for the first couple of days to be somewhat fruitless on the poo front, but like it or not, their bodies will try to pass one at some point. When the toddler feels the urge to push, it's incredibly common for one of the following things to happen.

- They panic and withhold the movement.
- They become upset and ask for a nappy.
- They slink away and soil their underwear undetected.
- They may continue with play and pass their bowel movement without any change in their demeanour.

In some cases, a little one will poo on the potty early into their journey, see it, then become upset. It's a strange concept for them to adjust to, and for many, this can then result in them displaying one of the behaviours above. How we respond to this aversion is vital. When it was obvious to me that my charge needed a poo, I announced, "Toilet time" just as I had the previous days.

"No!" came the reply.

> **Nanny Amies' Top Tip:** Irrespective of whether I'm training girls or boys, I teach them to stay seated for all movements. Not only is it confusing for boys to sit for poos and stand for wees, in terms of their balance, focus and ability, it's much less messy for them to sit down for wees, too.

"We can tiptoe like mice ... or hop like bunnies?" I modelled, offering them a sense of control.

Hopping our way to the bathroom, I helped the little one onto the potty and sat on the floor in front of them. Despite my camaraderie, they instantly became upset and stood straight back up.

"No poo!" the toddler said, while holding their bottom.

"You don't have to poo, love. Just sit down while I tell you a story", I reassured. I began talking, making up any old nonsense to keep them relaxed and seated. I knew that if we moved away from the potty in that moment, they would either withhold or soil their underwear.

I could see by their facial expressions that the poo was imminent. Yet the toddler stood back up and shouted, "Nooo!" No Poo!"

Nanny Amies' Top Tip: Avoid offering your toddler bribes for using the potty; you risk them producing a movement simply in exchange for a treat. This can limit the chances of them listening to their bladder and bowel.

If we lead with an emotional response, we may decide in this moment to offer a nappy (which becomes a safety blanket and habit), let them soil their underwear or simply move away from the potty at a loss of what to do next. I do get it! However, logic tells me that this is something they must learn, so I remained planted on the floor.

"I can see you don't want to do a poo, sweetie. You can sit on the toilet or sit back down on the potty?" This was about validating their fear but giving them a bit of autonomy too.

"No poo, Wara!", they cried.

Okay, time for a couple of toys from the potty basket to encourage them to focus on something other than the impending poo.

The toddler sat back down on the potty and began playing with the toys, and within seconds, they pooed. Phew! The toddler then quickly stood up, looked at it and cried, "I don't like poo. Bye-bye poo".

I very calmly said, "Wow, your poo is ready for the toilet now. Brilliant! Bye-bye poo". I asked if they'd like to flush it away. They very politely declined and allowed me to get them cleaned up. Always clean front to back after a bowel movement to prevent bacteria from making its way into the urethra.

This pattern happened for the next few days and with each protest, we worked as a team to get it in the potty. Was it easy? Absolutely not! Did it work? Hell, yes! After the first week of potty training, the little one was announcing their need for a poo while taking my hand and leading me toward the potty. It became a routine, an expectation on both of our parts and a potty-training win.

Potty-training snag list

So, your toddler seems potty trained. Great! But don't just leave them to it yet. I'd like to finish this chapter by pointing out how many things must happen for your child to be fully capable of using the potty or toilet independently.

1 They recognize the urge to go. They have to stop what they are doing and actually go.
2 Once in the bathroom, they must take down their clothing.
3 Once sat still, it's time for them to respond to the urge and pass a bodily function.
4 Once finished, they need to wipe themselves clean. After the clean-up, they need to pull their clothing back up.
5 They have to learn to flush the toilet. And remember to wash their hands.

Realistically, most toddlers will need help up to around four years and beyond. In my experience, a huge contributor to children struggling with potty training is that their parents drop their support after a few weeks or months of training. So, help them for perhaps longer than you think, especially when out and about. Don't worry, you won't need to babysit toilet trips forever. Your toddler will become independent in good time, when a solid foundation has been laid first.

Finally, if you are stuck in a little potty-training hole, I'll leave you with a quote from Henry Ford that I really appreciate.

"If you always do what you've always done, you'll always get what you've always got."

Good luck, you've got this!

CHAPTER 5
DAYS OUT WITH TODDLERS

All eyes on you

"Laura, the paparazzi will most likely be there, so make sure you both look the part. Oh, and the little one needs to behave!"

A boss once shouted this at me from across the kitchen before a family day out. Imagine the pressure! Taking a young child anywhere at any time can lead to rising stress levels. Will they need a nappy change at the stores? Will the queues be so long that you'll feel like abandoning ship? Argh!

Toddlers are fun-loving, excitable, loud, unpredictable and carefree – basically, they have an agenda that is entirely (and unfortunately) separate to ours as adults. On top of that, we have to give a lot of attention and focus for a child's health and safety when out and about, and this can be mentally draining. Young children also come with a lot of "stuff" such as nappy bags, buggy, toys and extra layers of clothing, so outings can be physically tiring too! It's because of these things that many parents confide in me how they avoid going out, especially heading out alone with their toddler and certainly avoiding big days out whenever possible.

I wholeheartedly admit that going out can be stressful and tiring, but there are so many benefits, not just for the toddler, but for you too. The fresh air, stimulation and movement all equate to a better night's sleep for your toddler and you. In our ever-modernizing world with digital devices and electric lights playing havoc with our circadian rhythms, going outside helps to sync the body clock. Going outside is what nature intended.

The benefits of going out

Fresh air and natural sunlight are beneficial whether you experience it from the comfort of your backyard, the local park or you travel further afield.

I'm hoping you know by now that I do understand why you may choose to stay indoors with your little ones. However, I very much hope that I can convince you to take little outings each day to help promote your whole family's wellbeing. Start small with short, local trips, and don't feel the pressure to do anything too ambitious if you won't enjoy it too. Being outside is beneficial.

- Being outside allows all our senses to engage with the wider environment. We are not designed to stay indoors all day. Being outside positively impacts our emotional and physical health.
- Eyesight development needs time in natural light and the chance to focus on real-life objects ahead of us. This is particularly important when considering the rising numbers of young children spending large amounts of time viewing two-dimensional objects on a screen.
- Being outside in open spaces offers toddlers more opportunities to develop gross motor skills (large movements using the whole body). This also increases the muscles necessary for fine motor skills, such as writing and getting dressed. Climbing outdoors will help your child to learn how to write indoors!

- Being outside increases spatial awareness. Awareness of the surroundings helps a toddler learn how to avoid hazards and to make safer decisions.
- Moving around outside improves both short- and long-term health. Movement results in a lower BMI (body mass index), a lower risk of diabetes, heart disease and asthma.
- Running, stumbling, bumping up against a tree or taking a tumble all increase a child's resilience. Of course, we don't want them to get hurt, but safe resilience building is one of the best gifts you can offer your child.
- Being outdoors, walking through the woods, climbing at the park or playing on the grass can promote problem-solving and imagination.
- Being outside inspires a love of nature.
- Fresh air and natural light are vital for sleep health.
- Exposure to the sun helps a toddler's body produce vitamin D, which helps to support the immune system and bone development.
- Fresh air and green spaces create a natural calming effect in the body, even producing the "feel-good" hormones like oxytocin and serotonin. Screen time, by contrast, can increase stressful feelings.
- Being outdoors can promote confidence. As children explore, they may try something new, take a risk, perhaps finally conquer that climbing frame or meet a new friend on the slide.

Planning ahead

Let's delve into how I prepare for going out. That's not to say I never feel stressed or always enjoy every minute of being out, but planning will make a huge difference to how an outing will go and how you manage the unexpected. I can hear you say, "It would be easy to go out if I had a nanny with me!" Well, reading this chapter is the next best thing! Here are the main things to think about.

Tiredness: Whenever possible, ensure that your toddler's sleep schedule is factored in. Tiredness will massively increase the likelihood of a tantrum, so try to have the toddler in their pushchair, car or back home as close to their usual nap time as possible. Inevitably, they might fall asleep in the pushchair, but stretching the toddler beyond what they are physically capable of handling can lead to stress all round.

Mealtimes and snacks: Think ahead about where to get lunch or take it with you. This might sound like stating the obvious, but you also need to pack snacks and water. And don't think it's only your toddler's behaviour and tolerance levels that will be impacted by hunger; get yourself some snacks packed while you're at it!

Spare clothes: I pack spare outfits into pouches or bags and store them at the bottom of the nappy bag or pushchair. They don't take up much room there, and they don't get in the way of me reaching for items that I may require more often. I also have spare nappy sacks that I can use to house soiled clothing.

First aid kit: Take a few plasters, antiseptic wipes and antiseptic cream or spray to comfort toddlers after a tumble and to prevent infections.

Exit plan: Have an "exit plan" in place for times when your toddler has a complete restraint collapse. Sometimes we must admit defeat and call it a day, so whether it's leaving a restaurant halfway through your meal for a quick breather or leaving the playground early, if you know your child is struggling, don't be afraid to cut it short. I genuinely couldn't care less about what others may think about me taking a toddler home who's physically and emotionally spent. In some instances, I'll even retreat while the youngster is still having a ball, ending their day on a high, as opposed to carrying them out of somewhere kicking and screaming.

Props: Whenever possible, I will take items that will make my life a little easier, whether I'm 30,000 feet above the Pacific Ocean or popping to the local playground – I call them props. Having also been tasked with keeping toddlers quiet and well-behaved in some of the world's poshest restaurants, I don't mess around when it comes to packing useful distractions. For example:

- **Books:** Depending on a child's age, I take a colouring book, sticker book, puzzle book or any reading or picture book that a child typically enjoys. Crayons or pens as well.
- **Play dough:** If I'm on a flight or in a restaurant, I may bring out a tub of play dough and a tool to help the toddler engage with the dough.
- **Small figures/animals/insects:** Any characters or animals can offer a chance to use imaginative play.
- **Construction toys:** A pouch of small building bricks can provide many options for a little one to explore.
- **Boats/cars:** Small, moving items can be well received. I have a lovely pirate boat with pirates and parrot.
- **Fidget cubes:** There are some wonderful items that offer children a chance for more exploratory play, appealing to their inquisitiveness, while remaining sitting.
- **Notepad and pencils:** The *hours* of Tic-tac-toe, Hangman or Dots and Boxes I've played ... Once children are four years and over, you can start challenging them with simple games like these.

Nanny Amies' Top Tip: If you don't have a high chair, consider taking a bumper seat. This can prevent the child feeling left out and getting bored and frustrated. If I'm going to a busy place with a toddler who will be walking, I will use a backpack with reins. This allows the toddler some freedom and the adult a safety measure in crowds!

Do you take screens?

While it is very common to use screens and devices to entertain a child, where possible, I avoid doing so out of the home. Screens limit a child's chance to interact with the world and those within it. They also limit chances to build patience and tolerance. If I am on a flight with children, I will pack a tablet of some kind, but even then it's the very last thing I offer. This thought will be daunting for many, and I do appreciate that screen time is a lifeline for many, so I will cover this topic further in Chapter 7.

> **Nanny Amies' Top Tip:** Having books and toys that are reserved purely for when you are out of the home means that they maintain some novelty. This can lead to extended play and a more content child, so don't be afraid to keep "Day out toys" hidden and away from the rest of your other toys. I love to have them in easy to grab pouches.

When to bring out the props!

If I'm in a restaurant or on a flight, I view toys and activities at varying levels of quality in terms of how well they grab a child's attention. This helps to ensure that you don't show your best hand from the get-go and have something left in an emergency!

For example, *you* are the first-tier option – playing eye spy, asking questions, pointing out of the window or telling stories. You can keep your toddler entertained for a little while without the use of any props or toys at all. If you go in with a screen first, nothing else will quite cut the mustard, and that either leads to the overuse of screens or a restless child.

Essentially, how we lead an outing will impact how the trip goes. While, of course, there are always unknown entities, the trips I took with toddlers at the back end of my nannying career were entirely different to those I took early on. Here's an early example ...

When the s**t hits the fan

Let's go back to my day out with the warning about the paparazzi. My bosses, their toddler and I were heading to a famous rock star's penthouse in the heart of a bustling city. I'd never been before, and I hadn't worked with the family for very long, so I felt a bit of trepidation.

The car journey had been long, but I'd managed to keep the little one entertained with nursery rhymes and the new views out of the window. We entered an impressive-looking building with an ornate, imposing lobby and made our way to a private lift with a button marked "PH". The whole time I calmly narrated our journey to the toddler to help them feel involved and remain in good spirits. My bosses really cared about how their child was perceived by others and told me on a regular basis that the responsibility of that perception lay in my hands.

> **Nanny Amies' Top Tip:** A child's behaviour is a perfect blend between nature and nurture, so all adults (and children) that spend time with a toddler will in some way impact their behaviour. So, choose who your little one spends time with wisely.

As the lift doors opened, I tried to maintain a demeanour that private nannies must learn to perfect – you need to create just the right level of involvement so that your young charge behaves within acceptable boundaries, while you remain mainly in the background. I thought of myself in that moment as an elite SAS nanny, lurking, watching, ready for anything.

As champagne was served, the toddler had made their way to the middle of the room while the adults were cooing over them. I stayed close by, but a little back, ready if needed. If I'd have had other SAS nannies there for back-up, the news over the earpiece would have gone something along the lines of: "I have the subject in line of sight, they remain in clear view. I, however, continue to go undetected!" (Then maybe add in a dramatic roly-poly to access cover from behind the neighbouring sofa!)

Suddenly, the toddler disappeared behind the sofa furthest from me. I had a decision to make. Did I head over there to assess the situation or wait a short moment to see if one of my bosses responded first?

In that split second, I heard a sound coming from behind the sofa that still haunts me to this day ... decision made! The imaginary radio chatter over my earpiece to my back-up SAS nannies sounded: "Action stations! Go, go, go! Subject requires immediate back-up!"

I walked quickly toward the sound at the same time as the rock star rose from the sofa, looking just as shocked as I felt! He *glared* at me, searching my face for answers about what on earth could have created that sound. I smiled nervously because the sound we had heard could only mean one thing – a nappy explosion!

The toddler waddled out from behind the sofa saying, "Poo" in the most angelic and innocent of tones.

In all honesty, it's difficult to know how to describe the scene, but I don't believe in sugar-coating things, so read on at your own discretion ...

As I crouched down beside the toddler, I witnessed the contents of their nappy streaming down their legs into their shoes and puddling onto the rug. I had dealt with a great many soiled nappies at this point in my career and I wouldn't bat an eyelid normally, but this was another level. I wasn't the only one to notice ...

"This rug is an antique! It is a 16th-century Persian rug worth more money than you'll ever earn and now it's covered in shit!"

The rock star's reaction to the nappy spillage could have been likened to that of a toddler tantrum! He was livid and not shy about letting me know. I happen to have very strong feelings about how we speak in front of a child, whose emerging language skills are developing by the second. While I had every sympathy for the rug, I was offended by the way the rock star was speaking to me, and in turn, my charge!

I looked toward my bosses in the hope of finding some support. They were still clutching their champagne, while understandably looking somewhat shell-shocked.

Despite this, I asked them, "Would you mind grabbing me the wipes please? I daren't move because I need the little one to stay still and not walk around!"

The room was filling with such a stench, and one of my bosses was now walking toward me with the nappy bag in hand and a face like thunder.

The rock star shouted, "You'd better have carpet cleaner in that bag!"

That's when they began ... my nervous giggles! This is something that started when I was at primary school and has never left me. During times of heightened stress or moments of angst, I simply giggle, and I mean, full on, tears streaming down my face. This is something I am not proud of, and honestly, it can offend people.

Through my giggles, I managed to turn to the rock star's wife and ask, "Is there a spare room and a towel we could use please?"

She was very sweet and calmly showed me, the toddler and my boss to the bathroom. The second the door closed, my boss started howling with laughter ... what a relief! With sore tummy muscles, I placed a fully clothed toddler in the bathtub and began removing the offending garments while singing their favourite nursery rhymes.

Nanny Amies' Top Tip: Singing helps to distract and entertain toddlers, and also helps us to feel calmer too. Singing can release feel-good chemicals, such as oxytocin and dopamine, both of which are essential to our emotional wellbeing. It doesn't matter a jot what you sound like while doing so ... when times get tough, get singing!

It was great to have the parent with me helping – if you need help, don't be afraid to ask for it! When we emerged from the safe haven of the bathroom, it was decided that it was preferable for all concerned that I took the toddler for a walk around the city while the adults finished their champagne. As I roamed the city appreciating the fresh air, I reflected on my time at the rock star's apartment and wondered if he and his rug would ever fully recover.

Your approach matters

Nappy explosions are just one of many reasons we may need to cut an outing short; behaviour is a common factor too. I'm often asked how I deal with challenging behaviours outside the home and, in essence, it's the same way I deal with them inside the home! Having consistent, predictable boundaries in place that you deliver with confidence is the key to damage limitation with tantrums and challenging behaviours. However, just like knowing what to pack for a day out, there are a few approaches that are worth having up your sleeve to counteract, or even avoid, challenging behaviours from developing in the first place.

Connection: Be sure to have "positive connections" with your little one through the day, offering them some descriptive praise or positive attention, especially when your child displays a behaviour you'd love to see them repeat. For example: "I love being at the park with you!"

I know this may sound cheesy, but your child's self-esteem is intrinsically linked to their behaviour, so give it a try! It's much easier to comment only on negative behaviours, so flip this on its head when possible.

Movement: Toddlers are not designed to sit still for long, so give them plenty of time to move around before taking a seat (in a car, high chair or on a flight). This can be done by running a lap of the garden, bunny hops, star jumps, climbing the stairs, etc. Also, once they've been sitting for a while, it may be time to pull into a park to take a quick walk, or go outside for a while if eating in a restaurant.

Involvement: Involve the toddler in age-appropriate decisions because offering choices can help them to feel empowered. It gives the child that developmental need for control within sensible boundaries. For example, "Would you like to sit on this chair or that one?" And "We can leave now or after one more slide? You choose?"

Giving age-appropriate choices works well, but adults must implement non-negotiable boundaries that keep children safe and healthy. For example, when it comes to crossing roads, I insist that youngsters hold my hand, irrespective of whether they want to or not. So many parents ask me, "What should I do when my child doesn't want to hold my hand over the road?" Hold it. Just hold their hand.

Language: Using clear, calm and concise language helps, leaving no room for misinterpretation. For example, "Could you please come down, it's time to go home" is less effective than a clear, "One last slide, it's home time".

If you are in a restaurant or another confined space, note that if all the toddler hears is "Stop!", "Don't touch that!" or "No!", they will become aggravated.

Countdowns: Offering countdowns as you approach a transition time can help to prepare your child for change. Whether it be getting ready to leave for your day out or getting ready to make your way home, keeping the toddler posted in terms of how long they have left to play can prevent disappointment. For example, "Five more slides, then we'll head to the car".

Outnumbered!

Things get trickier when you have more than one child to look after. When tasked with caring for three very active children, I knew I had to bring my A-game if we were to ever leave the house! Each child was very different, with all of them enjoying different activities, so it was challenging to plan an outing that equalled three happy bunnies.

Over time, I realized something important – while there's a lot to be said for museums, farms, adventure parks and other child-specific establishments, sometimes less is more. Those big days out seemed more likely to end in chaos, and I would be left feeling resentful. By the end of a big day out, I found myself wanting to say: "Let me get this straight … I've packed and carted around a bag of drinks, snacks, toys and spare clothes, planned the day, gone out of my way to ensure you've all had fun, absolutely exhausted myself running around in three different directions, keeping you safe all day, bought you each an ice cream … and now you tell me you'd rather have gone to the park!"

> **Nanny Amies' Top Tip:** Save the big days out for when you have back-up! Do not put yourself in a situation that is more trouble than it's worth.

The best outings were the simple ones. When charged with multiple children to care for on my own, my go-to outings were picnics. Oh, how I love picnics, and as long as the weather wasn't truly diabolical, we had them all year round!

Nanny Amies' Top Tip: As soon as you can, give each child their own backpack containing their individual water bottle, a snack, an extra layer of clothing, if necessary, a reading book and one small toy of choice. This lightens your load and the children are given age-appropriate responsibilities and opportunities to become valued and helpful team members.

For picnics, I would carry a blanket, the picnic and often a ball of some kind. We'd set up camp, play, eat and head home when the time was right. By allowing each child to choose an individual toy and book, they each felt that their own personal preferences were being met. By them carrying said preferences, I felt less like a carthorse and more like a valued team member. Picnics have worked for me in any role with any child. I also have fond memories from my own childhood of picnics with my family. Picnics on the beach, midway through a hike, midway on a long journey, you name it! There's always time for a picnic in my book! (Pardon the pun.)

Nanny Amies' Top Tip: Using your non-optional language and a confident tone, set out safe boundaries before you let the little ones move from the blanket. For example; "You can play between these trees and that path. If you hear me shout your name, I'll time how quickly you can run to me!"

Try not to feel a huge pressure to take your toddler on grand days out. I fear that social media sets an expectation on parents that's rarely achievable. What you see in a short video clip or a sweet little picture is not a true depiction of that family's entire day. Trust me – I've been the one taking the pictures of the happy family on a day out – you don't see the nappy changes, the tiredness, the coats and bags I carried.

With all of this in mind, particularly the amount of benefits a child receives from time spent outside, it's easy to see why I will head outdoors with toddlers, come rain or shine. Will I always love it? No. But will the toddler always benefit in some way? Abso-fresh-air-lutely!

CHAPTER 6
SOCIAL SKILLS

"They won't play with me!"

This chapter is where I become a real cheerleader, advocate and ally for toddlers all over the planet! It's incredibly common for parents to expect their children to play together or with their friends "nicely". There's no denying how helpful it would be if children could fully occupy themselves and play nicely together, at home or when out and about, without refereeing. However, unless your children are particularly laidback or you've spent a great amount of time working on this skill already, it's highly likely that you witness some form of conflict. So, what can we do to help?

Most children under the age of three are simply not capable of long bouts of cooperative play. For example, if you have siblings who are aged three and one, any expectation of playing well together can lead to frustration on both the parent and child's part.

However, just because your child isn't yet physically capable of a skill or behaviour, it doesn't mean that we should turn a blind eye to challenges or give up until they are older. Whether it be sibling rivalry, squabbles among friends or territorial displays over toys at playgroup, your child will require your guidance and support for their social skills to flourish.

What's play got to do with it?

Your toddler's ability to play with others is, as mentioned, directly related to their age. Their general behaviour is also a factor, which we have already looked at in earlier chapters. I want to talk next about play, as this is often overlooked.

One to two years old

For the first two years, children are developmentally geared up for solitary play. They are toy- or object-focused so, if they are playing happily with a toy, they will see no reason to share it. Toddlers at this age also lack awareness of other people's feelings. While you may witness the beginnings of them offering objects, food or toys to those around them, this is on their terms from a mimicry perspective and is largely repeated due to the lovely reaction it inevitably receives from family members.

For this age, you can model manners, turn-taking and sharing. Make this part of your play with them. Showing your appreciation for these things will help your child to process their behaviours. However, even if your under two-year-old child is quick to hand an object back and forth to you, it is still very early days, so manners, sharing and the understanding of other people's feelings shouldn't ever be expected of them.

Two to three years old

Throughout their second year, your toddler will start to notice and observe more of the behaviours of those around them. This is when they really begin to mimic the actions of others, especially during play. They will likely play near, or alongside, peers or siblings. However, while the proximity may be close, they will remain focused on their own play and won't be fully interactive with others – this is parallel play.

Your toddler still has very little impulse control. If they see a toy that they want, there's no reason in their mind why they can't have it, hence the birth of the "Mine!" phase!

- It's important to remember that while "It's mine!" sounds rude to an adult, to a naturally egocentric toddler who does not yet understand social norms and fairness, there's no thought outside of wanting what they see. They act on impulse alone.
- Shouting and shaming a toddler will not encourage them to develop the awareness of other people's feelings or belongings.
- Validation can be an effective way of supporting your toddler while setting a boundary around the behaviour. For example, "You love this slide! So does Sarah, it's her turn next".
- In the heat of the moment, it's about damage limitation. We obviously don't want "It's mine!" to end up in a brawl. Don't be afraid to back your words up with calm actions; for example, by moving to another area of the park.
- Talk about sharing on the way to the park or playgroup. For example, consider ways in which you can teach them that they don't own every slide in the borough: "Tim would love the slide, Ellie would like the slide, you enjoy playing on the slide ... "
- Have faith that when you don't make a big deal out of it, alongside of coaching and redirection (see page 51), this phase will pass.
- Finally, most parents sympathize with this phase, so park any embarrassment you might feel in the "not necessary" bay! And honestly, if they don't seem to understand, that is not your concern – this is a very common part of toddlerhood.

Nanny Amies' Top Tip: If your toddler behaves in an unkind manner, forcing them to apologize isn't going to teach them to feel remorse or care for others. Instead, model this for them. For example, you say to the other toddler, "Oh dear, I'm sorry, Sarah pushed you. Are you hurt?"

Three to four years old

This is the age when we start to see children taking part in associative play. They are now more likely to play with the same toys or equipment as their peers or siblings, while still holding on to their own specific play goals. For example, one child may use the slide as a slide, happily going up and down, whereas another may view the slide as the only way down from their castle ... a castle that they want to stand at the top of for a while!

At this age, individual characters get stronger and their language skills develop too, so it's likely that children will clash over play and tell you about it! They still require a great deal of support to achieve long-term, harmonious play. It's also very common for a child to mimic sharing at this age but not yet understand *why* they should share. This can really confuse parents and carers because on those days where a child is particularly tired or hungry, for example, they may not mimic any sharing at all. This may result in a "You know how to share!" comment from parents, or chastisement when really the child still needs a teaching moment.

Four to five years old

This is the stage you and your parenting friends have been waiting for! With a bit of luck (and a lot of coaching), you can take a little step back from constant refereeing because your child may now be able to partake in cooperative play.

They may be able to communicate and/or share the same play goals and which toys to play with, while displaying basic conflict resolution skills too.

Even as your child continues to grow and develop, it's important to understand that there are so many things that impact a child's ability to fully partake in successful cooperative play. For example:

- Illness
- Hunger
- Tiredness
- Past experiences
- Natural temperament
- Who they are playing with
- The support and role modelling they have experienced

Play dates from hell

I've witnessed a great many play dates in my time, whether I've been the instigator, the invited party, or at playgroups or parties with multiple children. Whatever the occasion, there are certain things that can almost guarantee a spanner in the works of peer and sibling play.

Picture the scene – you've planned to get together with another parent so that your children can play together. This is so thoughtful of you; *they* should have fun while *you* get the chance to sit with a cuppa and have an adult conversation! Whereas, in reality, all hell breaks loose and you are left wondering why on earth you bother!

Play dates can be wonderful things when approached with appropriate expectations. When we sink into deep conversation and that cuppa, we can unintentionally set children up for conflict. Let's unpick why this happens and how to avoid it.

Age: As discussed above, perhaps the most common reason that play dates (or play between siblings) don't always go to plan is due to the developmental phase of the children invited to play. Rather than leaving young toddlers to it, sit down with them, or close by. While this will naturally impact the flow of your adult conversation or to-do list, you will be able to keep an eye on any behaviours and redirect them before they go awry.

Time: Booking a play date that runs into a "trigger" time, such as before naps or meals. Don't be afraid to maintain your routine by explaining to friends or family that your toddler needs to rest at specific times of the day. If your child is in a patch of particularly challenging behaviours, either skip the play date if they are only free over lunch, for example, or cut it short when you know your child needs to rest.

Length: Play dates tend to run longer than a child of any age can cope with. An hour is probably more than enough for most toddlers. Keep an eye on your little one's social battery. It is okay to draw a close to a play date, even if they are having fun.

Snacks: Play dates can be a lovely time to share food or snacks. However, it's also easy to bend boundaries on sweets, cakes and foods that are generally high in refined sugar. This will cause a spike in blood sugar levels, and what goes up, must come down! Offering some fun foods is kind, but let's also offer fruits, veg sticks or savoury foods that will naturally fuel your child.

False threats: An absolute classic! Have you ever heard or said, "If you do that again, we're going home!" Meanwhile, the child in question repeats the behaviour another five times without being removed from the environment. Say what you mean and mean what you say. If the behaviour is challenging enough to warrant going home, take them home! In my experience, this helps them to process the consequences to their actions, and allows them to rest as needed.

Name-calling: If your child is behaving in a way that is inappropriate, you may feel like telling them that they are being ungrateful or rude. However, name-calling can actually make matters worse due to the impact it can have on your child's self-esteem. Be on the look out for calm, kind behaviours, any conflict resolution blossoming and sharing occurring while they are playing, and mention it. Connect with your toddler over the good stuff to build positive associations with positive behaviours.

> **Nanny Amies' Top Tip:** The phrase "Use your kind hands!" has become quite popular. While to my adult brain it makes perfect sense and sounds very reasonable, unless you have consistently taught your toddler what "kind hands" are, they won't get it. "Hitting hurts" is more effective.

I've learned much of this from experience ... I've let play dates run too long and regretted it all the way to bedtime. I've given toddlers cupcakes and apple juice to then have to deal with the downer that follows. It's simply not worth it!

"They won't play with me!"

Hearing this can break a parent's heart. It's easy to assume that children can make friends wherever they go, mixing with new faces, confidently mingling without any worries for what others may think; yet this isn't always the case.

A child's temperament, language skills and previous experiences of socialization will impact their approach toward peers and, in turn, how their peers react to them. Before I understood child behaviour, I thought that most children could attend a play park, chat to other like-minded toddlers and have fun. But making friends isn't that easy.

Nanny Amies' Top Tip: Imagine walking into a bar by yourself, full of adults a similar age to you, and the landlord says, "Go and talk to people! Just go over there and start talking!" Unless you've already had a bottle of wine or are naturally very confident, that thought would be quite worrisome. Now imagine your child at nursery or the park hearing "Just go and play with the other children". It's much easier said than done.

One child I looked after was happy to approach children they'd never met and share their ideas for play. However, they were not yet able to accept the times when those children didn't want to play exactly how they did.

The headstrong child wanted play to occur in a specific manner, and they would become incredibly frustrated if others didn't want to join in. They saw it as the other children choosing not to play with them and would cry, "They won't play with me!"

Typically, it would result in crying and them refusing to partake in any independent play, so we'd have to head home. On bad days, it would result in them lashing out, pushing others or screaming at them. I would apologize profusely to the other children and their parents before heading home.

I found this behaviour to impact my mood on outings too. I'd feel sad that the child couldn't relinquish their blinkered play style. We'd spend ages talking about how other children didn't always want to do what the child wanted to do, and no matter how many examples I offered, it made no difference.

Yet, the more I got to know them and the more time I spent with them, I realized that it wasn't just play with others that they struggled with. They had a lack of tolerance for change or things not going exactly how they had envisioned.

I felt that it was my role to offer up another perspective and help them to develop the skills necessary to form friendships and bonds with peers. While shying away from playgroups made life easier in that moment, it didn't allow my charge the chance to practise how to cope with those feelings. So, how did we get past this?

> **Nanny Amies' Top Tip:** Teaching young children "scripts" for different scenarios can give them something to fall back on when meeting new people. For example, "Hello, my name is Sam. What's your name?" or "I like to play hide and seek; would you like to play?"

Signs of neurodiversity

Before we go any further, I'd like to list a few things that can help us to determine if the behaviour a child displays is neurotypical or if they have some neurodiversity that requires extra support and strategies.

Sociologist Judy Singer coined the term neurodiversity in 1997 in a bid to describe the various ways in which people think and behave. Neurodiversity can bring wonderful character traits to life, as well as some challenging ones, so thinking of it from Singer's perspective is refreshing and wise.

Neurodiverse children may have autism, ADHD (attention deficit hyperactive disorder) or a number of physical or developmental disorders and/or disabilities. Physical symptoms are easier to spot and diagnose, while children on the autistic spectrum, for example, can fall under the radar. The following symptoms are taken into consideration by professionals when considering the root cause of a child's behaviours.

- **Social skills:** Neurodiverse children may miss or reject social cues such as smiling, eye contact or affection. They might need more time to adjust to certain social settings and require support in the use of emotional vocabulary.

- **Speech and language:** Neurodiverse children may experience speech delay, pronunciation difficulties, a lack of understanding of the spoken word or trouble fully expressing themselves.
- **Literal thinking:** Neurodiverse children may display a lack of humour and imagination and have more "rigid" thinking.
- **Learning challenges:** Neurodiverse children may struggle meeting milestones such as potty training and sleeping through the night. They might also struggle within some childcare settings and activities due to difficulty staying focused and following instructions.
- **Adaptability:** Neurodiverse children often need routines and activities to pan out exactly as planned. They might struggle with change and the unexpected.
- **Stimming:** Many neurodiverse children display repetitive behaviours such as rocking, clapping, arm flapping, pacing or humming. This can help them to block out sensory input and feel calmer.
- **Sensory overload:** Neurodiverse children may become over-stimulated by noise, crowds, lights, smells and extreme temperatures. Their brain can struggle to process large amounts of environmental stimuli, leading to an overload and breakdown of behaviour.
- **Dysregulation:** Neurodiverse children can have meltdowns while overwhelmed or over-stimulated. A meltdown is not the same as a typical tantrum, and they can cause major disruption and stress within the family home.
- **Hyper-focus:** Neurodiverse children can become fixated on certain items, toys or activities. They can take comfort and enjoyment in the repetition of engagement with their chosen focus.
- **Consistency:** Neurodiverse children often behave in similar ways irrespective of where they are or who they are with. For example, if a child becomes overwhelmed with a lot of noise at home, they will also struggle with a lot of noise at school. While they can learn to "mask"

some behaviours with age, there will be a consistency in how they approach daily life.

If your child displays some of these symptoms, it does not automatically mean they are neurodiverse, particularly while they are in the midst of their toddler years. Developmentally appropriate behaviours must be considered, so if your two-year-old child cannot offer an accurate description of how they are feeling, for example, please do not self-diagnose them with autism. If you have any concerns, speak with your doctor, health visitor and/or your child's nursery.

We are seeing more understanding of neurodiversity, which helps families of neurodiverse children to flourish. However, we still have the eye rolls from uneducated onlookers to contend with when families are struggling with certain aspects of neurodiversity outside of the home, so the next time you witness a child stimming or melting down, offer the parents and child a warm smile and give them space. Families with young children, in any circumstance, can run into trouble, both in and out of the home. Speaking from experience, having an audience or feeling judged makes it twice as hard as it needs to be.

Siblings

I once cared for two siblings, aged two and four years old, who fought so much that I decided that if I were to ever have my own children, I only wanted one! If I were to make it out of that job with any sanity at all, I had to help them develop a sibling bond stronger than the rivalry, but my goodness was it deeply ingrained.

Sibling rivalry is something that most families will experience on some level. Which level exactly will depend on your children's temperament, birth order, routines and how the adults in their environment react toward them.

Siblings are essentially individual children with their own developmental journey. We often expect siblings to play together, eat together, maybe share a room, possibly even a bathtub and certainly their toys, so this will inevitably end in chaos from time to time!

Add in that children are constantly vying for their parents' affection and attention, so this alone can be the catalyst to outbursts between siblings. In turn, how parents or the adults in the home respond to the rivalry can either help children to build bonds and form friendships or become arch enemies and never truly enjoy one another's company.

Back to my two charges. We waved Mum and Dad off for the day and before their car had left the driveway it began:

Four-year-old: "Hey! I want that toy!"
Two-year-old: "No, mine!"
Four-year-old: "Give me it, now!"
Two-year-old: "Nooo!"

The four-year-old child, enraged, picked up the TV remote and, before I could get to them, threw it at their sibling's head. As the two-year-old child screamed and clutched their forehead, I saw blood appear through their fingers. Exactly 30 seconds into my shift and we had need for first aid intervention. Enough was enough.

I tasked the eldest child with getting me a clean towel and ensured that they saw the outcome of their actions. As I held the towel on the wound, I described my actions, "I'm holding this here to stop the bleeding".

The older sibling was obviously worried and, in all honesty, so was I. The animosity between the siblings was growing, and if blood could be shed while I was in the same room, what might happen while I was preparing lunch or popping to the bathroom?

I had to put a plan in place for all the adults in the house to try to follow, which would hopefully help the siblings to accept one another. Our first step was to set some house rules around what we'd allow and what we wouldn't.

It's common when I ask parents, "What boundaries do you have in place at home?" for them to answer, "I'm not sure we have any". So, getting an idea in your mind of the behaviour you want to promote and the behaviours you won't tolerate is the first step. For example, you could use this list (or tweak it to suit your house rules):

AMIES' HOUSE RULES

In this house, we are kind.

In this house, we do not hit.

In this house, we listen to each other.

In this house, we do not shout.

In this house, we do not throw.

In this house, we work as a team.

House rules include the adult's behaviour too! As a parent or carer, it's vital that we are kind, we don't shout and we all model the types of behaviour we hope to see from children.

Part of this is resisting the urge to compare siblings. In this family, it was more common for the eldest sibling to be the instigator of scuffles, which resulted in a lot of, "Why can't you be more like your brother?" critiques.

Ultimately, a child of four years can't be anything other than themselves. By comparing them to another child, you only set them up for further resentment. At no point will a young child sit back and think, "Hmmm, yes, I should behave more like my annoying sibling!" Critical comparisons can also have a negative impact on a child's self-esteem. Low self-esteem will not help your child display more positive behaviours; in fact, it will hinder it.

Spending quality time with them both at the same time, modelling friendliness and sharing, was a game-changer in comparison to barrelling into their space at the first sign of conflict. Visualize that for a moment: children being largely left to their own devices until a frustrated adult gets involved in a time of crisis. Instead, imagine a calm adult sitting for a few minutes here and there "playing nicely" and offering descriptive praise and self-esteem boosting language too.

I like to consider behaviour as a cycle – the more we see or do something, the more likely a behaviour will become a habit. It's not until we really take responsibility for how a child behaves that we begin to see what an impact we can have.

Reactive behaviour

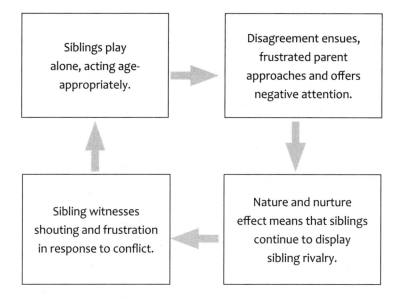

Siblings play alone, acting age-appropriately.

Disagreement ensues, frustrated parent approaches and offers negative attention.

Sibling witnesses shouting and frustration in response to conflict.

Nature and nurture effect means that siblings continue to display sibling rivalry.

Proactive behaviour

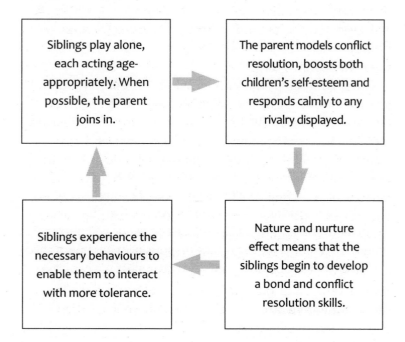

Siblings play alone, each acting age-appropriately. When possible, the parent joins in.

The parent models conflict resolution, boosts both children's self-esteem and responds calmly to any rivalry displayed.

Siblings experience the necessary behaviours to enable them to interact with more tolerance.

Nature and nurture effect means that the siblings begin to develop a bond and conflict resolution skills.

Building bonds

To make true progress on the sibling rivalry front, we must initiate ways in which we almost "manufacture" a mutual goal or shared happiness. The irony is that the things I'm about to suggest will likely be things you've instinctively avoided if you do have siblings who are at each other's throats.

Baking: Yes, it's messy. Yes, it requires planning and taking over the whole kitchen. However, baking is a wonderful activity to promote turn-taking, teamwork and the shared happiness of getting to eat your baked goods together.

Place a child either side of you with the bowl in front of you, offering it to each child when the time is right. Stay calm, remain in control, use clear simple language and let them know, "We can all bake together with our kind voices. If we become unkind, I'll finish up".

If behaviours do start to get fractured, try redirecting them with suggestions of jobs, problem-solving sentences and even a quick break before trying again. For example: "Tim, you'd like to do the mixing now ... Sarah, I'll count to five then it's Tim's turn."

Collections: Collecting particular items can be a wonderful activity for any child, but when we add shared collections between multiple children, we offer up opportunities for pleasant conversations, acts of kindness and that all-important mutual goal. For example, provide a box that lives in the garden and suggest that each time you go on a family walk or outing you'll collect some of nature's treasure. Suggest that when you have all collected enough, you'll build a bug hotel in the garden and see which insects move in!

The choice of collected items can be anything. The suggestion above appeals to my love of the outdoors, so choose something that you can also get excited by. If you can get involved and model teamwork, your children will find it easier to follow suit.

Making posters: Offer a large piece of card and a pack of pens, a few stickers and anything else that may inspire some creativity. Ask your children to create a poster for Mummy, Daddy or another family member that will mean they have to share the items available to them.

Remain close; perhaps you could even take a little corner of the card, modelling a kind act such as drawing a heart while saying, "Wow, Granny will *love* this!" Children love to gift family or friends, so this is a lovely way to promote that bond.

Make a memory box: Wrap a shoe box in paper and decorate it with stick-on gems and glitter to create a magical memory box. Over time, fill it with lovely memories, photos, ticket stubs and keepsakes that you can all look at from time to time.

For extra sibling brownie points, individually ask your children what they love about each other, write it on a sticky note, date it and add it to the box! Reading these things over the upcoming months and years will melt the heart of any frustrated or detached sibling.

There are so many options to try, these ideas are just to get the cogs turning! Remember that the more you do these types of things, the more chances your children have to build bonds. However, in the same breath, we do not need to come up with elaborate plans every day! Simply being aware of how you can positively impact this behaviour is helpful.

Watch your language: Irrespective of what you are doing, where you are and who you are with, your words count! Avoid labelling your children's behaviour toward one another where possible, particularly when in conversation with other adults within earshot of your warring offspring. Even though you'll feel they don't listen to a word you say, they do take on board all you say, so phrases such as, "All they do is fight! They never get on!" simply highlight your expectation of them.

If you don't believe your children can get on, neither will they! Therefore, sentences such as, "We tried baking together last week; the cupcakes were delicious!", irrespective of if it ended up in fighting, are much more effective. Vent by all means – you absolutely need to get feelings of anger and frustration off your chest – but wait until they are in bed or out of hearing range first!

Nanny Amies' Top Tip: Avoid boosting your child's ego. Creating an environment that boosts self-esteem is vital, but phrases such as "You are the best!", "You are the prettiest" or "You are the fastest" will result in a child comparing themselves to others as opposed to feeling equal to others. Name me one person with an overinflated ego who you enjoy spending time with ...

Helping children to share

When it comes to the most common catalyst of fighting – sharing – there are some practical suggestions I'd like to leave you with. Please bear in mind that developmentally, children under four will struggle to share naturally.

It's natural for adults to force children to share, as opposed to helping them figure out *why* sharing is a nice thing to do. Here are my tips to encourage harmonious play. I have seen over the past two decades that children who receive this level of support (generally speaking) can manage their social skills with a little more ease than those who don't.

1 **Don't rush in:** If there's no sign of violence, allow children the chance to figure out a disagreement between them. If violent acts are commonplace, this may take a little time to become an option for you. However, if children are displaying low-level rivalry, leave them to it.
2 **Do not take sides:** On the occasions where you have to intervene, if you side with one child over the other, you can unintentionally reinforce sibling rivalry.
3 **Use clear, simple language:** For example, "Aisha has the toy for now, you can have a turn when he's finished".
4 **The three Rs – routine, rest and rules:** Stick to your guns when possible and your child will be less likely to become overtired and more likely to develop tolerance of others.
5 **Model sharing techniques during play:** For example, you could say, "Please can I have a turn?"
6 **Model patience if they decline!**
7 **Offer a time limit or schedule:** If a child is purposely taking their time or "hogging" a toy, give them a countdown to let them know their time is drawing to a close. For example, "When the sand runs out, it's Olivia's turn", or "Alexa, set an alarm for five minutes … then it's Olivia's turn to have the doll".

8 **Ask open questions:** During conflict, ask open questions to give the children room to problem-solve. For example, "There's one car, but two children, how can we fix this?"

9 **Validate the child's feelings toward the specific toy:** For example, "I can see you're having fun with that toy. Your brother would like a turn too when you are done".

10 **Avoid immediately giving a child a toy if they try to take it from you:** Explain simply that you are not finished yet. Allow your child to feel frustrated with this during a supportive moment and to witness how you can maintain ownership of something respectfully.

11 **Teach your child how to ask politely for toys:** Model, as above, that other children won't always share.

12 **Limit siblings playing with favourite toys in front of each other:** If your child has a favourite toy, encourage them to play at the table out of reach of a younger sibling. Taking a prized possession to a playgroup or a soft play area where there are other children is setting your child up to become upset or frustrated.

13 **Talk about kindness:** Model treating others how we would like to be treated ourselves outside of the times they are being unkind themselves. For example, read books about kindness together.

14 **Children do not always have to share:** When children are engaged in play and have created a plan around a certain toy or resource, it's a big ask to have them stop because another child likes the look of something they had first. Yes, sharing is a kind thing to do, but balance is needed too. We don't want our children to be a pushover and relinquish their own preferences to simply suit other people's wishes.

Let's say that you are sat on the sofa, all snuggled up, excited to flick to the next chapter of this book and someone suddenly said, "Hey! I want to read that!". Would you relinquish it? I hope you are enjoying it too much to give it up that easily!

CHAPTER 7
SCREEN TIME

The good, the bad and the ugly

In the world of child development, the topic of screen time is controversial. However, in many family homes, screens provide a lifeline for parents being pulled in what can feel like a thousand directions. So, before we go a word further, please rest assured that this chapter is written free of judgement and with a true understanding of how difficult it is to juggle childcare, work, life, housework and all that lies in between.

In fact, because I know this topic carries a lot of guilt for parents, I will let you know from the get-go that I use screens while caring for children. But (you knew it was coming) ... I use screens wisely, in a way that works with me and not against me. Because, if you can believe it, some screen usage will make your job as a parent even harder than it already is!

Whether it be the TV, a tablet, a gaming console or your phone, children can be "easier" to manage when they are engaged with a screen. Yet, if screens are overused, they will easily become your enemy as opposed to your ally.

Nowadays, technology impacts so many aspects of life that children will benefit from learning how to navigate the internet and touch screen technology. However, no amount of IT skills can mask a lack of foundational, early years development. Toddlers need movement, real-life experiences, objects, fresh air, free play and interaction with the humans within their environment to fully develop.

I ask that you bear this information in mind as you continue through this chapter, and trust me when I say that I'm on your side. Like a best friend who'd tell you that you have spinach in your teeth, I will always tell you the truth, and that truth will come with helpful tips and words of encouragement too.

> **Nanny Amies' Top Tip:** If your toddler is currently having a lot of screen time, hold off making any changes until you've finished this chapter and created a plan. Your child might not want to relinquish any time spent with a screen, so the more confident you are, the easier it will be for the whole family.

There's such a contradiction between our ever-growing dependency on technology and the fact that we are still living creatures reacting to the world via our senses and instincts. As the title of this chapter suggests, I am going to go into the pros and cons of screen usage because it's not all bad. For now, I just hope to get the cogs turning on why it's important to consider:

1 how much screen time your toddler has
2 what type of content they are consuming

Commonly, in homes where parents don't have back-up or childcare, screens become the babysitter until the default parent is able to take over. In this case, it's even more important that screens are used sensibly to ensure that behaviours away from screen usage aren't being made worse. Also, a huge benefit to considering the time and content viewed is that you get to a point where you can use screens or turn on the TV guilt-free when you choose to do so.

> **Nanny Amies' Top Tip:** When it comes to what, and particularly who, your child is watching, ask yourself if you would be happy to have that character in your home. If they are disrespectful, speak unkindly or are constantly hyperactive, for example, are they really the best role model for your child?

What do developing brains need?

You may wonder what brain development has to do with screen usage. I imagine that many people (like I once did) will reach for the TV remote to help keep their little one busy. But, here's the thing: if screen usage becomes the mainstay of a child's entertainment, they miss out on many developmental opportunities.

Toddler brains need certain things to help them develop efficiently. It's the efficiency of our brain that will impact your toddler's ability to focus, socialize, manage emotional responses and ultimately achieve all the things that enable them to become happy and well-rounded individuals. Here are some examples.

Movement: Toddlers can make sense of their environment via the brain stem with movement. Also, it helps toddlers become healthy and capable, which results in the brain stem releasing fewer stress hormones. With fewer stress hormones, other areas of brain development can be prioritized. If the brain stem detects danger (this can be experienced on screens, with raised voices or severe sibling rivalry, etc.), a toddler's stress response will be prioritized. When the brain prioritizes a stress response, a toddler can become more reactive to frustration, anger and stress. Therefore, receiving a wealth of sensory information while being planted on the sofa can be over-stimulating to a developing brain.

Interaction: Toddler brains require conversation, eye contact and one-to-one interaction with adults and children, especially those who model appropriate behaviours and skills. If screen time overtakes actual real-life interaction, this can impact a toddler's communication skills and their ability to fully engage with others. I appreciate that for some children eye contact can be over-stimulating. However, experiencing genuine human interaction at a level that suits individual needs is still a necessity.

Experiences: Our brains need multiple opportunities and experiences to form a wide range of skills, connections, understanding and awareness. This is why human babies stay with their parents longer than any other animals do; our brains need time to create the connections via experiences. If you use screens to avoid your toddler having to deal with negative emotions, such as boredom, the toddler misses out on an opportunity to learn how to cope.

In a nutshell, experiencing life as human brains have evolved to, especially throughout the early years, is essential to a child's emotional and physical health. Climbing, doing, failing, waiting and experimenting are more beneficial to brain development than any electronic device could ever be.

Online play: Giving your toddler the chance to play in a wide variety of ways is so important. Interactive, hands-on play helps to form new connections in the brain as toddlers move and explore. This stimulates the brain, and the amount of effective brain stimulation offered early on will determine how many connections are formed and cemented. There are plenty of games available online claiming educational content suitable for toddlers. And yes, they can help your child to recognize numbers, letters and colours. Despite this, your toddler will benefit further from learning these things via first-hand experiences with three-dimensional objects and interaction from those around them.

The good

With all of this in mind, does screen time have any redeeming features that can help us to use it without worrying about negative impacts? Absolutely! I am not anti-screens, and I know from first-hand experience that they can offer benefits within family homes when used with purpose. Some of the benefits include the following.

- Screen time can provide parents and carers with a short break, resulting in little bit of breathing space to have that well-earned cuppa or focus on an essential task.
- Bouts of breathing space can help parents be more present when they come back into the child's space and when the screens have been turned off.
- When appropriate content is viewed, it can provide entertainment and mental stimulation. This is particularly helpful when the weather is really bad or if a parent is feeling ill.
- Screens can be a lovely source of educational content.
- Screens can expose children to scenes, topics, notions and thoughts outside of those within their own daily environment, teaching diversity and an understanding of different ways of life.
- Screens can encourage a highly active child to sit still and be calm for a few moments. This can be particularly helpful during the transition from naps to no naps.
- You can learn from what your toddler enjoys watching, choosing activities or outings to match. For example, introducing toy animals into their play, which they enjoyed watching, leads with a child's interests. This can then help them to engage and focus on things with more longevity than those that do not interest them as much.
- Having access to portable content can be very helpful for long travel times or trips to the doctor, for example.

Screen time and neurodiversity

If you are a parent of a child with extra needs, you will already feel extra pressure in relation to their behaviours, so screens can come with extra stigma. However, there are definite benefits to screen use for your child, which can make screens feel like a need as opposed to an extra. The list is long but a few examples are:

- Some neurodiverse children can struggle to navigate the world around them, and screens and headphones used outside of the home can provide a comfort blanket for both parent and child.
- Screens can help neurodiverse children to communicate and develop language skills.
- Screen content can often grab and hold a neurodiverse child's focus more than traditional learning styles.
- Many games and online learning platforms provide dopamine stimulation. Some neurodiverse children have a lack of dopamine, so this can help to improve wellbeing.

Even with these benefits (and more), it's still important to find the right limits for your neurodiverse child. Overuse of screens still comes with cons for neurodiverse children, so getting the balance right is key. Let's look at that next.

The bad

Honestly, I don't win any friends when I broach this topic, but I feel that offering a balanced view is essential, especially on a topic as widely debated as screen time. So, what are the negatives with screen time for toddlers?

- Toddlers can become expectant on when and where they receive the screen. This can lead to power struggles, outbursts and challenging behaviours. If screens are as normal as having breakfast, imagine telling your child that there's no breakfast today.

- Children can be heavily influenced by content that does not set a good role model. For example, some creators may be rude, have bad manners or show dangerous behaviours. If a child watches a lot of that creator, they can mimic their actions and behaviours.
- Screens are designed to grab and hold a child's attention, which can mean that tasks, chores and personal care routines outside of the screen can seem boring.
- For a lot of screen time, toddlers are sitting still, which can lead to a sedentary lifestyle that impacts their overall physical and mental health.
- Handheld devices can be easily overused, for example, in pushchairs or everyday outings, which severely limits a child's interaction with the world around them.

The ugly

Research is ongoing into the negative impacts of screen time, but researchers are telling us that there are some potentially serious side effects of a lot of screen time. After reading this section, you may wonder how, as a professional child carer, I use screens at all while caring for children. Simply put, the ugly, serious stuff listed below doesn't have to be a side effect of screen usage. If we are aware, we can avoid the things on the following list from occurring.

- If used close to bedtime or upon waking, screen time can impact a toddler's body clock and melatonin levels (the sleepy hormone that aids good-quality sleep). A lack of sleep can impact behaviour, development and wellbeing.
- Some content can make real-life risk assessments more challenging. For example, a character falls off a tall building

in one scene and is unharmed, and this might encourage your toddler to jump off a tall structure.

- The overuse of screens can increase the risk of depression, anxiety and other mood disorders due to the contrasts between real life and digital life.
- Some content can desensitize children toward violence or inappropriate behaviours. As children grow, they may then make decisions that are either dangerous or damaging to their reputation.
- It's incredibly easy for young children to become addicted to screens, which makes life when they aren't watching a screen very difficult.
- If children watch enough of a certain character or online personality, their thoughts can be influenced or limited by that person.
- A child's accent can change. A sure sign that they are hearing another voice more than their parents'.
- Screen time can increase cortisol (stress hormone) levels due to the sheer amount of information the toddler's brain must process, including lights, noise, voices, screen changes and movement.
- A lot of modern content is now fast-paced to hold a toddler's attention. Content that has scene changes every few seconds requires the brain to repeatedly refocus attention. This can dull the appeal of toys and day-to-day experiences that do not offer the same level of change. When a child views a large amount of fast-paced content, the development of their attention span can be impacted.
- If children watch streaming channels, there is a never-ending supply of content available to them. Without a definitive cut-off or end to the programming, this inevitably increases their viewing time.
- Looking at screen glare, blue light from screens and flat screens instead of three-dimensional objects can have a negative impact on eyesight development.

- As children watch content on a screen, dopamine (a feel-good hormone) is released. Children can feel very frustrated or sad when the screen is then turned off.

> **Nanny Amies' Top Tip:** Consider using a DVD that has a set amount of content, meaning that when it's finished, it's finished. That way, there isn't an endless supply of content available.

Is your toddler addicted?

Screen addiction is a real occurrence in an increasing amount of family homes. This can lead to family discord and stress. Even very young children can experience screen addiction.

HOW TO SPOT SCREEN ADDICTION

Have you observed any of these behaviours in your child?

- Irritability when not using a screen.
- Anxiety or anger when asked to stop using a screen.
- Anxiety or anger when told they can't use a screen.
- Hiding their screen usage.
- Needing more and more screen time as the days and weeks pass.
- Only happy or calm when using a screen.

Children's content, whether on TV or online, is designed to become a firm part of family homes. Companies mass-produce merchandise, games and clothing, all in your child's favourite TV characters, adding to the pull of screen-related content. This means that it's easy to see how more and more youngsters are showing symptoms from the list above. While the thought of screen addiction may worry you, I must assure you that it is possible to positively impact a child's relationship with screens. Leading with the old cliché, the first step to recovery is admitting that they have an addiction.

Accepting that screen addiction is not a child's responsibility is also an important step. While your child may be the one asking for their tablet or your phone and displaying challenging behaviours if they don't receive it, it's parental boundaries, routines and actions that will help them create new habits.

> **Nanny Amies' Top Tip:** Do not try to convince your toddler that the TV or their tablet isn't fun. We know that it is! Validate their desire for screen time, while holding a boundary. For example, you could say, "The TV is your favourite; we'll go to the park before we watch anymore".

Goodnight tablet

When I began offering overnight care, I unknowingly opened myself up to a world of exhaustion, harder days and some very long nights! There's "tired" and, as every parent knows, there's, "I've been up all night and then had to care for them all day" tired.

In one home, the toddler was at the helm of the family ship, steering the adults in whichever direction they wanted. For the record, this is a lovely thing for strong-willed toddlers to do while at the park, playing with their toys or at the zoo, for example. However, when it comes to decisions about meals, bathing, teeth brushing, bedtime and other important aspects of daily life, I can't get behind toddlers being in full control. They do need us adults to help them with their daily care routine.

This youngster simply didn't want to embark on the mundane aspects of life, which led to lots of pushback from morning until night. By the time bedtime came around, their parents were tired and worn down.

This had led to giving their two-year-old child a tablet at bedtime, as it meant the toddler would lay quietly and contentedly with the device, while their parents could rest up in preparation for the battles to come the following day.

While the little one did lay in their bedroom and seemed to settle with their tablet, it did not mean we were in for a peaceful evening. Come midnight, the toddler would scream and seem genuinely distraught, which resulted in parents (or me) rushing in, the lights going on, food being offered, more screen time and general chaos, if truth be told. Despite the toddler being given everything they wanted, they were clearly not happy.

Nanny Amies' Top Tip: To finish screen time while hopefully avoiding any tantrums, first get down to your toddler's level. Then comment on their programme or game and engage with them. Use matter-of-fact language to let them know what will happen next. For example, "After this show finishes, we'll turn this off". If the toddler becomes upset, offer them a choice: "Do you want to turn it off, or shall I?" then follow through, irrespective of their upset. They will learn to adjust with practice.

The impact of screens at bedtime

There were many factors leading to our tired and fed-up family being awake at midnight. Let's look at the impact of the screen first. Consider how we react to light, noise and activity – even as adults we perceive them as a cue to wake and do something. So, screens are very confusing for us at times of sleep, and this is especially true for toddlers whose brains are still developing. While our bodies may be tired at bedtime, our brains are stimulated by the content. So, the toddler's brain wasn't fully relaxed when they fell asleep. Offering them a tablet when they woke up was just adding more stimulation to the mix.

We can also add in that the tired toddler most likely had raised cortisol levels due to the lack of routine. They had overstretched wake windows (see page 142), which resulted in their body fighting sleep.

> **Nanny Amies' Top Tip:** Create a box that contains engaging toys and digital devices and keep this box out of eyesight until your child demands screen time. If devices are permanently left in plain sight, toddlers will struggle to detach from them.

How much is too much screen time?

Personally, I don't think there is an exact science to answer this question. While there are recommended figures out there for you to find should you want to go look, I feel that the amount of screen time each household offers will depend on parenting styles, work commitments and just life! Nonetheless, in the same breath, I do believe there is such a thing as too much screen time. So, I'll list some points here to help explain how I prevent screens being overused.

- **Create natural screen breaks:** I put some boundaries in place that will create natural screen breaks for my toddlers. For example, no screens at mealtimes and no screens in the bedrooms and the bathroom.
- **Turn off the TV:** Many parents like to have the TV on all day as background noise. This is understandable as being

with young children all day can feel lonely. Unfortunately, it can have a negative impact on attention spans, as children tend to flit between play and watching. Instead, I use music, story books and podcasts as they ease the silence but offer only audio information.

- **Set a routine:** I integrate screen time into a predictable part of the daily routine. Typically, this is twice a day, for example, pre-lunch and pre-dinner, and this way meals signal the end of screen usage.
- **Plan:** Make a plan before the screen is turned on. I set a clear boundary and expectation on how many episodes a toddler can watch or the amount of time they get.
- **Use "now and next" phrases:** Help your toddler to understand what they need to do before they can access a device or screen, by using "Now and Next" phrases. For example, "Now we'll do a puzzle; next we watch TV".
- **Toy rotation:** Consider packing up, putting away and swapping toys around to help keep the novelty of certain items going. This can lead to longer play times and less demand from the toddler for screen entertainment.
- **Free time box:** Create a box that contains engaging toys that are kept out of reach until your child demands screen time. This may contain stickers, sensory dough, favourite books or game, a construction kit ... anything that will interest your child when they ask for screen time. The idea is that this box is extra-special. For example:

Child: "I'm bored! I want the TV!"
Parent: "The TV isn't available; you can have your free time box or choose something else."
Child: "I don't want my free time box or something else! I want the TV!"
Parent: "I can see you'd like the TV; I'll let you know when it's TV time."

- **Screen-free days:** Perhaps not for the faint-hearted, but consider having screen-free days. The easiest way to do this is to spend as much time outdoors as possible on this day. But don't be afraid to own a "There's no TV today" boundary.
- **You:** Use screens to your advantage, such as while you are preparing a meal, as opposed to whenever your child requests it.
- **Consistency:** Stick at it. If Tuesday's rules are different to Wednesday's, your child will not be able to remember or stick to screen time rules or routines. Keep it simple and consistent for them.

Nanny Amies' Top Tip: Dedicate a corner of a room as a screen-free zone. This may have cushions, a den/tent, a poster or anything that creates a new environment with books and toys in it. In the same way that we immediately pick up the remote when we sit on the sofa, children benefit from having a new association to a "zone" that doesn't carry an association to the TV or tablet.

Screen time for survival

While caring for multiple children within a family home, aged three, six and ten, my thoughts and approaches toward screen time were well and truly pushed to the limit. They each had different preferences and interests, and when it came to the school holidays ... well, I did not come up for air! So, screen time felt like a necessary tool some days. Energy had never been a more cherished commodity, one that dwindled rapidly with each passing hour. However, I set some rules, irrespective of the complaints from my young charges. Monday to Friday we had to partake in the following before a screen was so much as mentioned.

- Brush teeth
- Wash face
- Get dressed
- Have breakfast
- Free play and/or reading

Please don't think this stopped them from asking me from time to time. If a child didn't push back against their boundaries, I'd be worried. But it mostly worked. After some free play, we'd head out for fresh air or an activity of some kind, again showing them what our priorities were before returning home for lunch. This is when I would happily offer screen time, safe in the knowledge that they had moved, experienced at least a smidgen of what nature has to offer, acted out independent thoughts and conversed with humans.

Once lunch was ready, the screens went off. They weren't always happy about that, and sometimes I had to offer countdowns. Occasionally, I had to confiscate the TV remote. But our morning routine remained, irrespective of moods and reactions. We then mirrored something similar in the afternoon. This totalled two predictable slots of screen time each day that worked with me, not against me.

One weekend, we watched a movie together, which was a rare treat as I usually used their screen time to get my jobs done. As the movie ended, right before I announced that screen time was about to end, the middle child said, "Right ... that's enough TV for me; time for a puzzle". I was flabbergasted. They had recognized their need to move away from the screen.

Nanny Amies' Top Tip: If reducing screen time is your goal, consider how you also approach tantrums or the pushing of boundaries. While the screen is a catalyst, your toddler's behaviour always requires a confident and calm response.

"But ... without screens I can't get anything done."

One of the most common reasons for screens being used so much is for that guaranteed peace it affords parents. Toddlers can't manage much independent play at a young age, but this can improve over time. However, if toddlers view a lot of low-quality content that impedes the development of their attention span, independent play will take longer to achieve.

If children were able to calmly play and entertain themselves for long periods of time, I believe there would be fewer screen addictions. At the risk of sounding like my beloved Nanna, "What do you think parents did back in my day?" Not that long ago, screen usage was only accessed via the TV. Is it the birth of handheld screens that has resulted in independent play becoming a dying art?

> **Nanny Amies' Top Tip:** If you do want your toddler to have screen time, the TV is a better option than handheld devices. TVs are fixed in one spot and less immersive so children stand a better chance of detaching from the TV than they do from a personal device.

The art of independent play

To help encourage your toddler away from screens, let's look at how we can foster independent play. The journey toward independent play depends upon your toddler's personality, the environment and how you interact with them.

Temperament trait: If your child is high in distractibility and sensitivity (see page 265), they may need a little more support with independent play than a child who is low in these traits.

Age: A child under two will find it very difficult to achieve independent play for more than a few minutes. But this skill will increase as their attention span grows.

> **Nanny Amies' Top Tip:** If you notice your child cast aside a toy after only a few moments, offer them a "play extension" prompt, which will increase their interest in it. For example, "Oh wow, that blue car is so fast ... is the green one faster?" or "You took such good care of dolly, maybe she's hungry again?" This helps to increase their attention span.

Keep them close: Most children will want to be close to you (it's their basic survival instincts), so have them play near you. Avoid phrases such as "Just go and play!" or "Go away!" If I'm cooking, I will bring a few toys to the kitchen for them to play with. Does it take twice as long for me to cook a meal? Yes. But does the toddler learn to play well on their own after a few months of this? Generally speaking, yes.

Environmental factors: The environmental factors have a huge impact on how a child explores and extends their own play. So, with a few important considerations, we can create areas that encourage play as opposed to stunt it. This isn't about having a huge house – my house is tiny. We are not aiming for insta perfect here! Here's what you can do:

1 Create an area that is safe and free from ornaments that are at risk of being damaged. Phrases such as "Don't touch that!" and "Get off that!" will be frustrating for you to repeat and frustrating for your little one to hear.

2 Ensure the toys available are not too advanced for the toddler's age, overly complicated or hard to manipulate. This will lead to frustration and ultimately frustration stunts play.

3 Offer "open-ended" toys that can become anything your little one imagines them to be. Open-ended toys can look dull to adults as they don't do much, but that's the whole point. Items such as wooden blocks, figures, dolls, food, jugs and animals allow a child to base an idea from the ground up and let it evolve, depending on mood and thought process. Offer toys that flash, sing and move of their own accord sparingly. While these toys have their place, they can replace your child's imagination and ability to focus on less entertaining things. Without imagination, determination and focus, they'll struggle to entertain themselves for long.

4 Start the toddler off with a play scene or theme to inspire their imagination. For example, build a tunnel from blocks and place a car inside. Or offer a picture book alongside similar toys to the characters or storyline and display them together to encourage exploration that way.

Create new habits: Our daily routines and habits will impact a child's ability to focus, wait and occupy their own mind. For example, being outdoors in a pushchair with nothing to look at but the trees, birds, cars and passers-by is a wonderful way for a little one to be content without some form of manipulated stimulation. If they are given a device to hold for every pram ride, car trip and meal out, they will expect that each time and not learn how to occupy their own thoughts. I know it's challenging to get shopping done or eat a meal in peace without the aid of a device, but for what you gain in compliance, you lose in terms of your child's patience and tolerance toward everyday tasks.

Parenting style: I'm sure it will be of no surprise that your role in your child's play is crucial in their early years. While the whole reason you want, or even need, them to play independently is to enable you to get things done, initially you have to take time to teach and support your child to do that.

Sitting on the floor with them for a few minutes before you start your task can boost your bond, leaving them feeling content and more likely to play alone. "High-quality attention" like this increases a toddler's confidence, self-belief, happiness and contentedness. Without these things, independent play is very difficult!

Consider your language carefully. Phrases such as, "Why can't you just play with your toys!" are ineffective compared to, "This toy is so interesting, it can ..." I get it – this takes time and energy that you may not have, and for that I'm sorry. But effort now will bring more independent play later.

PRACTISE TOGETHER

Independent play does not happen overnight. It's the same as anything – the more practice and opportunities a toddler has to build this skill, the more likely they are to crack it. Here are some of my top tips:

1   Choose a quiet five-minute slot in the day where you can focus on play.
2   Sit on the floor beside your toddler to start them off.
3   Once they are engaged in the toys, slowly increase the physical distance between you. For example, look interested in something else, but come back to them if they seem to be losing interest.
4   Gradually build up the space and time. For example, "I'm just popping for a glass of water; I'll be right back".
5   Be honest and trustworthy! Go get your water and return just as you said you would.
6   If your child gets upset and you return instantly, they learn that they aren't safe unless you are there. So, be close by, as needed, while they learn this new skill.

7   Once you get to the point where you can be busy with a separate task and your little one approaches you, smile at them! Say hello and give them a hug. They will be more likely to return to their independent play.

8   Practise every day!

Choose what they watch wisely

While your child is building their independent play skills, the chances are screens will still be used, so let's ensure that the content they view is of a quality where you can achieve that guilt-free click of the remote. Just because a programme claims to be educational, doesn't mean it actually is, sadly. The easiest way to find out is to watch with them.

- Ensure the characters are kind, friendly and respectful, including their tone of voice, words, attitude, facial expressions and behaviour.
- Diversity is a wonderful thing, but if they are watching a lot of content that originates from another country, try to ensure the language used translates to their first language or any second language they may be learning. I recently witnessed a toddler, whose language was emerging, watch content where the main character said sentences such as, "He had apple snack for". While this is a wonderful attempt at the English language, it isn't the correct way to state that a child had an apple for their snack. Learning how to talk is hard enough, so removing language barriers is advised.
- Ensure the subject matter is appropriate and not scary, violent or of an adult nature.
- Avoid a never-ending stream of content, irrespective of its quality. You can have too much of a good thing.

- Avoid content with fast-paced scene changes.
- If it's a game, choose an app that focuses on exploration and open-ended play. Avoid games that don't accomplish anything meaningful.
- Ensure that the presenters speaks slowly, repeat phrases and pauses, allowing your child time to process the information on offer.

> **Nanny Amies' Top Tip:** Avoid using screens as a reward as this will sensationalize it. Just plan it into your day, as mentioned on page 125.

Enjoying screen time

A great many parents, grandparents and carers use screen time because screens can be a wonderful addition to the home. Watching films and favourite shows together can be lovely, quality time. When screen time does occur, I insist it is just that, and that children sit comfortably, focusing on the screen with purpose, enjoying well-chosen content. I hope that screen time becomes your ally. I genuinely want what's best for your little one, which includes playing the role of the protective bestie.

CHAPTER 8
SLEEP SUCCESS
Bedtime battles

Sleep is one of our most basic human needs at any age! Our bodies and brains need it for good health, wellbeing and overall development. Sleep deprivation is something that many, if not all, parents experience and, sadly, makes caring for children much more difficult. While we all have our own views on children's sleep habits, no one can deny the importance of it. Until you have experienced painful, ruptured sleep night after night, you may never truly cherish sleep the way you do when you have attempted life without your necessary quota.

Positive sleep habits are a gift to prioritize and cultivate. The irony is that the less sleep you get, the less likely you are to sleep (and think straight). So, my aim with this chapter is to help you promote sleep in a way that suits your individual family's needs by explaining a few key aspects of sleep health, and tips that have worked for me.

Nanny Amies' Top Tip: Just as every child is unique, so are their sleep habits. Try not to compare your child's sleep to other children's. You can't ever know what goes on behind closed doors, so focusing on your own household's routines and habits will be more effective than comparisons.

Sleep deprivation was so mind-altering for me that I was forever changed when I began my journey as a live-in nanny. I once naively thought that dinner, bath and a bedtime story were enough to send a little one off to sleep for the whole night. Oh, if I could give my younger self one piece of advice, it would be, "Dinner, bath and a bedtime story alone is *never* enough to create a healthy sleep pattern".

If your current routine consists of just this, and your little one *is* currently sleeping well, it's likely that you are covering other essential aspects of sleep health too. Sleep is complex, impacted by many different factors, and I believe that's why so many families struggle to achieve the restful nights they long for.

Getting sleep right starts during the day

A solid bedtime routine is only a drop in the ocean when we consider all that impacts a child's sleep habits. From the moment they wake to the moment they close their eyes again – it all counts. I do worry that may sound overwhelming, so let me be clear: it's not that you must be on high alert or "Mission Sleep" for 12 out of 24 hours, it's just important to know that what we do during the day will help (or hinder) how well your toddler and you sleep at night.

Humans are mainly diurnal, which means that contrary to many animals who are nocturnal, we are predisposed to be awake, foraging for food and keeping alert to dangers during the day. We then hunker down to sleep and restore energy levels through the night. Our bodies are set up to release hormones that aid us in our diurnal habits – cortisol upon waking and melatonin while asleep.

Sadly, modern life is very different to that of our ancestors, who heavily relied upon their diurnal behaviours. This means that there are now many variables that can interfere with our daily rhythms, confusing the difference between night and day, light and dark, noisy and quiet. As an intelligent species we have continued to push technological boundaries that can, at times, confuse our bodies that night is, in fact, day. Electricity being the main culprit (lights, TV, etc.) and more recently the invention of handheld devices that offer wake cues such as light, noise and movement close to our faces.

With the creation of refrigeration and supermarkets, we also have 24-hour access to food, something that wasn't an option to us (except with breastmilk). Eating is a wakeful behaviour, so eating during the night can confuse our body clock. One of the biggest turning points for me, in my bid to help children sleep better and for longer, was looking back at how our ancestors evolved to achieve sleep and realizing how our most basic instincts still contribute toward our modern-day sleep health.

The 24-hour cycle

Our circadian rhythm – an invisible clock which has a 24-hour cycle – supports our inner functions, such as our digestive system, body temperature, metabolism and sleep patterns. It is very much linked to light and darkness; being exposed to natural light early in the day signals our circadian rhythm to begin the cycle, in the same way that dimmed light signals the body to wind down in preparation for sleep, like the sunset would or the light from a fire in our cave 2,000 years ago.

There are many things that we can do to set our bodies up for sleep success, things that our ancestors would have done. For example, getting up and out in the morning, regardless of whether or not we need to "forage" for food.

Being exposed to natural light is just one aspect of helping our inner clock respond to a 24-hour cycle – we must also move, interact with others and eat. From the perspective of life within the cave, we'd only stay inside all day if we were injured, ill or hiding from predators. However, modern life has created houses so enticing and comfortable that more and more families are opting for time at home as opposed to time spent outdoors. This, alongside modern-day ailments such as social anxiety, the rising costs of family entertainment and the pull of technology, means that the current generation stays home more than any other has done before.

Nanny Amies' Top Tip: A child's circadian rhythms develop gradually – from around two months old they begin to produce the melatonin hormone which supports sleep functions. So, exposing them to light cues during the day can help set the foundation of healthy sleep patterns. It's never too late to start this if you have a toddler.

Just by looking at our natural circadian rhythm, it's easy to see how sleep can be such a challenge for so many modern-day families. However, there are a few other aspects worth your consideration too. Let's take a look.

Rhythmicity level

We all have different levels of "rhythmicity", which will influence not only how much sleep we require, but when we require it. For example, you may require more sleep than your partner, but less sleep than your friend, and the same can be said for children. A child who is highly rhythmic will quickly display signs of irritability and emotional distress if they do not get the right amount of sleep (or food), whereas a child low in rhythmicity may cope relatively well with an hour less sleep than usual. Realizing how rhythmic your individual child is can help you map out your day and, therefore, nurture their nature.

Boundary-pushing

Does your toddler resist going to bed or to sleep? The tricky thing is, if your child is fighting sleep, this doesn't necessarily mean they don't need to go to bed – behaviour has a big impact on how parents administer routines. In my experience, behaviours need handling as a separate issue to sleep. For example, while a tantrum may ensue due to a parent announcing bedtime, the tantrum shouldn't mean that bedtime is put off. We will look at this in more detail soon.

> **Nanny Amies' Top Tip:** If your toddler attends childcare, where possible try to match up their schedule at home to the childcare setting. Anchoring naps and mealtimes is a fantastic way to help their circadian rhythm tick along, undisturbed by inconsistencies.

Sleep pressure

Upon waking, our bodies release cortisol (a hormone which helps us stay alert to our surroundings) to support our need to forage and defend ourselves. With movement and activity, the level of cortisol we experience lowers as time passes, meaning that by bedtime we start to feel less awake and hopefully more tired as our body prepares for sleep. As our cortisol levels drop and that feeling of tiredness has kicked in, it means our "sleep pressure" is at the optimum amount, increasing the chances of us drifting off into a peaceful sleep (if we are in our sleep space at that time). And this, in my experience, is one of the leading causes of sleep disturbances because if we aren't in our sleep space prepped for sleep, our body assumes we are still outside our cave (perhaps we've not found enough food or we are fleeing a predator). As a result, the body delivers a boost of cortisol to keep us going.

We are given that extra cortisol when we are past tired and become overtired.

In a toddler, this leads to hyperactivity, irritability and confused circadian rhythms. It has also led to hundreds of parents telling me, "They are just wired come 9pm, they don't even seem tired!" In busy homes with busy schedules, this is a common occurrence, especially given the fact that this information about cortisol is only discovered when a parent or carer researches sleep health.

Young children are unable to recognize the symptoms of tiredness within themselves. While there will be tell-tale signs such as yawning, rubbing their eyes, pulling at their ears or becoming emotionally frayed, clingy and maybe even lethargic, they will not be able to say, "I am tired". So, it is our job to (try to) stay one step ahead.

"Stay in your bed!"

I challenge anyone to care for a toddler all day (let alone day in, day out) and not want to crawl into their own bed quicker than you can say, "Good night, sweet dreams". On reflection, waving off my little toddler friends as they left a nursery with their parents was a breeze in comparison to nannying and settling my charges into bed after being with them all day. I either shared their bedroom or occupied the neighbouring room, and will never ever forget that feeling of being ripped from a deep sleep by a wailing toddler … who was the very reason that I was in a deep sleep in the first place. So, when I tell you that I get it, I really do.

I soon had the realization that getting the toddler into their bed was only one part of the puzzle; ensuring that they remained in their bed was another! At the end of a busy day, all I wanted was to tuck them in, kiss their foreheads, wish them sweet dreams and walk away, before patting myself on the back for a job well done. Let me tell you about one toddler, where this was far from reality …

With one little charge, bedtime became the busiest, most stressful part of the day. It was while caring for this toddler that I named bedtimes "Bedlam", due to how I'd feel in response to the palaver that ensued. They would hop in and out of bed quicker than a fiddler's elbow and while their energy levels seemed to peak at that time of night, mine were at their lowest.

I couldn't understand it – we didn't stop all day. Fresh air, trips to the park, playing, swimming (they had their own pool and I made it my mission to teach them how to swim, so we did so every day). How could this tiny little person not only have so much energy but also be so persistent with it? I tried rubbing their back, telling them more bedtime stories, later bedtimes, more swimming, more fresh air, you name it ... bedlam was seemingly my destiny each and every night. And while bedtimes continued to be the bane of my existence, I also faced their early rise and sleep disturbances through the night too.

Before too long I was a shadow of my former nursery nurse self. I didn't know if I was coming or going and noticed a severe drop in my zest for life! No matter how often I chanted, "Stay in your bed!", they would do the opposite and get up, pulling at the baby gate in the doorway to their room, laughing, crying or shouting until I returned for what felt like hundreds of times each night. In the end, I would have to sit perched on the floor with my arm awkwardly squeezed between the cot safety rail, patting their back until they finally succumbed to sleep. I was (not so slowly) cracking.

"There must be something we can do!"
As I've touched upon, being a professional, live-in nanny means that you are there to make a parent's life easier, remaining upbeat, helpful, energized and ready to work at any given moment. But in this case, I could feel my ability to uphold my end of the deal slipping. I woke tired, went to sleep tired, ate breakfast tired and struggled on, always

tired. Until one morning, after a particularly bad night, I got my insomniac of a charge ready for the day and attended the breakfast table where their parents, refreshed from a great night's sleep (and rightly so, my role was 24hrs support), sat sipping coffee and reading the morning paper.

"Good morning, Laura! How was it?"

Try as I might, on this morning, I could not feign professionalism. "It was horrific, we've had about four hours' sleep in total," I sighed.

"Oh dear! Well, the little one seems perky enough, that's good," they replied.

"Yep, but I'm not sure how to manage ....." Cue my tears. There, at that beautifully set breakfast table in front of my two bosses and little charge, I began to sob. Everyone but me was silent.

"There *has* to be something we can do." I blubbered. "There must be a way to get them to sleep for longer!"

And in that moment, it dawned on me: I needed to research sleep disturbances in a bid to ensure the toddler was getting enough sleep and to rid me of my misery. That was the beginning of a new start and just the thought of figuring out a way to help us get more sleep made me feel a touch brighter.

Nanny Amies' Top Tip: It's not defeatist or weak to admit you need help. Almost every problem I've helped to solve over the years has stemmed from conversation, brainstorming and research. Talk to those closest to you, seek support and know that you are not the only one who's struggling. As the saying goes, "It's okay not to be okay".

I began reading blogs and websites that kindly offered up information on toddler sleeping habits. This is what led to me going on to study sleep, as I realized I knew so little about a topic that was so essential to life as a live-in nanny (and being human).

I soon learned that the toddler in my care was, in fact, not suffering from insomnia and instead was simply overtired. In my attempt to wear them out, I was pushing them past their ideal sleep pressure. I was creating a surge of cortisol that meant they were somewhat chemically fuelled to gleefully hop in and out of bed to their heart's content. Not only that, but increased cortisol levels can result in restless, wakeful sleeps and early wake-ups – I'd created a monster! So, job number one was to shorten their wake windows (the amount of time spent awake) in line with their age.

At two years and two months old, this toddler's ideal wake window was somewhere in the region of five hours. I'd been keeping them up for at least seven hours. For example, they'd wake around 5:30am or 6am, then nap between 1pm and 2pm. They would then finally drift off to sleep close to 9pm, which, on top of a great deal of exercise each day, meant their hormones were fighting the very thing I was so desperately trying to encourage.

Wake windows

Wake windows lengthen with age and will differ for every toddler. The windows in the table on the next page are guidelines for you to trial, discovering what timings work best for your little one depending on their natural temperament and daily routines.

> **Nanny Amies' Top Tip:** While trialling timings, routines or approaches, don't be tempted to try something new every day. It takes around five days to adjust to new habits, so consistency will be your best friend in your bid for more sleep.

Age	Naps	Wake windows
3–6 months	Around 4	Awake for 1–3 hours
6–12 months	2–3	Awake for 2–4 hours
12–18 months	1–2	Awake for 3–5 hours
2 years	1	Awake for 4–6 hours
3 years	0–1	Awake for 6–7 hours (or 12 with no nap)
4 years	0	Awake for 12 hours

This information was enough to make a big difference, but there were other important aspects of sleep health I had been missing too.

Sleep cycles

Thinking back to our unplugged, living-off-the-grid ancestors, a lot of their behaviours and routines will have been based on survival. Sleep will have been the time that they were at their most vulnerable. This is useful to know because right before we drift off, our brain takes notice of all the sensory information available to us, including sight, smells, sensations and sounds. Your toddler will cry out if they notice a shift in the environmental information around them, just as they are designed to! This often happens at the end of their sleep cycle.

We are supposed to have very brief, periodic half-awakenings throughout our sleep to ensure that our "cave" is still safe. This is an inbuilt safety mechanism and a very clever one at that. No matter the routine, sleep environment, parenting style or age of child, we can never eradicate all overnight wake-ups because of these little "safety" checks.

However, we *can* try to ensure that the checks are brief and followed quickly by another sleep cycle.

Sleep cycles, like wake windows, lengthen with age. For example, a six-month-old baby may experience a 45-minute sleep cycle, whereas a toddler of three years may have a cycle lasting around 60 minutes. Sleep cycles consist of various stages, with the main ones being REM (rapid eye movement) and non-REM sleep. Essentially, light and deep sleep.

Nanny Amies' Top Tip: During REM sleep, toddlers can be fidgety, display shallow breathing, their eyes may flicker from side to side, and they can seem generally restless. However, this isn't the time to intervene and soothe them "back to sleep". It's a natural stage of sleep they will pass through independently. Dashing to soothe your toddler while they are experiencing REM sleep can mean they have difficulty linking sleep cycles together independently as they grow. If they are actually awake and/or need your support, that's different, and do get in there.

What this translates to is that anything your little one experiences right as they drift off ideally needs to be readily available upon their safety check. So, for this toddler, each time they drifted off with me sat right beside them, "Shhing" and patting their back, their instincts kicked in due to the environmental change, leading to blood-curdling cries throughout the night, bringing me back to my watch post by their bed. My job was to teach them a new sleep association.

Sleep associations

A sleep association is what it says on the tin: something that we associate with sleep that signals to our brain that it is time, and safe, to sleep. So, I must start this section by saying that it is **more than okay** for you to aid your toddler off to sleep! Rocking, patting, singing, stroking their hair, feeding and anything else that comes naturally to you could never be classed as wrong. In keeping with the theme of this chapter, that's exactly how our ancestors would have got their offspring to sleep.

Co-sleeping

Our ancestors would have likely slept together side by side, which, as we know from modern-day co-sleepers, can greatly reduce night wakes. While co-sleeping, those safety checks are met by the close presence of a parent, often resulting in sleep cycles being linked more quickly due to the consistency of the sleep environment. However, whether it be due to raised awareness on sleep safety or simply a personal preference, a huge portion of the population now choose to sleep separately from their children.

Sleep safety is a vitally important topic and if you would like to know more, I urge you to visit The Lullaby Trust website (see page 271) for valuable, comprehensive information on how to create a safe sleep environment for your little one.

Swapping one sleep association for another is not as simple as flicking a switch and ta-da! a child suddenly associates something other than their parent with sleep. Luckily though, it is possible with the right amount of will, patience and consistency.

Sleep training

Sleep "training" has a terrible reputation. I think this is because of the misconception that sleep training equals leaving a child alone in a room to cry themselves to sleep. Sleep training is actually an umbrella term that covers all aspects of sleep health, yet even when I've gone on to list all that this training involves, I've still had parents on social media scold me, believing me to be cruel and neglectful. In light of this, I ask that you read the following information with an open mind and you take from it what feels most helpful to you.

Sleep environment

The very first thing I'd consider when working as a sleep consultant is a child's sleep space. We need to think about the temperature (ideally, a room needs to be between 16–20°C/60–65°F), lighting, bedding, safety and noise levels. We are aiming for that cave-like environment – calm, cool, dark, quiet and safe.

Melatonin (the sleepy hormone) is produced overnight while we are in a darkened environment and helps us to achieve restful sleep, so be sure to avoid night lights with bulbs that prohibit the production of this home-grown sleep aid.

> **Nanny Amies' Top Tip:** Blackout blinds are a must, both for at home and away. Having travelled the globe with families, you will never catch me on a flight without my portable blackout blind that adapts to any window! You can also buy blackout fabric and use double-sided Velcro on your window as a cost-effective option.

Daily routine

Next up, I'd look at a little one's routine to ensure that their wake windows (see page 142) are in line with their age and sleep needs. Those wakeful hours will need to include moving, exploring and interacting in ways that are stimulating for your toddler's brain (which will, of course, look different for each age group).

I like to anchor a toddler's meal and snack schedule not only to help their body clock predict the rhythm of the day, but also to ensure that I am feeding them effectively before a stretch of sleep.

The hour before bedtime is a very important aspect of sleep health. A predictable chain of events in this hour can signal that your toddler is getting close to bedtime. Over time this leads to less pushback as they begin to understand that is their norm.

If a little one's sleep environment and routine are age-appropriate, it means their sleep pressure (see page 138) is most likely set at the right level. If it isn't, I usually ensure that they are primed for sleep with the appropriate wake windows before attempting any further sleep-training methods. It is important to know that no method will work if a toddler's routine or environment is out of sync.

Tweaking sleep associations

If a toddler has a sleep association that cannot remain in their sleep space all night – for example, a parent, a bottle of milk or a screen – I recommend a weaning schedule to help them adjust to achieving sleep without it. The weaning schedule is included on the following pages to map out the necessary steps as clearly as possible. However, I always insist that parents use the map only as a rough guide. Please feel free to adapt the times and approaches offered in the chart that follows, so you feel comfortable moving forward. The only way we can positively impact sleep patterns is by being consistent, so feeling happy and confident with your approach is of utmost importance. This example is based on a parent who currently rocks their little one to sleep.

Stage	Goal	How	Why
Stage one (allow 5–7 days)	To achieve as much sleep as possible.	1 Use wake windows and current sleep associations to promote sleep. 2 Use the stirring technique (see page 152). 3 Once the little one is asleep, place them into the cot carefully – feet, then bottom, before laying their head down.	The more sleep that your toddler gets, the less likely they are to wake through the night due to raised cortisol levels. They may still wake for habitual feeds.
Stage two (allow 5–7 days)	To achieve as much sleep as possible. To ensure one-to-one quality time is offered every day to your toddler. To introduce habit-stacking.	1 Without screens and distractions, spend time before bedtime with your toddler. Come down to your little one's level, make eye contact, offer physical touch such as hugs or hand-holding, and read a book together or play with toys. 2 Add a new habit to help promote sleep, such as adding in a soft teddy to the routine or rhythmically patting their back while rocking them to sleep.	Securing your bond during waking hours helps a child feel safer and content. It also highlights the difference between night-time and day-time behaviours. Habit-stacking layers a new habit over the top of an old one and can help bridge the gap between their old and new association.

Stage	Goal	How	Why
Stage three (allow 3–5 days)	To help little one drift off in their cot. (You will remain present throughout this process and largely play it by ear depending on little one's reaction.)	1 Stand next to the cot holding them. When they are close to sleep, stop rocking but continue to pat. 2 Just before drifting off, place them into the cot and continue patting. 3 If they become upset, assess. If upset peaks, pick them up and continue rocking and patting. 4 Repeat until your toddler drifts off in their cot with you patting them.	Your repetition, calmness and predictably will help your toddler to trust this process and their cot. If we take the toddler away from the cot due to crying, we risk reinforcing the concept that the cot isn't safe. Rather than have them lead your behaviour, we are trying to flip this and have you lead theirs.
Stage four (allow 3–5 days)	To help the toddler develop the skill of independent sleep.	1 Once your little one is in the cot, relaxed and close to sleep, stop patting but remain close. 2 If they become upset, place your hand on them with limited movement and assess. If upset peaks, return to patting. 3 Repeat until your toddler drifts off in their cot without you patting them. 4 You may need to reset when you first attempt this. For example, pick them up, cuddle and try again when calm.	We are trying to create a sleep environment that will remain the same upon their wake-ups. For example, no patting. If they can get used to drifting off without patting, but with you there, it's a very supportive way to offer them the chance to develop this independent habit.

Stage	Goal	How	Why
Stage five (allow 3–5 days)	To help the toddler drift off on their own.	1 By now, your toddler will understand that you trust their cot and that each wake-up results in them being comforted and returned to the cot. 2 When you have a good sleep routine in place, offer a little rocking and then place your toddler into their cot awake.	This is the final piece of the puzzle in terms of your toddler being able to link sleep cycles more independently. While there will always be instances of illness or sleep regressions, moving forward your calm presence should be enough for them to re-achieve sleep in their own sleep space.
Stage six (allow 3–5 days)	To remove yourself from the sleep environment. (There is no right or wrong way to do this. Remember the three c's: calm, comfort and consistency!)	What you do next is your call. Once you've placed them in the cot, choose to: • Pat for a few minutes before leaving the room briefly, before reentering to pat them further. Repeat until they drift off. • Immediately leave the room. Return to pat them, if necessary. • Sit in their room until they drift off, offering a calm presence.	Leaving your toddler's room for very short intervals will allow them time to adjust to being in there alone. This can be for five seconds in the beginning, building it up by a second per night, if need be.

Use a sleep clock

Once I began getting the hang of various sleep issues, I was able to implement helpful strategies that aided the whole family's sleep patterns. While caring for one toddler, they went through a spell of waking really early, so I introduced a sleep clock that simply differentiated between night and day. Stars dimly lit the screen overnight while a sunshine brightly shone at a chosen time of day.

Alongside this clock I taught them to wait in their bed and call out "I'm awake now, Laura" as soon as the sun on the clock began to shine. Once I heard them, I would ensure that, regardless of my energy levels, I went into their room looking happy to see them and proud of how they had waited for the sun. This built a lovely association to staying in their bed and made a huge difference to those early wake-ups.

Nanny Amies' Top Tip: If you introduce a sleep clock to your toddler's sleep environment, ensure that you have realistic expectations. For example, if they currently wake at 5am, setting the clock for 7am will not mean that your child will magically wake at (or wait until) 7am. Start by setting it for the time they currently wake and add on five minutes every five days until you reach a more acceptable wake-up time.

However, thanks to a developmental leap (in this instance, an advancement of their language skills), the toddler went through a phase of waking at 11pm each night. Despite their sleep clock still being covered in stars, they would ever so politely shout, "I'm awake now, Laura!" at the top of their lungs. Now, if we bear in mind that my bedtime was 10pm, at 11pm I was in no fit state to be popping in there with a smile, praising them for waiting in their bed for me to arrive! Nope, this just wouldn't do. Cue the "stirring" method.

The stirring method

I held off on my own bedtime for a few nights, ready to go into my charge's room at 10:45pm, 15 minutes before their newly scheduled wake-ups. Once by their bed I would either gently rub their back or stroke their hair – very carefully! – with the view to "stir" them and induce an independent fidget or turning over. The idea behind this method is that you gently lift them out of their current stage of sleep in the hope that they then sink back down into a deeper stage, missing out on the wake-up. It worked a dream (pardon the pun).

Within a few nights of this, the wake-ups stopped. Had I turned lights on at 11pm or offered wakeful behaviours such as food or heightened interaction, I would have risked setting their body clock to continue waking at that time. Keeping things as sleep-related as possible (which I know isn't easy) is the most effective way to prevent habitual wake-ups from forming.

Some things are out of our hands

You can be 100 per cent focused on sleep patterns and really conscious of the types of things that lead to wake-ups, yet still experience phases of disturbed sleep. This is simply because some things are out of our control. For example, illness, teething, neurodiversity, nightmares and night terrors can all lead to restless nights. Night terrors occur when a child suddenly shifts from one stage of sleep to another and their body wakes, but their brain doesn't. They can look awake and terrified, but they aren't aware of what is happening. All this can impact the sleeping habits of a youngster, even those who have settled into a wonderful sleep pattern previously.

Sleep regressions are usually out of our control too. Some lovingly refer to these as sleep "progressions" due to the cause being an advancement in a child's development. When a toddler develops a new skill, you may notice that their sleep becomes disturbed. This is due to them cementing the newly learned information and creating a "busy brain". Even the potty-training journey can disrupt sleep – whereas previously they may have urinated in their nappy without a second thought, once they develop bladder control, they will wake in response to it becoming full.

While developmental leaps and illnesses are out of our control, it is important not to give up entirely and have your toddler decide when the day starts. I'm sure you do not need me to tell you that, no matter how much they try to convince you, 3am is not the best time to get up and at 'em!

> **Nanny Amies' Top Tip:** Babies are not born afraid of the dark. This fear stems from scary content, stories, experiences and imagination, so don't assume that a nightmare requires turning all the lights on. In fact, when it comes to nightmares and night terrors, less is more. A calm, supportive approach, with no shaking them awake or questions and conversation about the dream (unless initiated by your child), will gently aid them back to sleep. The stirring technique can work wonders for night terrors.

What can you control?

Regressions and sleep disturbances caused by illness can go on to outlive the original cause. This is the reason for many of my Telephone Clinics! Toddlers wake and then food, tablets and everything but the kitchen sink is offered. A new body clock pattern gets set. So, what starts off as something short term becomes a habit.

Because of this I always encourage parents to ask themselves, "What can I control?" in relation to their toddler's sleeping habits. For example, if a child experiences a regression and begins waking in the night, we cannot control the developmental leap, but we can control how we respond. If a toddler begins waking at 5am, we cannot control their wake-up time, but we can control the environmental factors at that time.

This is why, if I am confident that all aspects of the sleep health and routine are being covered, I activate "night-time robot" mode between 7pm and 7am. Meaning that if a toddler were to get out of bed, for example, I will be as dull as dishwater while very calmly putting them back in. I will not provide entertainment, or debate or negotiate. I am simply calm and I attend to their needs gently but in ways that do not stimulate extra brain activity.

What if they ask for a snack? I ensure the meal schedule is set so I can confidently close the kitchen after the last meal and reopen it again for breakfast. I do offer water throughout the night, but nothing that contains sugar.

> **Nanny Amies' Top Tip:** Sometimes it is okay to wake a sleeping toddler. If they have had their quota of daytime sleep and you are at risk of their afternoon wake window being too short, cap their nap by gently introducing wakeful aspects into their sleep environment, for example, light, noise and gentle movement.

How you enter your toddler's sleep space is particularly important because they thrive on having an impact on those around them. At this age, they are also seeking more autonomy too. If their behaviour turns you into an all-singing, all-dancing, food-offering, fun-loving play pal, your family will become less diurnal and more nocturnal! Be as fun and as interactive as you can possibly muster between the hours of 7am and 7pm, then flip it in reverse for bedtime. Be calm, quiet and robot-like to send a clear and supportive message that the night-time is for sleeping and daytime is for being wakeful.

Dealing with sleep is far from easy and, wow, is there a lot to digest in this chapter, but I very much hope it can help you all get some more sleep. Sleep deprivation will convince you that there is no light at the end of the tunnel, that you'll never sleep again and that everything is hopeless. But I'm here to tell you otherwise – there is hope and a lovely night's sleep waiting just around the corner, in a cave-like environment.

Sweet dreams.

CHAPTER 9
DUMMY DEPENDENCY

*The dummy fairy has their
work cut out here*

READ ME FIRST!

This chapter looks at how to say goodbye to dummies and how to help reduce the habit of thumb-sucking. If you are reading this book well in advance of your little one needing to say goodbye to their dummy, I want to start with some preventative tips to help you avoid a negative dummy dependency from forming.

1   Limit language and attention surrounding dummy use (even if you do rely on it heavily).
2   If you pack spare dummies for days out, etc., do so calmly and quietly.
3   If your little one drops or loses the dummy, do not rush to reinsert it straight away.
4   Avoid telling people that your child "Needs the dummy!"
5   Remove the dummy during play time and times of calm.
6   When your little one becomes upset, consider other modes of comfort before offering the dummy.

7 When your little one wakes up from a nap or sleep, and you remove them from their cot, consider leaving the dummy behind and allowing it to remain in their sleep space.

For those of you beyond the preventative stage, this chapter is for you.

Before I delve into the pros and cons of dummy use, I must start by saying that I personally offer dummies to the children in my care. I think they are fabulous tools and I wholeheartedly recommend the sensible use of them. But it's all about that word: sensible. It's quite hard to be sensible when it comes to a little one who is upset and in need of comfort. For me, I wish that dummies came with a bit of background information, a character reference perhaps. In the same way that you'd interview a nanny before hiring them to care for your child or how you would walk around a potential nursery to check that it's the right environment, learning about dummies (which are essentially a rubber bung used to quell your little one's tears) is a wise move.

DUMMIES BY A DIFFERENT NAME

There are so many different names for a dummy – I've heard pacifier, sucker, binky – and I'm sure there's more that I haven't heard of! In this book, I'll be using the word dummy, as that's the UK term I use in my work.

In my experience, the whole family tends to develop a dependency on dummies, and understandably so! They can soothe a crying infant and the iratest of toddlers, so why wouldn't you use such a thing? Well, as you asked ... because, as with anything else, dummies are often overused. There's a "con" for every "pro". What a family can reap in comfort can, in some instances, bring challenges too.

One of my favourite roles as a live-in nanny was getting to play "fairy". I played the dummy fairy, tooth fairy, potty-training fairy ... all of them were a joy for me as I love to make use of the creative streak I inherited from my mum. Children tend to get on board with something more easily when it's delivered in a fun, positive manner. Throw in a bit of fairy dust and there's not much you can't achieve.

Why do toddlers like dummies so much?

At around 32 weeks into pregnancy, babies begin to develop an innate sucking reflex; this is nature's way of helping them to prepare for life as a newborn. Some of them suck their thumbs in the womb. Once outside of the womb, their sucking reflex enables them to feed. The sucking reflex and urge to feed can be so strong that even directly after a full feed an infant may cry out for more, as if they were never fed. This is very stressful for parents, unsure of what else to offer their baby. This is where the dummy comes in to save the day – the first dummy was designed to act as a substitute for the infant to use when nutritional needs had been fully met or to briefly soothe the sucking reflex if a feed wasn't immediately available.

Modern advice is that dummies are not offered until around the fourth week after birth to ensure that they do not interfere with the development of a baby's latch on the breast or bottle. Babies born prematurely may be given a dummy soon after birth to encourage the suckling reflex to develop outside of the womb where it didn't have time to do so prior to birth.

Over the years, the designs of dummies have adapted and become readily available. Advertising and product placement has led to many parents believing that having a dummy is an essential part of early childhood. (Which to some, they absolutely are.)

Team this with how empowering dummy use can be for parents who have fed, rocked, sang to and changed a crying baby, who then experience a dummy's almost magical calming effects. It's easy to see how they become a firm aspect of daily habits.

It's important to say here that how we as adults offer dummies, talk about dummies and behave around dummies will go on to impact how a little one feels about them, long after the reflex to suckle diminishes.

> **Nanny Amies' Top Tip:** If your little one didn't take to a dummy, don't worry! It's common for babies to reject the offer of a dummy and leave parents desperately wishing they hadn't. But what you lose in your armoury of comfort early on, you gain in not having to remove the dummy from a toddler who's become very attached to it. Same goes for parents who choose not to offer a dummy.

"I need the dummy, where's the dummy?!"

Voluntary feeding kicks in when your baby is around three or four months old, so after this, they no longer need the dummy for its intended use. Being aware of how you do use a dummy moving forward can be super helpful. This is especially important as baby becomes a toddler and vital as your toddler becomes a pre-schooler, when the habit can have negative side effects.

Illness and injury aside, how much comfort does your toddler *truly* require from the dummy? If a toddler so much as whimpers and they are instantly plugged with a dummy, what message does that send? What about if the dummy is constantly available or constantly in their mouth? Now, don't get me wrong, this is fabulous in terms of reducing parents' stress levels but, sadly, it also reduces the opportunities for toddlers to develop any emotional resilience. Without resilience, they will struggle to deal with big emotions. Big emotions will always be felt, so learning how to cope with them is very important.

I've been in family homes where a panic-stricken parent paces the floor shouting, "Where's the dummy?!" because their toddler knocked over their tower of bricks and the parent was apprehending their tears. Or "I need the dummy!" from a toddler, pushing their plate of food away. Our language and actions can allow a youngster to believe that unless they have the dummy, they cannot cope.

I know that over-reaction to crying and dummy usage is often down to a parent's sensory overwhelm. Sometimes it's due to anxiety and even depression, so please do not misunderstand my no-nonsense approach to this topic as a lack of caring. Just consider that you are your child's whole world, their oracle, the introduction to life, and that means that, initially, they only know what you teach them.

Nanny Amies' Top Tip: If the mere thought of your toddler crying increases your blood pressure, I urge you to learn more about their emotional development. Crying, while horrible to listen to, is a normal and healthy way for a toddler to express their frustration or dislike of something. Their tears do not automatically mean trauma. If crying creates a trauma response in you, first, I do wish I could offer a cuppa, a listening ear and a hug but, second, it may be worth trying to delve into the reasons why.

Pros and cons of dummy use

Before we look at ways to reduce dummy usage, I would like to mention some pros and cons. Knowledge is power, so when (or if) you decide to embark on the mission of dummy removal, it's helpful to have as much information as possible. Information can enable us to move forward with confidence, and in the same way that parents initially nurture the use of a dummy, 99 times out of a 100, it's a parent who must steer the ship toward dummy-free times.

Pros	Cons
• Soothes an emotional child. • Helps with reflux. • Can settle little ones more quickly than without. • Can reduce risk of SIDS (Sudden Infant Death Syndrome). While research is ongoing, there are many things about SIDS that we simply don't know. Statistics show that where dummies are used, SIDS is less likely. • Parents feel empowered as they have an effective tool. • Unlike thumb-sucking, a dummy can be removed safely. • Can help prevent tooth decay because saliva reduces plaque. • Can help to ease ear pressure on planes. • Provides relief for all during triggering times.	• Toddlers can very easily become dependent on a dummy. • Parents can easily become dependent on dummies, which leads to anxiety if it's lost. • Child may become reliant on a dummy and struggle to self-regulate without one. • Can cause wake-ups if dummy falls out while asleep. • Can impact breastfeeding. • Can create tantrums if a dummy isn't readily available. • Can impact jaw and tooth development (use flat or orthodontist dummies to reduce this). • Can increase the ingestion of germs if not sterilized or cleaned regularly. • Can increase risk of ear infections due to constant ear pressure change. • Can have a negative impact on speech development. • Can have a negative impact on social skills and play skills. • Dummies have addictive qualities.

Many parents already know the cons of dummy use, so those who choose not to offer their child a dummy may wonder why, or even how, they become such a firm aspect of a toddler's daily life. That's because of the pros. When a dummy works well for a family unit, more will be purchased. They will be integrated throughout nappy bags, along with one in the car, two in the cot, one in mum's coat pocket and you may even find the odd one rattling around in a toy box somewhere. Often, parents don't realize how dependent they themselves have become on the dummy, until that is, they begin to see some of the cons overtake the pros.

Parallel dependency

From a development perspective, a toddler is not able to consider the aftermath to making choices which aren't necessarily healthy or sensible. They respond purely on impulse and how they feel in any given moment. Therefore, when it comes to making decisions about their own dummy use, they can't.

Nanny Amies' Top Tip: Many neurodiverse children rely on dummies past the age we may "typically" view as appropriate. If your child still relies on a dummy, families can make long-term dummy use work – have a chat with your dentist to protect your child's dental health and do what works for you. However, if you are hoping to reduce the dummy usage, you may want to consider one of the various sensory oral chews on the market. They come in an array of colours, shapes and textures and can be a wonderful alternative to dummies.

From the perspective of the parent who has developed a parallel dummy dependency, perhaps they remember that their child had severe reflux or that they had a "Velcro" baby who never calmed without an array of tactics being used. It's possible that they follow a gentle child-led approach and enjoy a free-flowing household, free of rigid boundaries. Ultimately, parents are hardwired to feel uncomfortable when their child cries. Therefore, it can be very difficult to not offer up the one thing that is guaranteed to calm them. However, there comes a time when, no matter how difficult, we must consider life without the dummy.

When should we remove the dummy?

Just as with a "recommended" amount of screen time, I'm not going to delve into a specific or official recommended age in terms of saying goodbye to the dummy. The time to say goodbye will look different in every home and is very much dependent on individual circumstances. Instead, I will list what I feel to be a few valid reasons for saying goodbye, irrespective of a little one's age.

- An important reason for me is if a dummy is limiting the opportunities for a toddler to form words. If a dummy is in situ for large chunks of the day, it can impact tongue placement, freedom to make sounds and to communicate in a way that's unique to them.
- If a dummy limits the way a little one interacts with their peers or their imaginative play, it's got to go. Toddlers should have the opportunity to play and explore with all their senses and available skills. Play is where they learn how to function, create and execute plans, build their imagination and express themselves. With a dummy in their mouth, sadly these opportunities are more limited.

- Dummies can cause tantrums, tears and stress, which is the complete opposite of their purpose! If a toddler is addicted to their dummy, they will struggle to regulate their emotions without it.
- You notice that the dummy is having an impact on your toddler's mealtimes. Some children are so attached that they will not relinquish the dummy during meals, therefore impacting their solid food intake, possibly leaving them reliant on milk feeds past the age when nutritional needs require solids.
- If your toddler wakes up distressed in the night because their dummy falls out, it's now a nuisance and having a negative impact on sleep patterns. If your little one is over one year in age, can roll over independently (reducing risk of SIDS) and the dummy creates a lot of stress, is it really worth keeping? Basically, if the dummy is causing more tears than it's preventing, it no longer serves its purpose.

> **Nanny Amies' Top Tip:** Upon your little one waking, consider leaving the dummy somewhere in their sleep environment or separate to where you'll spend the day. Allow them the chance to adjust to daytimes without it. Use the information offered in Chapter 8 to help you ride out what will be a day or two of adjustment.

Is there a wrong time to get rid of the dummy?

Yes! Try to avoid removing a dummy while you are on the cusp of a big change such as a house move, holiday or potty training. If your little one is ill (although a blocked nose can sometimes lead to a toddler giving up the dummy independently, if you are lucky), experiencing separation anxiety or teething, it's worth waiting until things are calm and normal within your home.

Parents can often feel pressured to remove the dummy due to external forces. Whether it be nursery, society, grandparents or maybe a friend's child that just got rid of theirs, you may feel very keen to get rid of dummies. My advice here is to decide upon the right time for you and your family, rather than being pushed into it against your will.

> **Nanny Amies' Top Tip:** The next time your toddler becomes upset over an inconvenience (not an illness, pain or moment of true fear), which let's be honest, should be any minute now, consider waiting before offering them the dummy. Can you offer physical comfort, a distraction or a sip of water instead?

Are *you* ready to remove the dummy?

Remember that from your child's perspective, not only has the use of their dummy been encouraged and promoted, but they also won't (and can't) understand why it's now being discouraged. So, you must be ready to confidently remove it, and part of that confidence will come from choosing the right time and removal method.

As well as this being a huge adjustment for your child, you will have to retrain your own behaviours, particularly during times of stress and conflict. The dummy often becomes a safety blanket for parents as well as children, so finding new ways to offer comfort and support is great preparation. You will need to make sure that all adults in your little one's world are on board and ready too. Your plan will not work if granny has a hidden stash of dummies at her house (I have witnessed this first-hand).

It usually takes about five days to break a habit (five consistent and consecutive days). While five days may feel like a long time, in the grim scheme of things it will be over in a blink. Most parents do report that weaning away from dummies wasn't anywhere near as bad as they feared.

> **Nanny Amies' Top Tip:** If your toddler takes out their dummy, calmly remove it from sight or pop it to one side. Out of sight is out of mind, and the more you can do this, the less dependent they will be on it.

A story about language development (and a fairy)

Many moons ago, I cared for a toddler who used their dummy 24 hours a day. I had noticed that one of the parents seemed to encourage the dummy use. Whenever the toddler discarded their dummy during play, the parent would either quickly reinsert it or say, "Where's your dummy?" This resulted in its overuse and at times when, I'm sorry to say, it wasn't even close to necessary.

As the toddler made their way toward their third year, it was clear that they were struggling to pronounce certain sounds. For example, the "s" sound would be pronounced as "l", making words like snake become "lake", or sausage become "laulage". While it's perfectly common for toddlers to mispronounce words, a constant switch of the same specific letters may require a little attention.

Children can develop speech delays, lisps and communication difficulties without the use of a dummy, but when a toddler has a dummy 24/7, it certainly doesn't help them with the correct speech formation.

I dared to broach the topic of speech therapy and dummy removal. I can still feel the burning of my cheeks now when I think of those doting, proud parents scolding me, "Who the hell do you think you are to tell us that our child is anything less than perfect?!" Gulp.

I tried to explain that it wasn't a criticism – I'd only mentioned it because I cared. I said that early intervention is vital in these instances, but they were having none of it. That was until six months later when their child began at a private, educational nursery setting a few hours a week. The manager called the parents into the office to speak about their three-year-old child's progress and development, so the proud pair popped on their finest regalia and set off to hear what they assumed would be a glowing report.

The next I knew doors were being slammed and I heard the shrill call of, "Laura! Where the hell are you!" Double gulp!

As I entered the kitchen, one parent was sat at the table crying, while the other paced the floor. Storming toward me, a pointed finger close to my face, one shouted "Why didn't you tell us that our child's language skills were not where they should be for their age! And you call yourself a nanny?"

"Erm … I did. I suggested speech therapy and you got very upset with me."

"Well, you should have insisted because now the manager of that nursery tells us that our child is not speaking at the level they would expect and that will not do!"

"The dummy has to go!" cried the parent still sitting at the table, and in that moment, it dawned on me that this was less about development and perhaps more about image.

Cue the dummy fairy

Pushing my feelings to one side and hell-bent on proving that I wasn't an entirely useless nanny, I immediately planned a visit from the dummy fairy (AKA me). The plan was to make moving on from the dummy as fun as possible. I sourced balloons, bunting and a basket, and set out a trail of arrows plus glitter in the garden for the whole family to follow. When we arrived at the last arrow, there was the shrine to the dummy fairy.

The three-year-old child was really excited to see the balloons attached to the basket and the pretty bunting blowing in the breeze, plus the parents hadn't seen the shrine prior to that moment, so they "Oohed" and "Aahed" at the appropriate times, which really helped the little one to embrace the moment. So much so that they excitedly plopped the dummy from their mouth (and the one in their hand) into the basket. I took a balloon, handed it over to them and explained that when we come back, the dummy fairy will have taken the dummies and replaced them with a special gift.

Off we went, back into the house, before I snuck out to exchange the dummies for a lovely new bedtime teddy and grown-up water bottle. Upon my return, I suggested that we go look to see if the dummy fairy had come back. The toddler skipped back out, delighted by the sight of the exchange which had occurred within the basket. And so, it was done. Bye-bye dummy.

Earlier that day, I checked that there were no dummies left in toy boxes, under pillows or in the car, as it would have been a disaster for the little one to find one after the dummy fairy visit. The first hour after the exchange went very well; there was no mention of the dummy and the toddler was pretty easy to keep busy.

However, as we neared bedtime and tiredness arose, the house began to show signs of mourning. A bit of a "Where is the dummy when you need one?" type of vibe was emerging, mostly from the parents. I urged the parents to think ahead, to consider what a huge change it was and how it will be easier with each passing day. But bedtime was a scene like no other. The toddler, who had never gone to sleep without their dummy, really struggled. Trying every behaviour, button-pushing, tantrum and trick in the book, one parent finally caved as their child said, "Come dack dummy fairy. Please come back".

The parent suddenly presented a dummy they'd stashed away. After just ten minutes of pushback, they had caved.

Nanny Amies' Top Tip: I highly advise that once you have said goodbye to the dummy, you do not reintroduce it. Once it's gone, it's gone! By offering it back, you'll make the next time you try an even steeper incline to climb.

How to say goodbye to dummies

When you are getting ready to say goodbye to the dummy, start by planting little seeds of thought that will allow your child to connect to the fact that the dummy won't be around forever. For example, "Soon you won't need a dummy anymore".

These little seeds should be offered infrequently and without any pressure; it's just a gentle way to begin emotionally preparing a little one for the change ahead. If they try to debate or insist that they still need it, try not to enter into negotiations or to convince them to get excited about a visit from the dummy fairy. Just make short, matter-of-fact statements and move on quickly. There are some lovely picture books out there that can help to prepare your little one too.

Nanny Amies' Top Tip: If you have decided it's time to say goodbye to the dummy, avoid asking questions such as, "Are you ready to say goodbye to your dummy?" This makes it appear optional and immediately puts you on the back foot if your child says a firm, "No!"

So, lets now look at the various ways you can help your toddler (and the family) to say goodbye to dummies.

Option one: Weaning

During times when your child would usually ask for or be given the dummy, try to hold off even if just for a few minutes. Use other strategies instead such as hugs, singing, distraction or postponement. This is a case of thinking outside of the box and requires a strong will, both of which are entirely possible! For example:

- If your little one associates the sofa and TV with having the dummy, get outside or away from the triggers that will remind them of dummy use.
- If you cannot get outside, consider postponing dummy use with a phrase such as "I'm popping to the toilet, as soon as I'm back, I will get your dummy". Even delaying it for just a few moments initially will begin to make a difference if they are used to having regular and instant access to it.
- Offer a sensory activity such as play dough or kinetic sand to help them connect to a different medium.
- Tell a little white lie, "Ooh, I'm not sure where it is, let's look".

> **Nanny Amies' Top Tip:** When you postpone dummy use, it might be 60 seconds of hell, but you'll survive, as will your child. Building up their resilience to longer bouts of time without it will really help when a final goodbye occurs.

Option two: Use at sleep time only

This method is a halfway house to giving up. The dummy now lives in your child's sleep space and is only used for naps and/or bedtime. By limiting the dummy use to sleep time, you allow your child the chance to develop a tolerance to life without it, while still leaning on its benefits for sleep patterns. When you feel the time is right, start to remove it from the sleep environment as well (see other methods).

Option three: Bedtime weaning

Once your little one has drifted off with the dummy in their mouth, consider removing it and placing it close by so that they can get used to not having it during the lighter (REM) stages of sleep (see Chapter 8).

If a dummy falls out during the deep sleep stages (non-REM), they won't be as aware. Learning how to sleep without a dummy will prove helpful once it's gone permanently. If the dummy falls out and wakes them, try to resist the urge to instantly re-plug it. Your behaviours will guide your child and re-plugging will reinforce the need for it, unfortunately.

Bedtime can be the most daunting aspect of the dummy removal process and is usually the one thing that worries parents the most. So, once it's time to fully let go, stick to your usual bedtime routine and try not to mention the dummy unless your little one broaches the topic first. If your toddler mentions the dummy, answer any questions they may have as honestly as possible. Validate their feelings, sympathize and offer comfort as calmly as possible. We are aiming for that balance of support and leading them confidently away from the upset.

It is okay for your toddler to be upset for a short while, and they may even struggle to drift off the first night or two, but I am yet to meet a child who hasn't adjusted to a new norm. Initially, you may need to offer a little extra support at bedtime to help them lay in their bed calmly, and that's okay. Personally, I don't make extra allowances that aren't conducive to the sleep habits or routines already in place. For example, I wouldn't offer food, tablets or other beds for them to sleep in because they missed their dummy.

Option four: Faulty dummy

You have the option of making a dummy ineffective by making it "faulty" and so less appealing. To do this, carefully pierce it with a sterile pin. Initially, the hole will be very small and your little one may not notice much difference. Over the course of a week, gradually make that hole bigger, which will render the dummy largely useless as the amount of suction it offers decreases.

You can take this method a step further by snipping off the very top of the dummy, being sure to dispose of the small piece without your little one seeing it or having access to it. This approach needs to be taken with care to ensure the health and safety aspects of the dummy are not impacted.

In some cases, you can leave a "broken" dummy with the aim of your child finding it and making this discovery independently. They may bring it to you to report its condition and offer a chance to throw it in the bin and say goodbye from a practical stance. If you have multiple dummies dotted around, gradually snip each one over the course of a few weeks.

Option five: Plant it!

A creative way to say goodbye to the dummy is to have your little one help you dig a hole in the garden (or a plant pot indoors) and plant it. Invite your toddler to pop their dummy in, before covering it with soil and watering it. At your earliest opportunity, remove the dummy and replace it with a flower or plant. You can even hang a little gift from the plant or place one close by on the soil. Have the plant or flower ready, as leaving it too long can create a negative association and you want this experience to be exciting.

Option six: Choose a special occasion

You could align the removal of the dummy with a special occasion and enlist the help of Santa or the Easter Bunny. Children can feel more open to the idea when a well-known character gets involved. For example, they already have a positive association to Santa, so recruiting him can work wonders! Grab yourself a fun gift bag and leave a note from your chosen "helper". For example, "Dear Maya, this bag is for your dummies. When I come back, I'll swap them for a new toy! Love from Santa".

Option seven: The dummy fairy

As in the story earlier, using the dummy fairy can be fun and effective. Injecting a little bit of magic into what can be a tough transition is a gift. Choose a day and time that works best for you, then this is how you do it:

1 Choose something to replace the dummies with as a gift from the dummy fairy – perhaps a new teddy to sleep with at night or a water bottle to use during the day.
2 Write a letter, addressed to your toddler (see next page).
3 Place the letter where the other post lands through the letter box or pop it by your toddler's bedside for them to find upon waking. Consider a trail of fairy dust (glitter) to help engage them.
4 Act normally and let your toddler spot the letter. Then ask things such as, "Oh wow, what is this?" "It has your name on it! It's for you!" "I wonder how it got here?"
5 Read the letter using an excited tone. The letter should be worded simply and as clearly as possible to ensure your toddler can process what is happening. Be prepared for questions and the need to further explain what it means.
6 Help your toddler to collect the dummies and to follow the letter's instructions!

1 Fairy Lane,
Magic Glen,
MG1 2DF

Dear Mateo,

Could you help me collect some dummies for the babies?
You'll find a special bag in your garden. Pop your dummies in there and I'll leave you something special when I come back to get them!

Thank you soooo much!
Love from Twinkle! Xxx

Option eight: Go cold turkey

This is what is says on the tin – the dummies are simply no more. Whether this occurs after or without weaning, it's a case of collecting up all the dummies and saying goodbye to them. This approach is not for the faint-hearted and can provoke some challenging behaviours. However, in many instances, it's a short-term pain for a long-term gain.

> **Nanny Amies' Top Tip:** If you are trying this method, when you say goodbye to the dummies, do it early in the morning to allow your toddler time to adjust before bedtime.

I believe it's important for children to be offered something that symbolizes that the dummy has gone. Having them help you to collect them and see them go is a great way to do this. It allows them to play a role, feel included and have some say over the process. Working as a team as opposed to this being entirely adult-led will almost always work in your favour.

Thumb-sucking

A family I worked with had a little one who had always sucked their thumb. As we know from earlier, this is a behaviour that can start even before birth, so can be a well-established habit. Thumb-sucking is a common and natural behaviour. As it stems from an instinctive reflex, it can get to a stage where toddlers aren't even aware they are doing it.

In an ideal world this behaviour will cease before adult teeth arrive because continued thumb-sucking with adult teeth can impact both jaw and tooth alignment. You might also need to think about hygiene implications – is the hand they are sucking clean?

This family were particularly focused on cleanliness, and the older their toddler got, the more they tried to get them to stop. The parents would constantly chant, "Get your thumb out of your mouth!" or comment on how unsanitary it was (understandable if we consider the number of germs a toddler can collect on their hands). However, because thumb-sucking stems from a comfort-seeking behaviour, anything that increases anxiety or worry will likely increase the child's urge to suck their thumb, so I offered up an alternative perspective.

The parents were open-minded to change, and once I explained that any form of shouting, shaming or criticism of this habit would push the toddler to do it more, they were fully on board. Team "No More Thumb-Sucking" was formed and we tried to follow these simple rules until we began to see a decrease in the toddler's habit:

1 We tried to help the toddler to become more aware of when and where they may be sucking their thumb. We talked about thumb-sucking outside of trigger times and let them know that we were going to work as a team to try to keep thumbs out of mouths.

2 We let the toddler know that, as we grow, the only thing that should go in our mouth is food, and that having a thumb in our mouth can impact the way our teeth grow.

3 When the toddler had their thumb in their mouth, we would calmly point it out with simple phrases such as, "Your thumb is in your mouth sweetie, pop your hand down please".

4 We spoke about the importance of hand-washing and explained how soap bubbles were like ships for the germs to travel down the plug hole in.

5 We introduced a fidget cube and offered that at certain times of the day when the toddler would typically suck their thumb, like screen time, for example.

6 We would gently pull the toddler's thumb from their mouth once they drifted off to sleep. While inevitably it would end up back in there, every little helps!

7 We avoided nagging or drawing a lot of attention to the behaviour.

8 We silently removed the toddler's thumb from their mouth if we felt we had already mentioned it enough that day.

What if subtle isn't helping?

If your little one doesn't respond well to subtleties, you may need some physical props to help redirect their focus. For example, pop a children's plaster on their thumb, one with a character on, and ask them to keep the character dry. Perhaps you could draw a smiley face on their thumb and offer descriptive praise when you see it's still there (because if they suck their thumb that smiley face will fade).

There are nail varnishes on the market that are designed to make fingers taste terrible. The thought of painting a rancid-tasting varnish onto a youngster's hand doesn't sit well with me, so I haven't tried this. However, this is a personal feeling, as opposed to advice, as these varnishes have been on the market for years and must work well for many.

If your child is four years old (or over), you can ask them to wash their hands every time you see them with their thumb in their mouth, as that gets boring really quickly!

Finally, consider creating a reward system that offers more attention, connection and rewards for non-thumb sucking behaviours. This may be stickers, collecting marbles in a jar or adding bricks to a tower to see how high you can get in a day – anything that highlights their efforts and times when you notice that they are not sucking their thumb.

Be patient and consistent because behaviours formed in the womb will not dissipate overnight. Children need lots of opportunities for new habits and conscious thoughts to replace those subconscious behaviours.

Trust in yourself

Your journey toward becoming dummy-free will be unique to your family unit, so it really does not matter how your friends or family have navigated this milestone prior to you. For example, if you have an infant who's still very much in need of a dummy but also a toddler who ideally needs to say goodbye to one, that will be something to navigate in a way that's right for you and yours.

Whatever the journey, lean on logic and consistency. Ultimately, you should trust in yourself to make the right decision. If you doubt yourself or your toddler's behaviour in response to dummy removal, you may think you have made a huge mistake. If you feel that's a possibility, I urge you to read all the chapters in this book before attempting to go dummy-free. By becoming more confident with other areas of your toddler's behaviour and wellbeing, I feel sure that you can then lead your child confidently through this process, having faith that you have made a sensible decision.

CHAPTER 10
EATING HABITS

"They won't eat that!"

Children's eating habits are often one of the most emotive aspects of the parenting journey. Even for a toddler who will eat most things that you put in front of them, dishing up nutritious meal after meal is a huge parental (and financial) commitment. A constant pressure looms as children require food, multiple times a day, day in, day out. That's a lot.

For families who have children of a more selective nature, mealtimes can be stressful, disheartening and worrisome. An internal torrent of questions such as, "Have they eaten enough?", "Are they getting enough vitamins?" and "Why won't they eat what I give them?" can play on a loop. The thought of children being hungry or not getting enough vitamins can drive parents to distraction, bringing many to my inbox, which has given me an intimate view into many family's eating habits.

Despite homes all looking different, family dynamics being diverse and every child having their own food preferences, throughout my career I have seen many similar habits and issues. By sharing this with you, I have high hopes that this chapter can offer practical tips and information that may ease your worry and, dare I say, help to widen your child's eating horizons too.

I feel like this chapter could read as particularly "firm". This is due to how my views and experience with children's eating habits have been formed. While many children have genuine food aversions, a common cause of selective eating, in my experience, is environmental factors. So, I always try my best to describe practical ways in which we can create an effective environment where healthy eating habits can flourish.

The No. 1 goal

Before I go into any detail, I wanted to mention something that is easily missed: **A child's relationship with food is more important than what and when they eat.**

This is quite a bold statement, so let me explain why. If a child feels comfortable around food, they are more likely to eat a varied diet. If a child associates the feeling of hunger with sitting down to eat a meal, they are more likely to eat well. If a child witnesses those around them enjoying a positive relationship with food, they are more likely to establish positive eating habits themselves.

We are social creatures, so eating together as a family not only promotes healthy eating habits, it also cements bonds. I know those dishes pile up and you might want to tidy the kitchen or even eat with the adults later but, even if you just have a mini portion, modelling a confident, happy and communal approach to mealtimes is so beneficial.

As your toddler grows up, the relationship they build with food at home acts as a security blanket when they are offered new foods or novel eating experiences outside of the home, such as school dinners or eating at a friend's. They are able to fall back on their past experiences and trust that food is safe, even if they don't enjoy the taste or texture of certain products. When children do not have that positive relationship to fall back on, the opportunities to try various foods can be limited.

It's common during the baby-weaning stage for food to become more about filling them up (often with the hope of achieving more overnight sleep!). Things like variety, food groups, textures and smells can get overlooked.

Thinking back to our ancestors, the fear of hunger is instinctive. Parents can experience emotional distress when they think their child is hungry, and heaven help us if a toddler says those powerful words, "I'm hungry". The thought of them being hungry is, of course, an uncomfortable one, but what if "I'm hungry" actually means, "Mum (or Dad), I could murder a bag of crisps!"?

Little snack monsters

The natural feeling of hunger is, in fact, a wonderful thing in a bid to create healthy eating habits. Developing regular peaks and troughs in a child's appetite is key to them enjoying their food at certain times of day. At the risk of pointing out the obvious, it's starvation, malnutrition and neglect that we must prevent, not low-level, normal hunger.

And just in case you are sat in self-doubt while reading this, you don't purchase a book on child behaviour if you are a neglectful parent. While I can't comment on your cooking skills, I can tell you that caring about your little one's food intake puts you firmly into the "good parent" category in my eyes!

> **Nanny Amies' Top Tip:** Toddlers are inconsistent eaters, so try not to focus their nutritional requirements solely on one meal. Consider their food intake within a 12-hour period and over the course of a week. It's okay if they do not demolish every meal, every day.

It is very common in today's world for any and all hunger to be immediately snubbed out with easy to grab, packaged snacks. This can lead to toddlers who then graze all day, AKA little snack monsters. But "What's wrong with grazing?" I hear you cry. "Toddlers only have small tummies!", some will say. And you are right, they do. So why would we fill them up at every opportunity with anything other than nutritious options?

Using snacks as intended – as something to bridge the gap between two meals – isn't an issue. Leaning on processed snacks as a main source of sustenance can be.

A child-led approach

Many modern parents now aim for more of a child-led approach to eating, ditching routines and opting to follow their toddler's preferences in a bid to help them "listen to their bodies". Some might suggest that encouraging a meal schedule is archaic, whereas this old fossil is here to tell you that allowing your toddler, who has zero impulse control and no idea about healthy choices, free access to snacks will only work in your favour if the options available are wholesome, fresh and healthy. Until your toddler has matured to the point where they can make wise choices with regard to their food intake, I highly recommend placing gentle boundaries around crisps and biscuits.

It comes back to the huge amount of misunderstanding that sits on the fence between the gentle parenting trend and permissive parenting reality (see page 6). This may be too honest, but I can feel my pulse rate quickening at the thought of people calling me archaic while following their toddler's lead toward a processed diet. If fresh fruit, vegetable crudités, protein, dairy products and wholefoods are the main options available, toddlers will be more likely to listen to their bodies and that really is a wonderful thing. A child-led approach can be wonderful in these instances. But we cannot expect a toddler to listen to their body's true needs where processed snacks, which are high in sugar and salt, are concerned. That becomes more about craving specific flavours than seeking out nutrients.

I appreciate that fresh foods are more expensive, that they have a shorter shelf life and that not all children will eat a huge array of fruit and vegetables. It's far from easy to offer up wholefoods in comparison to packaged snacks. However, this does not negate the fact that processed foods should be limited to appropriate portions. I'm not suggesting no crisps or biscuits, but I am suggesting that your toddler shouldn't be the one in charge of how often they eat them.

Snacks	Meals	Toddler personality
On the go	Eaten in a fixed place	Active
On the sofa	In a high chair	Enjoys freedom
Offered with conviction	Offered with uncertainty	Responds to facial expressions
Relaxed	Stressful	Responds to environmental cues
After a nap	Trigger times, if tired	Mood impacts eating habits
Give freedom to move	Restricted	Will push back against rules
Offer a distraction	Lonely (if sat alone)	Very social
High in sugar and salt	Tend to be less seasoned	Sugar and salt are addictive
Predictable, if packaged	Unpredictable, when food varies	Finds security in the well known

Why are snacks so appealing?

Snacks are appealing for many reasons. Heck, even as an adult, as I approach the kitchen cupboards, I have to ask myself, "Am I snack hungry, or truly hungry?" Often, the "hunger" is merely boredom or procrastination. A wise person once told me, "If you don't fancy tucking into an apple, it's likely not true hunger".

Let's look at this from a toddler's perspective. In the previous table, you can see how a toddler thinks about snacks vs meals, and how that fits with their natural personalities!

Sensational snacks

It's helpful to think about how and when we offer snacks. We can, without realizing, place them on a pedestal and make them "sensational". Think about when you give your child an ice cream on holiday or they get crisps watching a film. Snack packaging is often colourful, fun and it rustles. It all makes snacks exciting and even more appealing. If you would like to de-sensationalize snacks, try the following.

1 When possible, offer snacks at the table. For example, crisps on the sofa and pasta at the table is huge in terms of associations, so the location of snacks can help to level out the playing field. Thanks to a traumatic choking incident during my first week as a nursery nurse, I only ever offer food to a child who is seated. Walking and running with food of any kind isn't an option for children in my care.
2 If your little one will only eat processed snacks, empty the package contents onto a plate or into a bowl that they are served their meals in. This can bring snacks more in line with the appearance of meals and vice versa.
3 Consider offering their favoured snack on a plate alongside a small portion of vegetables, fruit or a wholefood (such as cheese). Over time, try upping the portion of fruit or

wholefood while simultaneously offering a touch less of the processed snack.

4 Join your toddler at snack time and model the eating of fruit or other healthy food options.

5 Consider how many processed snacks your toddler genuinely needs each day. Know that it's okay to say no to snack requests that aren't a healthy option at that time.

6 Avoid offering snacks mid-tantrum or in a bid to calm your toddler down. Associating snacks with feelings of increased happiness or calmness means you'll have dopamine hits to contend with, as well as the habit.

7 If you have the time, consider making some home-made snacks. This allows you to keep a close eye on the ingredients included. This can also be a fun activity to do together.

8 Avoid offering a processed snack after a meal refusal. If snacks are offered at the peak of hunger, they'll taste that bit more delicious!

9 Finally, if your child cries until you give them their favourite biscuit and then stops crying the second you do, don't be so sure that this is entirely an eating habits issue. Have a read through Chapter 2 if you haven't already.

"Yuk! I don't like it!"

It's all well and good me suggesting that you offer up wholefoods, but what happens when you do and your child displays pure disgust as they push their plate away? As I'm sure you can imagine, I've been there, done that and have the "Like it or lump it!" T-shirt. However, before I get to the "Like it or lump it" stage, I ensure a few important factors have been covered first.

I hope that my no-nonsense Yorkshire ways translate to comedy value as opposed to child cruelty. Something I was told often as a child was, "There are two choices for dinner

... like it or lump it", and this was always said with love. My mum was not running a restaurant and money was tight. My sister and I were not emotionally scarred because mum chose what she wanted to serve up. Some of the 1980s approach to parenting was pretty great.

When I worked in a nursery, I got used to seeing 15 hungry toddlers sitting at communal tables wolf down their lunch. It did not prepare me for how a single toddler may do the complete opposite at home. I am sure many parents wonder, "Why will my child eat everything offered to them at nursery, but nothing at home?"

Nanny Amies' Top Tip: If your child eats everything at nursery but not at home, this is very common. It's likely behavioural and/or environmental, and not a sensory processing issue or innate food aversion.

One toddler was not backward in coming forward when it came to telling me exactly what they thought of my cooking – it was enough to give me a complex! Add this to the fact that their parent was worried about how restricted the meal options were becoming and it was time to act.

It must be said that while the parent was concerned about their little one's food intake, their snack cupboard was being restocked on a daily basis. I'll never forget how the snacks were all adult-sized. The toddler was happy to eat chocolate bars, family-size bags of crisps and don't get me started on an entire packet of biscuits.

By the time I offered my best, homemade shepherd's pie at the end of a long day of snacking, there was no interest. Luckily, I'm not one to shy away from a challenge, so I got to work on creating a plan to help them rely less on chocolate and instead enjoy a wider range of foods.

Make a shopping list

Just as any good plan does, mine started with a list. I wrote a shopping list of items that my charge would help me gather from the store; I wanted them to see how a meal was put together from start to finish. If you have the time, you could make a picture list to help them find the foods in the store. Either draw a simple image or cut photos of food out of a magazine. This helps children become engaged with the shopping as opposed to running riot down aisle three.

Nanny Amies' Top Tip: To encourage a love of vegetables, try this "growing" carrots tip. Get some tiny baby carrots and have your toddler help you plant them in a pot, filled with soil. Water them together, and on day three, swap them for large carrots (ideally, with tops). Have the toddler help you pull them up, then wash them, chop them and serve them for dinner. Ensure family members appear very happy with the "home-grown" carrots.

We had fun gathering our supplies and went home to wash, chop and mix our ingredients. I decided to make a lasagne because this toddler enjoyed pasta with tomato sauce. I was aiming for the meal to be ready for 5pm, so at 3pm, snacking ceased. I was home alone with my charge that day, which made it easier as the parents did tend to offer snacks.

The toddler really enjoyed the preparation – especially seeing the cheese on top of the lasagne melt while it was in the oven (they loved cheese!). Honestly, they were excited and really happy to see that the dish was ready when I reached into the oven to get it with my silly, giant oven gloves. Reaching for a quick tickle in the oven gloves certainly helps to lighten any pre-dinner mood!

I served a portion for myself and a smaller portion for my charge. The hungry toddler shovelled their spoon right into the centre of the chopped up lasagne, keen to try it! I desperately tried to act as normal as possible. I imagined reporting, "They ate a whole portion of homemade lasagne!" to my boss on their return.

Right at that moment, the parent walked in. They entered the kitchen, stopped, looked at the bowl of food, scrunched their face up and said, "They won't eat that!"

I was stunned. The toddler threw their spoon of lasagne down and shouted "Yuk!"

My boss then opened the snack cupboard and handed their toddler a family-size bag of crisps. Years and years on, whenever I see that brand of crisps, I think back to that moment.

"They'll only eat pasta with this specific tomato sauce, Laura," my boss said, while waving a jar of sauce at me.

"I promise you that the lasagne would have at least been tasted if we'd have all acted normally", I dared to state. My boss, admiring my optimism, laughed. Sadly, optimistic I was not.

> **Nanny Amies' Top Tip:** Never underestimate what a powerful influence you have over your child's opinions, thoughts and habits. I am certain that the lasagne would have been demolished had the environmental factors remained effective and positive in that moment.

We only have one job

When it comes to the serving of food, I believe we only have one job, and that is to serve healthy foods at appropriate times. What happens once we have delivered our side of the deal is out of our hands. This might be a difficult belief to put into practice, but time and again, I have seen this work. With toddlers, the key is to set them up for success with appropriate boundaries and then take a step back to allow them to make their own decisions. I aim for this balance by:

Setting a routine: I create a predictable meal and snack routine which leaves around two-and-a-half hours between opportunities for a toddler to eat. For example:

Breakfast	7am
Snack	9:30am
Lunch	12 noon
Snack	2:30pm
Dinner	5pm

Work with their development: Once a child is older than one, eating three meals a day and is gaining weight, I prioritize solid food over milk feeds. I start with a solid breakfast option as opposed to a bottle of milk, for example. A large drink of milk in the morning can hinder appetite for food.

Role model: I sit down and eat with the child and model the behaviour I hope to see. This gives us a wonderful opportunity to show that foods are safe and to be enjoyed.

Create boundaries: I create gentle boundaries around a toddler's food intake, which looks like saying no to a second bag of crisps or sweet treat, for example.

Keep things low pressure: I avoid direct pressure to eat certain foods. While it is my decision on what to serve up, it really is their decision to eat what they choose from the plate.

Offer new things: I will offer a toddler regular opportunities to be exposed to various foods. This doesn't always have to be via their own plate either; we might paint with a floret of broccoli or feed cooked peas to the birds. It's common that children are sheltered entirely from the foods they don't like, which while I understand why, it severely limits the chances of them ever warming to them.

Ask them: Of course, I will ask them, when possible, "What shall we have for dinner today?" Getting a toddler involved in choosing a menu from time to time is a great thing!

Age-appropriate portions: I start with small portion sizes, with the view for the toddler to ask for more should they want it. Overwhelming them with big portions will create negative associations and essentially become an uphill struggle from the get-go.

Offer trusted foods: I will always ensure there is at least one "trusted" food on their plate – plain pasta, for example. This is so the toddler feels safe in their mind that there is a food they can eat and it will help them enjoy that meal.

I don't offer a back-up meal: Controversially for some, the meal prepared is the only option presented to the toddler. But as long as all the other things within this list are acted upon, this works well in my experience.

Present food calmly: Apart from the odd ice cream on a summer's day or snacks for movie night, I avoid using food as entertainment. This reduces the chances of food being leaned upon during times of boredom.

Stay one step ahead: If a meal is delayed or I can see the toddler is genuinely hungry, I will offer a drink and something that won't detract from the upcoming meal. For example, having a bowl of prepared vegetables, fruit, cheese or some unsalted crackers ready to go, means you still have a quick option to hand, but one that doesn't interfere with dinner.

Get the toddler involved: When I had the time and energy, I would invite my charge to help with at least one aspect of the food prep. This may be washing, chopping, mixing … anything which gave them a sense of involvement. Being able to lean on these facts once sat at the table is powerful.

For example, "Thanks so much for helping me chop these carrots! They are delicious!"

Be predictable: I do these things every day, so it doesn't take too long for little ones to fall into a rhythm.

***

Nanny Amies' Top Tip: Think outside the box when eating together. For example, as opposed to saying, "Eat your sweetcorn", consider, "Can you find the yellow food?" or "Why do you think it's called *sweetcorn*?"

***

One of my proudest moments as a nanny was when a youngster, who had avoided vegetables like the plague, picked up a floret of broccoli and said, "Look, I found the broccoli I chopped!" then popped it in their mouth. I quickly got over the shock and mimicked their behaviour, "I found some too! Yum!" I can now report that, years on, broccoli is their favourite vegetable.

Why won't they eat?

Irrespective of routines and approaches, all children will display a certain level of inconsistency toward their eating habits. Please don't think for a second that every food item I offer a child is immediately and enthusiastically gobbled up! Even a child with the most insatiable appetite for foods will sometimes skip a meal or not eat the amount we'd hope, and there's lots of reasons for this.

As with all the other behaviours covered in this book, understanding why a child may choose not to eat sometimes is important as it helps alleviate worry or concern. If the approach toward a child's eating habits is led via emotion, we are less likely to implement logical strategies, and logic really is key to developing healthy habits.

Before I list some potential reasons why a child may not eat, I hope it goes without saying that if you have genuine concerns beyond your child being a little picky or, if your child is consistently not eating well, speak with your doctor.

Nanny Amies' Top Tip: Offer foods around 15 times before taking a break or giving up on them. Continued exposure lets a child know a food is safe to try and gives them a chance to become familiar with it.

Here are some of the common reasons why your child may not eat what is offered to them.

Nature: Young children are predisposed to enjoy sweeter flavours. This is nature's way of helping them feed from their own mother's milk. They will actively reject anything with a very bitter taste thanks to innate self-preservation. Some theories suggest that a toddler's tastebuds only home in on bitter tastes at around 18 months. This was evolution's way of preventing the child from eating poisonous berries as they began to venture a little further away from cave mummy or daddy.

Tiredness: Tiredness can really impact a child's appetite, especially if they become upset or irritable. A predictable meal schedule alongside anchored naps can really help to prevent meal refusal due to tiredness.

Not hungry: Simply put, they may not be hungry. This is particularly true for grazers or little ones who still drink a lot of milk. If appetite isn't given a chance to grow, a toddler is unlikely to eat a meal offered to them. Also, some toddlers fill up on two meals, instead of three.

Illness: Illness, teething, tummy bugs ... all of those pesky things which make day-to-day life that bit harder can have a major impact on appetite. This might be a time when I relinquish my rules around snacking (while keeping one eye on ensuring habits don't form because illnesses are short-lived in comparison to eating habits).

Power struggles: Sometimes a clever little monkey will simply dig their heels in as they have figured out that meals are a great way to gain power within the household, especially if parents plead, beg, bribe or offer heightened attention to their meal-refusing toddler. If you feel this could be the cause of your little one's meal refusals, acting nonchalant is key!

Experience: A toddler may have had a genuine negative experience with a food item that has stayed with them. To this day, I still cannot eat a particular flavour of yogurt because while eating one at the age of eight, the fruit inside was mouldy! (Shudder!) It's okay to veto the odd food item, but sticking with this example, I will eat other flavour yogurts because others were always available to me. Again, it comes back to exposure.

Atmosphere: Try to consider how you like to sit down to eat. If the room is busy, noisy and stressful, your appetite may be capped, whereas if it's calm and others are sat down with you, you may be more inclined to eat. It's the same for your toddler.

Portions: If your toddler is offered a lot of food and leaves some on their plate, it may look like they've not eaten much. I have witnessed tots eat a lovely amount and be subjected to cajolement to eat more simply because the original portion was a tad too large. You can always offer more, if needed.

Sedentary lifestyle: If activity is limited, appetite can be also. This is another reason why I will get out and about with a little one every day. Movement, particularly outside, is a great appetite booster. (It's also worth considering the impacts that a sedentary lifestyle can have on a child who meets or exceeds their calorific needs too.)

Dislike: It is perfectly acceptable for anyone, young or old, to not like a certain item of food. A genuine dislike for a particular flavour or texture shouldn't be overlooked. (Put coriander on anything and I simply cannot eat it.)

Food aversion: For various reasons, some children will have an innate food aversion that they simply have no control over. ARFID (Avoidant Restrictive Food Intake Disorder) can result in children not feeling hunger or being interested in food. In these instances, families require specialized support aimed specifically at their needs.

FOOD ALLERGIES AND INTOLERANCES

Due to physical symptoms such as rashes, swollen lips, itchy eyes or upset tummies, it can be obvious when a toddler is allergic to certain foods. Therefore, parents will naturally avoid foods that impact their children's immune systems. However, food intolerances can be a little tougher to spot because they don't have the same extreme reactions. For example, a certain food item may just result in feeling nauseous, which can lead to toddlers avoiding certain foods themselves.

How we respond to any instance of selective eating, irrespective of the cause, will somewhat contribute to how often it occurs. While the most obvious solution may seem to be sticking to the foods that we know a toddler will eat, unfortunately over time, this can lead to children becoming very set in their ways.

Nanny Amies' Top Tip: If you are worried that your toddler isn't eating enough, keep a food diary (quietly) and record everything they eat and drink. It's easy to think that a child hasn't eaten much, when in actual fact, over the course of a day and week, their calorie intake is often much higher than we assume. Remember to record all drinks, especially if milk, fruit juice and smoothies are a regular tipple.

However, it is important to state that selective eating isn't always the issue. Some children will eat until someone physically stops them, and again, this is something I've witnessed first-hand.

Over-eating

I was lucky to host many a play date during my time as a nanny, which provided great opportunities to observe the behaviours of many children. One particular play date started very differently to any other, and that was with a stern warning from the parent of the child we were hosting: "Laura, under no uncertain terms is Luka to eat or drink any refined sugar! He's on a very strict diet".

I was surprised to hear this as we had hosted Luka many times and what he ate had never been an issue. I assured the parent that the only thing on the menu was chicken breast, potato and broccoli, with fruit to follow should Luka want it.

Lunch came and went, Luka happily munched on all the available food, and I breathed a sigh of relief when it was time to go play. Upon opening up the toy cupboard, I asked what they would like to play with and my charge immediately spotted a game that involved guessing the flavours or scents of little tablets in small, unmarked plastic pots. (I'm quite certain this game wouldn't be on the market today and looking back, I'm surprised it was then!)

The game included flashcards, with the idea being that if they thought they smelled or tasted orange, for example, they'd then pick up that card. Once I'd helped set them up with the game, I popped into the neighbouring room to put some laundry in the machine.

A minute later, I went back into the room. Multiple pots had their lids off, emptied of their contents. I saw Luka stuffing the flavoured tablets into his mouth, his cheeks round like a hamster's. It was an incredible sight to behold and truly shocking to see his reaction to such flavours ... he was completely out of control. This highlighted the pitfalls of placing children on restrictive eating plans. When it came to Luka's parent collecting him at the end of the play date, I had to brace myself for their reaction. I thought it was quite a serious matter, and I hoped I could convey to the parent that Luka genuinely couldn't stop himself, and perhaps needed a bit of support with that.

In turn, the parent proceeded to tell Luka, "This is why you're *massive*, Luka!" and threatened him with no pudding for a week. It was a sorry sight. I could see the parent only wanted to help their child become a healthier version of themselves, but I could also see Luka's head hanging in shame. Sadly, this all-or-nothing approach rarely works.

More practical solutions

I really hope that there has been the odd lightbulb moment in this chapter that can help you understand your little one's eating habits. In a bid to help further, I want to add some final points and practical solutions that have helped me to support many families in the past. Please feel free to take my suggestions, tweak them and make them fit in with your family unit and individual child.

Language use: Our language use is so important when it comes to food. It's so natural for us to say phrases such as, "Eat your veg, it's healthy!" But to a child who is largely unimpressed by such foods and unaware of actual health implications, these phrases won't always pack a punch. Phrases such as the ones below can be more effective.

- "Red foods make your heart beat strongly!"
- "Green foods help us fight the bugs!"
- "Your teeth are for crunching! What food can you crunch?"
- "Your tongue is for tasting; what foods can you taste?"

Fun: If mealtimes are currently stressful, the suggestion of adding fun to the mix may have you closing this book! However, children love fun, so consider using props that build a positive association toward mealtimes. This could be offering table mats aimed at children, fun cups, pretty napkins, cutlery with favoured characters on or anything else that will bring a smile to your little one's face while at the table. In some cases I will play nursery rhymes, unless I have a little party animal on my hands who would rather sing and dance as opposed to eat!

Presentation: If we consider that we often take the first bite with our eyes, how we present food is important. Obviously, not all meals can be a big production, but creating a scene or a smiley face with food can help. For example, you could slice mango and place it on a plate in the shape of a face and ask, "I'm going to eat the mango monster's nose ... how about you?"

Nanny Amies' Top Tip: There's more than one way to serve many foods. For example, carrots can be served raw with a dip, roasted, honey-roasted, boiled, in shapes, sticks or mashed. I've known children who love raw carrots but detest them boiled, so try lots of ways to see what they enjoy most and to avoid boredom.

Break it down: Children can really enjoy constructing their own meals when given the right ingredients to do so. For example, offering them bread, cheese slices and butter may encourage them to explore more than they would if it were presented as a cheese sandwich.

Self-esteem: I feel that it's really important for a child to understand what they are capable of because, if they feel generally capable, they are more likely to try something new.

Therefore, try to comment positively on their table manners or anything in relation to their eating habits when you can.

Self-serve: Use your child's ever-growing desire for independence to your advantage by having some foods out in bowls with serving spoons. This can inspire a child to at least pop something on their plate, and this all helps in a bid to increase that exposure.

Story time: Consider telling your little one a story at mealtimes to act as a distraction from any unwanted foods. It could be traditional or use your imagination – remember that no one's watching apart from a youngster who adores you!

New food plate: You may choose to pop an empty plate or bowl next to your child's meal which can be used if they show dislike for an item. By placing the item on that plate, it reduces the pressure to eat it. This can also be used in reverse, by popping a small amount of new food on the plate and letting them know they can touch it, taste it, smell it or even lick it if they so choose!

Nanny Amies' Top Tip: One important rule I uphold is that we respect the chef, always. It's okay not to like something, but it is never okay to call something I've cooked gross or disgusting. Modelling a more respectful phrase allows a child to stretch their vocabulary. For example, "You wouldn't like to eat that, no problem". Or, "That isn't your favourite, you can leave it".

Teddy bears' picnic: Consider sitting some favoured teddies or toys on a blanket and having a carpet picnic together! Sometimes having food away from a table is less pressurized and injects a bit of fun into proceedings. The same goes for a traditional picnic outdoors (see page 92).

Play: Children learn through play, so use it to your advantage. You could pretend to run a restaurant and design menus together, colour in pictures of food or make papier-mâché food items. Design your own pottery, make your own napkins, bake together ... the options are endless.

Bridge the gap: This is a wonderful technique used to gradually increase a child's tolerance and exposure toward the concept of new foods. You lead with two trusted foods to create a "new" food. This can help to broaden the range of flavours, textures and combinations. For example:

Trusted food	Bridge the gap	Trusted food	Goal
Toast	Melt the cheese onto the toast	Cheese	Accepting a new texture
Breadstick	Dip the breadstick into some chocolate spread	Chocolate spread	Accepting a new appearance
Cornflakes	Mix cornflakes into yogurt and let it set in the fridge	Yogurt	Accepting a new flavour

Nanny Amies' Top Tip: Avoid planting seeds of doubt by pre-empting any dislike. For example, "I know it's not what you usually eat, but give it a try". Offering food in a confident, low-pressure manner, which doesn't alert them to any potential cause for concern, is helpful.

Desensitization: A great technique is to hide vegetables in plain sight while gradually increasing the exposure to them. If that sounds like a contradiction, here's what I mean:

- Chop a few mushrooms (for example) into minuscule pieces, barely visible, while leaving some slices big and obvious to spot. Add them all to a pasta sauce (homemade or in a jar).

- Offer a side food plate, as explained above, and say, "Don't worry love, pop them there" if they spot the large slices and don't want them.
- In this method, the toddler is exposed to the mushrooms but under no pressure to eat them. Even if they pick them out and move them, it is starting to build exposure and trust.
- The toddler will likely not notice the tiny pieces, so learns to trust the flavour and texture.
- Over time, gradually increase the size and/or amount of the mushrooms.

Hiding foods is an easy, short-term solution to help increase a meal's nutritional value and to ease your worry. However, it doesn't help to build that all-important relationship with food. The point of this technique is to offer your toddler some control over their food choices, while also boosting nutritional intake.

Same approach, different day: Repetition is where success lies, yet repetition is difficult in times of stress. Your child needs regular opportunities to work through any negative emotions they may have toward certain eating habits, while you must have faith in yourself to make the right decisions for them, regardless of their pushback.

Selective eating is a common struggle within family homes, and one I am asked about all the time, so please don't feel alone. If you do need more support, there are many organizations and resources at the back of this book (see page 272) that you may find helpful.

CHAPTER 11
EMOTIONAL DEVELOPMENT

"Here, have some chocolate!"

We all know that raising a toddler is about sleep, nappy changes, helping them to walk, etc. What we don't hear so much about is their emotional development. For every practical skill we teach a child, they also need to learn about patience, tolerance and most importantly resilience to be able to execute day-to-day life effectively.

Emotions get shoved to the bottom of the pile while practicalities like feeding and tantrums rise to the top. Add in caring for any number of children and simply surviving the day becomes a priority. However, the irony is that if we focused more on a toddler's emotional development, stress levels wouldn't become the all-consuming, overbearing force that they so often do.

Emotional development offers children the chance to become aware of their feelings, to process them and, in turn, to learn how to cope with them, good or bad. However, emotional development is, in my experience, the most overlooked aspect of child development there is. I know this from working with so many families, and from my own practice too.

Nanny Amies' Top Tip: My first tip is to suggest that you don't dismiss the importance of emotional development. This isn't "new age, hippy, wishy-washy stuff"; this knowledge will aid your child throughout their whole life.

"I just want my child to be happy"

It goes without saying that you want your child to smile, to be content and to enjoy their life. What I want to talk about in this chapter is that true, inner happiness is really a by-product of emotional development. It's not about the number of toys or the size of your house. Inner happiness is the master key to living a contented life.

We can only be truly happy when we have self-belief, the ability to problem-solve and some resilience. We must be equipped to face adversity because, without that, any happiness we gleam from an object, an experience or even a person will be fleeting.

It might seem a bit strange to be talking about toddlers and adversity but bear with me. On a basic level, adversity starts from the moment we realize that we are a separate being to our parents. Or we might notice that an object is out of our reach. Therefore, adversity evolves with us, as do the growing feelings of negativity, unfortunately. Essentially, there's always something just out of reach.

Parents are hardwired to respond to a toddler's cries, and rightly so, but we also have to be careful about what we are teaching them. For example, if a toddler cries because they can't reach something and a parent instantly gives it to them to quell the tears, they learn that tears solve problems.

I've been in homes where toddlers can speak in clear, full sentences, but when it comes to an inconvenience, they instantly fall back to screams or tears. And why not, when they've learned that it works for them? The thing they can't reach is delivered without so much as a please, thank you or even a smile. Again, I must stress that I get it! You love them and your eardrums, so you are solving your own problems by delivering the item they can't reach.

But what if we were able to override that immediate desire to quell tears and, instead, help even the youngest toddler begin to build up a tolerance to frustration?

Nanny Amies' Top Tip: If your toddler sees something out of reach – a drink, for example – and motions toward it, model, "Drink, please", followed by a short pause that allows the information to be processed. You can also model an appropriate response while handing the drink over, "Yes please". This helps them learn how to express their needs verbally.

To teach, we must first learn

Becoming a parent is physically and emotionally challenging (before we even get to the lack of sleep!). It can highlight any personal vulnerabilities we may possess. If, like many of us, you weren't taught how to recognize emotions, process them and manage your stress levels, then how are you to be expected to teach a toddler those things?

If you can teach yourself how to recognize, process and respond to stress and strong emotions, this will be a skill you can then fall back on in times of true stress and upset. This starts by noticing your feelings. Notice the next time you get cross at an inconsiderate driver, slam something down on the worktop, raise your voice, swear or feel unhappy in any way, and consider what physical impact that is having on your body. Perhaps you can hear the pulse in your ear or can sense a tightening of the jaw muscle. Maybe your tummy has knots in it or you feel like you just have to get out of the house.

When we begin to take note of these physical changes, with practice we can then start to anticipate the bubbling over of our emotions by using grounding techniques, which allow our brains to recognize we are not under threat.

Grounding techniques (which I also cover in relation to toddlers on page 212), can really help if your brain is used to perceiving a toddler tantrum, for example, as a stressful threat. If you are entering your fight or flight mode (see page 24), that could explain why your body may react physically to certain behaviours your little one displays. Once you can fully recognize your own emotions, you can even begin the journey of emotional development alongside your toddler, if need be.

> **Nanny Amies' Top Tip:** I have done a huge amount of work on myself over the years. Do not be afraid to consider the origins of your own behaviours and reactions. Understanding yourself will help in terms of mental health and your family's overall emotional wellbeing. Whether this be reading a self-help book or talking to a therapist, the impact can be positive for the whole family.

For me, the more I've learned about child development, the more patience I've been able to bring to my job. Being able to take a quick step back and consider how I am feeling and reacting is, in my opinion, one of the most effective ways we can aid a child and their emotional intelligence. Being able to decipher between an emergency or an inconvenienced toddler is a great first step.

Same emotions, different expression

When toddlers begin to talk, they will naturally begin to express their feelings, which is a wonderful thing! Even if it leads to complaints or whining, a toddler using language to express their emotions is certainly preferable to a physical expression. However, while under the age of five, when toddlers experience a heightened emotion, it's likely that they will naturally resort to crying, screaming, hitting or throwing. Which is where we come in. Knowing what your child is emotionally capable of is of the utmost importance.

For example, if you have a little chatterbox on your hands, one who can express themselves well verbally, do not expect them to always be able to rely on their communication skills during times of negative emotions. If you expect to rationalize with them verbally in the heat of the moment, it can add fuel to the already burning fire, and lead to further frustration on your part if you expect them to stop and talk it over. I know this because my own expectations of little chatterboxes were once too high. They are still toddlers.

A wonderful insight to consider is that your child feels the exact same emotions that you do, but they have much less brain development, life experience and understanding of social cues to lean on in times of need. For example:

Adult reaction	Emotion	Toddler reaction
Mutter under breath	Anger	Throw a toy
Smile	Happiness	Squeal and giggle
Ring a friend or family member	Loneliness	Scream in a bid to connect
Vent verbally	Frustration	Shout and cry
Resolve it logically	Fear	Scream and cry

I'll be honest, sometimes I wish I could throw myself on the floor and sob. And it's amazing that your toddler can express themselves so freely! Yet, your toddler isn't choosing to act in the ways that we as adults know we shouldn't – for now, that's their capability.

Having a focus on emotional development will help your toddler to build up more of the self-control that buffers their reactions. It also gifts them with a developing tolerance. Tolerance is the equivalent of having a raincoat in the cupboard ready for a rainy day – it helps to prepare us for what's to come. Ideally, then, life challenges and stress become a little more like water off a duck's back, and a little less like the hole that can sink the ship.

Creating the right foundations

The majority of work on emotional development must be done during times of calm. I realize that may seem a little odd. However, while a child's emotions are heightened, they won't be able to make much sense of how they are feeling in that moment. Imagine trying to learn something new while your heart is racing and you are screaming or crying – it's impossible! Your toddler will learn best when they are emotionally regulated.

When your toddler is emotionally dysregulated (the moments we are trying to help), these times are more about damage limitation, rather than teaching them a lesson. With this in mind, the first tool you have available to you is you. Consider the ways in which you can promote emotional intelligence and model how to cope under pressure. Some examples include the following.

Model	How	Benefits
Patience	Talk about how you feel during times of tension. For example, if you spill a drink, say, "Oh no, I spilt my drink. Let me get a cloth to clean up".	When children see their parents cope well with stress, they are more likely to cope better themselves.
Emotional awareness	Show that you understand why you, or they, are feeling something. For example, "I feel upset because I spilt my drink and I was really thirsty".	Role modelling understanding helps children to connect the dots between their emotions and actions. It can also help them understand the fact that others feel them too.
Emotional maturity (We aren't expecting them to show maturity yet, but role modelling it can be beneficial.)	Take action to help yourself move through an emotion. For example, "I'm going to make myself another drink and be really careful this time".	It's important for children to slowly learn that it's normal and perfectly okay to feel anything – we can't help how we feel, but it's how we deal with our emotions that counts.
Reflection	Think back and reflect on your own reactions, considering whether or not you'd do the same given the chance or try to stay calmer. For example, if you lose your patience and shout, apologize. Say, "I'm sorry I shouted, I felt cross that I had spilt my drink".	This lets a child know that it's okay to need more practice and to try again. It's also a great opportunity for your toddler to feel valued; if you apologize to them, it shows you care about their feelings. Feeling valued is a huge preventative factor against mental ill health.

Important: We don't want to offer children these insights into our own feelings in a way that pressures them to make us feel happy or them guilty. It's a fine balance. Don't use phrases such as "You made me feel ..." to avoid this.

Nanny Amies' Top Tip: Try to be on the lookout for your own feelings. This could be a loss of humour, irritability, feeling quiet, withdrawn, wanting to hide away, negative thoughts and not wanting to meet eye contact. These things suggest you need a little breather, and being self-aware can help you introduce coping strategies to ward off major outbursts.

What do emotions feel like?

So, how do you help a toddler learn about their emotions? When it comes to teaching a little one about their feelings, there are four main factors we can lean on for help.

1 Identify and label emotions.
2 Apply a basic understanding of what each emotion feels like.
3 Identify a connection between an emotion and an action.
4 Repetition. Toddlers require regular exposure to all emotions to cement their learning and understanding of them.

It can help to break it down in our minds to assist ourselves convey these lessons, for example:

Emotion	What does it feel like?	What does it look like?	When could it occur?
Anger	A pounding heart and wanting to scream	A scrunched-up face and clenched fists	Someone takes our toy
Happiness	Being grateful for a moment	Smiles and head held high	We see someone we love

> **Nanny Amies' Top Tip:** You can back up this learning by using each other's face to display a feeling, or a mirror to show what that face looks like. Emotional flashcards and books aimed at emotions are a go-to prop for me, also.

These lessons aren't to be taught in a "classroom-style" environment; it's more about toddlers experiencing them holistically and in their truest form. For example, if your toddler is smiling while you push them on the swing, be sure to note that, "You are smiling. You look happy to be on the swing". Or, "Henry took your car, you look really sad about that".

You can extend these lessons by offering up questions to help the child consider the feelings of others too. For example, as you are reading a story, say, "Oh, she looks really upset ... I wonder why". You could add an edge of slight concern in your tone to show you care. A very young toddler will not know why or even what "upset" means yet – this isn't about them scoring ten out of ten on the emotions pop quiz, but more about the beginnings of a cog that will one day turn into their emotional awareness machine.

What can hinder a child's emotional awareness?

As you may have surmised, I have been in homes where a child's emotional development has been somewhat derailed by certain environmental factors.

I worked for one lovely family who didn't want for anything financially, but honestly, laughter, smiles and gratitude were in short supply. Yes, the parents doted on their child – it was clear to see the amount of love they had, but they couldn't hack the tough stuff and when I say couldn't hack it, I mean truly. They admitted it to me on my first day and I assumed they were exaggerating.

"Laura, we don't cope well when the little one screams. We'll leave that to you."

Feeling needed, I initially took this as a sign of trust and validation in my position there. Yet, in practice, it was difficult to witness the complete change in both parents' demeanour once the toddler began to cry, whine or display anything other than joy. They either panicked, became really angry, leaving the room while slamming the door, or they offered their tearful toddler some chocolate. There was zero-tolerance on their part for a typical toddler outburst.

"Here, choc choc makes it better, doesn't it?", they'd say, as the toddler went down from 60 to zero the second the chocolate came out of the packet.

I was beginning to worry about the toddler's diet (the amount of chocolate offered on any given day was astronomical) and I could not fathom how the parents didn't worry too.

However, perhaps worse than any spike in blood sugar was one particular morning of complete lack of parenting … and I do not say that lightly. The toddler and I had been awake for the majority of the night due to them being unwell. I took them downstairs to try some toast.

Now, one thing I have never forgotten in my role as a nanny is knowing that no matter the bond I create with a child, nothing beats a cuddle from mum. I texted the parent to say how the night had been, hoping they would come to see their toddler.

When one parent finally emerged, they dashed into the kitchen looking frantic! Worried I'd caused them to worry, I tried to reassure with, "I think we are through the worst of it" and "They'll feel much better for a cuddle".

However, the parent dashed right past the toddler while shouting, "Rufus!" at the top of their lungs.

Wide eyed, looking under tables, opening the back door to try again, "Ruuuufus! Laura, have you seen the cat? I cannot find my cat!" they shouted from the pantry.

"Your child is unwell", came my stern reply.

"I haven't got time to listen to them, Laura. I need to find my cat."

In that sleep-deprived and emotionally charged moment, as I stood between a screaming toddler and their frantic parent, I realized that, even with the best strategies in town, the adult behaviours that the toddler was witnessing would be a stronger influence than any emotional development they may have been exposed to from me.

In that moment, I felt very vulnerable too because I couldn't understand the parent's behaviour. There was a lack of essential boundaries and that felt scary to me, and I imagine had the same impact on the toddler. No matter the scenario, children need boundaries and structure to feel safe. These parents also needed support to build their own emotional resilience before they could teach their child.

How do we build resilience?

Resilience is a protective layer of emotional armour that safeguards our mental health. Having a reserve of resilience to fall back on helps us stand strong when we are faced with challenges, upset and hard times. Everyone struggles with something – whether it be a toddler with a puzzle piece or an adult who can't find their cat. Without resilience, we can become anxious, deflated and feel like the world is against us.

The great news is that you can use simple strategies to help your child build this all-important armour. Here are a few ideas to help get you started.

1 Help the toddler to set goals and develop new skills. These can be developmental milestones such as colour recognition or potty training, alongside extra skills like learning how to complete a jigsaw puzzle or putting their own coat on.

2 Build the toddler's confidence by noting the good stuff and their efforts. For example, "I love to see you try to fit the jigsaw pieces together!"

3 Ensure the growth and security of bonds and loving relationships. Offering high-quality attention every day is a great way to show a toddler they are worthy of love and support. Feeling worthy at home also acts as a preventative measure when they start meeting people outside of the home who do not necessarily value them like you do.

4 Offer the toddler chances to make good decisions. For example, if they discard their toy at the park, "Hmmm, should we leave teddy here at the swings or take teddy home with us?" These are the type of decisions we don't even think about as adults; we simply rush to pick teddy up and leave, but allowing your toddler a touch of supervised responsibility can be a great thing.

5 Allow the toddler to experience disappointment and teach them how to cope with it. Let your toddler feel disappointed that you ran out of ice cream (no last-minute trolley dashes required here!). Let them feel disappointed that you can't go to the park today – it's in these windows of disappointment that you can allow them to problem-solve. For example, "We can't go to the park today. What shall we do at home instead?"

6 Avoid rescuing your toddler from negative emotions in a bid to prevent tears. I do know how those tears can impact your overall mood, but allowing your child the opportunity to pass through them will mean fewer tears in the long run. Appeasement can create a short-term win but has long-term impacts when used too often.

Resilience can be developed over time with continued opportunities to bounce back after feeling upset, angry, frustrated or scared. Knowing that it's normal to feel these things and that we can return to feeling safe, happy or content afterwards without the use of treats, food or screens is more beneficial than any quick fix could ever be.

The harsh reality is that your child will always come up against people who don't care about them or situations that don't go their way. Whether it be the toddler at playgroup snatching a toy, a school bully or some creep at their place of work, avoiding certain places and people will not help. Resilience and inner happiness will be their superpower for dealing with whatever comes their way.

Nanny Amies' Top Tip: Here is a simple, everyday way to help develop resilience and curb frustration. For example, if your toddler is getting frustrated with getting dressed, doing buttons, opening lids or drink bottles, try this together during play time. Waiting until it's time to get dressed or until your toddler is thirsty will increase the need for that skill and in turn frustration at being unable to achieve the desired goal.

Grounding techniques

Raising a happy toddler is about giving them the skills they need to thrive out in the world one day. If we can get our heads around the fact that adversity will, at some point, appear in our toddler's life, we surely must help them prepare for it. This is about future-proofing your little one's wellbeing.

In the same way you baby-proofed your home in preparation for their arrival, think of this like the emotional equivalent of plug socket covers and stairgates!

Grounding is essentially what the name suggests: it allows us to feel safe, with our feet firmly on the floor and our brain calm. Without any form of grounding, we can continue to panic, and panic gives our brain permission to rely on survival instincts, such as fight or flight. Toddlers need to learn that they don't need this if they miss out on the last cookie. There are a great many ways in which we can ground ourselves.

Hands and voices

Gentle, rhythmic clapping and singing can help a toddler to focus on the here and now, as opposed to the emotion beginning to take over their thoughts and actions. Obviously, we don't want to clap in their face while fully ignoring their upset, but this option can be helpful, especially when compared to strategies that are appeasement-led.

Music is another option to have ready. Music that has a similar beats-per-minute to that of our resting heart rate can be very calming. Having a lovely playlist to hand that contains songs that can help relax a toddler means that if you aren't in the mood to clap and sing, modern technology can certainly be used wisely. I love classical music that has been adapted to lullabies.

Which five things?

This is a well-known technique that many adults, particularly those suffering with anxiety, are taught to help combat intrusive thoughts. It can help your toddler "snap out of it", for want of a better phrase. It works like this: invite your toddler to focus on five things they can see, four things they can touch, three things they can hear, two things they can smell and one thing they can taste.

The order and what they choose aren't important – it's the fact that their brain is forced to be present and to absorb the environmental information available that helps to calm. For very young toddlers, I do this on a simpler scale too. For example, "Can you feel how soft teddy is? Mmmm and he smells so lovely!" or "Feel how cold this water is as it goes all the way down to your tummy". Back up your phrases with actions and body language to help a toddler engage in the visual element.

Breathing

In a true moment of panic, our breathing becomes shallow, and once we feel safe again, our breathing calms, returning to normal. Therefore, breathing techniques can be used during stressful times to override any perceived or even real panic. Again, we need to teach this outside of times of stress, and then model it during the heat of the moment. For example:

- **High five:** This technique can help toddlers to have a physical prop to help them draw in and then release their breaths. Hold up your hand in a high five position, breathe in as you trace your fingers upward and breathe out while coming back down the other side.

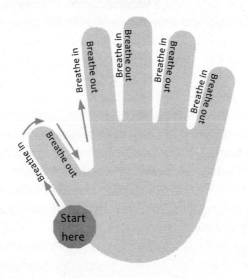

- **Flowers:** Pretend to hold a flower up to your nose and make an obvious sniffing motion before pretending to blow the petals away. Offer your pretend flower to your toddler to mimic the behaviour. You can also do this with a little windmill. If you have some pretend food, you can ask them to smell the food and blow on it to cool it down too.

- **Animals:** Animals can offer a great amount of inspiration; for example, be a bear smelling some honey before roaring out their breath.

These techniques can be modelled during play and, while they may seem like a lot of effort, they can work. They also help me feel calmer too!

When effort pays off

Let me share with you one story about when I was caring for a toddler whose emotions ran particularly close to the surface. It was important for their emotional wellbeing (and my sanity) to ensure that feelings didn't overshadow all the day-to-day activities. I was always trying to find that fine line between validation and "Let's crack on!" This toddler was very aware of their surroundings and also extremely switched on to how others were feeling.

> **Nanny Amies' Top Tip:** A sure way to know if your child is particularly sensitive is how they react to stories or programmes that have worrying or sad parts. If they really struggle to finish a story that's begun to sound a little sad, consider ways in which you can support this, as opposed to dodging all sadness or worry.

I must state that experiencing heightened emotions is not an issue in itself. This lovely toddler knew how to make people laugh and smile, and they certainly had no shortage of positive attention and truly enjoyed their interactions with others. It was relatively easy for me to offer covert lessons on emotional regulation to support them. My focus here was on emotional reactions that became disruptive, reducing what a child is willing to do, see and experience.

When the child reached the age of four, they were tasked with being a ringbearer at a wedding. With such an important role came a grown-up outfit, shiny shoes, new hairdo and a lot of anticipation!

Waiting outside for the bride's arrival, excitement levels peaked. My charge began to act a little ... well, silly. They pulled at adults' clothing, made high-pitched sounds, danced around the flower girls, treading on toes and, to be honest, looking like an accident about to happen. Essentially, excitement was getting the better of them, and while this was only to be expected in that moment, just before they were about to walk down the aisle in front of everyone carrying the rings was far from ideal!

The young ringbearer's parent sternly asked them to calm down – you know the technique, not wanting to create a scene but hoping to convey exactly how serious you are in that moment (it's all in the eyes). To everyone's surprise, the youngster stood motionless for a short moment, took a deep breath and said, "I just need to breathe and count. One ... two ... three ..."

They calmed down beautifully, just as the bride arrived, and went on to carry the rings down the aisle like a pro! This toddler had prior knowledge and practice at being able to calm themselves down and could draw on it when needed.

Nanny Amies' Top Tip: There are many times during the day to spend quality time with your child, even if you are out at work for much of it. Find the windows when you can be beside them and take that moment as a chance to talk about how we feel. For example, teeth brushing, bathing, bedtimes and dinner times. Leave phones in another room while focusing on eye contact and verbal interactions. This will also help to boost your child's sense of belonging.

Fear and anxiety

I am asked a lot about this topic and it sits very close to my heart. First, I would like to state how important it is to distinguish between fear and anxiety. In a world where people like me constantly promote emotional awareness, unfortunately it is common for parents to swing a tad too far, saying their toddler has anxiety. It is also common for parents to fall into the, "That may emotionally scar them" camp, and try to remove anything remotely challenging from their child's life. Things that induce stress do not automatically spell disaster. Some children are naturally more sensitive, but that does not denote anxiety. As you'll see on page 265, some children have intense reactions toward certain things, but again, that does not denote anxiety either. Anxiety is a medical condition covering various disorders. It is only classed as anxiety when it significantly impacts your day-to-day functioning. It's perfectly normal for toddlers to show some fearful behaviours. However, if they appear particularly anxious, withdrawn, show a loss of appetite, display physical symptoms such as an upset tummy, struggle to sleep and/or become very emotional, it's worth speaking with your doctor.

What can we do as parents today? Let me give you an example. If your toddler sees a dog barking, recoils and says, "I don't like it", they have essentially shown a natural awareness and respect toward something which looks unpredictable, noisy and potentially harmful. If they can walk away relatively calmly and either not mention it again or repeatedly come back to thoughts of said dog, we can chalk this down as natural "fear".

If your toddler constantly checks for dogs, asking if there will be a dog where you are going, asking about dogs at bedtime, refusing to go to a place where a dog may be, showing a loss of appetite or essentially displaying behaviours that are impacting day-to-day life, it's more likely that this is some form of anxiety that needs some extra support.

The key here is how we respond when a child first shows a fear-based behaviour. If, when a child first recoils in response to seeing a dog, their parent immediately crosses the road, avoids dogs at all costs, rings friends ahead of a visit asking, "Can you make sure your dog is locked in the garden when we get there?", and tells everyone how scared their child is of dogs, what started as a natural respect or fear can actually develop into something more deep-rooted.

These are the steps I follow if a child in my care displays fearful behaviour toward something.

1 Stay calm, be patient and remember how impactful your facial expression can be. Relax and smile.
2 Do not immediately veer away from the fear-inducing thing (dog, hand-dryer, etc). Instead, stop and look on calmly.
3 Offer up some factual information. For example, "The dog barks instead of using words like we do. He's talking to us".
4 Focus on the facts. The dog has barked, fact. But this dog is on a lead and we are safe, another fact.
5 Allow for a short observation to process information.
6 Use positive language toward the thing they fear. "The dog's tail is wagging so quickly! That means he's happy."
7 Validate the toddler's fear but move on. "I can see you are worried about the dog. We are safe. Let's keep walking."
8 Read books about the thing they are fearful of or watch TV shows that feature it. Knowledge and familiarity will help.
9 Perhaps get a toy dog or teddy to help increase their exposure gently.
10 Try to expose the toddler to the thing they fear via real-world opportunities (your neighbour's lovely gentle old dog, for example).

Yes, feelings are important, and being aware of how we feel, as the theme of this chapter suggests, is vital, but our mindset toward how we and others feel is as important as the feelings themselves.

Nanny Amies' Top Tip: You do not have to convince your child to feel something other than the emotion they are expressing. Listening, validating and moving on is more helpful. Imagine if you told me, "I hate ironing!" and I said, "No you don't, it's fab! Come on, crack on!" It's better to acknowledge what they are feeling than to try to persuade them otherwise.

Fear is contagious

The reason this topic sits close to my heart is because I'm a natural-born worrier, and my mum, bless her, is too. I have a vivid memory of my mum taking my sister and me to a fireworks display. This was actually a great opportunity for exposure as I was terrified of thunder and lightning, so loud noises, in general, made me feel very uneasy.

I can still feel my mum's tight grip on my hand as the fireworks were flying into the sky and she said, "Don't look up! If they fall back down to the ground, they'll blind you".

I am chuckling as I write this! My mum is a wonderful mum, but honestly, who ever heard of a fireworks display where you are only allowed to look at your feet? Turns out my mum wasn't so keen on fireworks and, in a bid to do something fun, became very nervous herself while there. I remember her words every time I see fireworks!

Whether you are trying to overcome a fear yourself or only just discovering the importance of your child's emotional development and resilience, I hope this chapter has helped. I will finish up by saying that no matter how difficult it can feel to teach these important life lessons, I promise you that your child will benefit greatly from learning them at home with you, as opposed to trying to figure it all out for themselves later in life.

CHAPTER 12
SPEECH AND LANGUAGE

"C c c cat"

Being there while a child learns how to talk and express themselves is one of the most wonderful parts of working with children. Hearing those early babbles turn into words is always a highlight of my job. We tend to have expectations of a toddler's ability to communicate; for example, understanding that babies can't talk, but expecting a three-year-old child to be able to tell you what their favourite animal is. So, what if things aren't going as you expect?

Some children learn to talk with ease, whereas others may experience a speech delay, develop a stutter or have challenges processing the language available to them. In this chapter we will look at how speech develops, how we nurture their language skills and how that has an undeniable impact on a child's overall ability to communicate.

Why is communication so important?

All living creatures communicate with their fellow species, whether covering the very basics of survival or to socialize with one another. The way humans use language has moulded us into a story-telling, humorous, forward-planning, unique species that interacts far beyond the most basic of human requirements.

For toddlers, communication on any level helps them to get their needs met. It also helps them to cement bonds with their parents, which, in turn, supports their chance of survival but increases their overall chance of flourishing within their environment.

Essentially, our potential to learn how to communicate effectively offers children a better chance of a strong future with more opportunities to build relationships, study, enjoy hobbies, work and hopefully become well-rounded individuals. Our language use also gives others a valuable window into our thoughts, mood, character, likes and dislikes, which, when others know these things, enhances our experiences. Simply put, talking makes us, us.

> **Nanny Amies' Top Tip:** Opportunities to boost your toddler's communication skills are all around you. Whether you are outside or indoors, talking about what you can see, hear and feel every day will help your toddler to process and understand the world they live in.

How do toddlers learn to communicate?

Right from the day they are born, children absorb communication via facial expressions, tones of voice, body language and touch. They may begin to contribute, practise and enjoy basic levels of verbal communication from as early as eight weeks old.

As babies begin to coo, they will hopefully receive a positive reaction and some form of returned communicational contribution from their parent. Whether that be a smile, some eye contact, a coo back or some loving words. When this happens, babies begin to look for that interaction, thrive from it and create an almost tennis-like rally between themselves and those within their environment. Coos progress into babbling (stringing sounds together), babbling develops into words and words then form short sentences, before children begin to speak more fluently. How we respond to these early interactions paves the way for all future interactions. However, learning how to make sounds and form words is only one part of our communication skill set; we must also understand what it is that we hear in order to use language to our advantage.

> **Nanny Amies' Top Tip:** If you have any concerns with regard to your toddler's communication skills or their hearing, don't hesitate to reach out to your doctor.

Language development

There are two main areas of language development: receptive and expressive. Receptive language usually develops first and includes: listening skills; understanding what we hear; processing visual information; the ability to follow instructions and to understand questions; along with the ability to predict what may happen next. In a nutshell, receptive language covers the things we hear.

> **Nanny Amies' Top Tip:** If your child doesn't follow instructions, don't automatically worry there is an issue with their receptive language skills. Age, behavioural habits and environmental factors should also be taken into account first.

Expressive language includes the use of words, gestures or signs in ways that enable us to express ourselves effectively. This is our ability to answer questions, make choices and use language practically in all areas of life. In a nutshell, expressive language covers what we say.

The first year of life is when receptive skills are beginning to form. A child starts to recognize sounds and the visual elements of language, such as facial expressions. Toward the end of that first year, your child may be able to wait to see if and how you respond to them, beginning some turn-taking. From 12 months, their speech has likely progressed to simple words and they may be able to request objects by their name. This object recognition is backed up with our words or sounds, so how you interact with them matters. For example, if a toddler says, "Brum, Brum!" while reaching for a toy car and their parent says, "Here's your Brum Brum", the car will continue to be referred to as a Brum Brum.

You will probably know that by now your toddler has realized they can use their voice to gain attention or make a stand. It's also highly likely that they understand much more than what they can yet verbally express.

As we progress toward two years old, your toddler may be able to respond to a question such as "Where's Teddy?" and back up their answer with a gesture or movement toward said teddy. They may begin to produce multiple words but will probably also show frustration that they cannot fully express themselves yet.

Next comes the ability to follow a two- or even three-part instruction, for example, "Please go to the kitchen and get your drink", along with being able to name and point to body parts. Your toddler may be stringing short sentences together and becoming more progressive in terms of being able to have simple conversations with you or their peers. They will begin to pronounce their words with some degree of accuracy, but not every word.

Around three years old, a toddler will continue to develop and perform more intricate sentences, as well as narrating what they are doing or being able to tell you little stories, recall events from the past perhaps and to express themselves, their wants and their needs more effectively.

It's important to know that some children will do these things a little later and some perhaps a little quicker than the brief milestones mentioned here. As with any other part of your child's developmental journey, it is unique to them.

> **Nanny Amies' Top Tip:** Children who have extra needs, hearing difficulties or who are neurodivergent may require extra support and specialist strategies beyond the ones described within this chapter. Though I very much hope that the information provided will offer everyone at least some food for thought.

Things that impede language development

While we've established that language development refines with age, there are, of course, things we can do to aid and also unintentionally hinder how a toddler's communication skills progress.

Pronunciation: It's very common for some form of mispronunciation to be delivered during the toddler years. In the rush of day-to-day life, perhaps you won't even blink when you hear, "dink pease" as opposed to "drink please", for example. As cute as these little mispronunciations are, when we reply with, "Here's your dink", we reinforce the child's current articulation of those words.

It's also common for words to be skipped entirely from a sentence, letters to be dropped from a word or certain sounds to be exchanged. While this is all very much a normal part of language development, if we mimic a child's attempts instead of modelling the correct language use, we reinforce incorrect verbalizations.

Overuse of words: Every parent and childcare provider has sounded like a broken record at some point, for example repeatedly saying, "Time to get shoes on" as you are trying to leave the house! If annoyance for this habit isn't enough to deter you from repetition, perhaps knowing that the overuse of words can also negatively impact your little one's communication skills will.

For example, if we are trying to teach a certain word, it could be very easy to say it again and again. After all, the experts say that repetition and consistency are the best ways to help a child learn, right? While this is true for creating new habits and other skills, saying single words or phrases in quick succession time and time again can create a "white noise effect", with the child zoning out. It also removes the need for a child to copy or mimic the word back.

Overuse would look like, "Look a cat! Can you say cat? The cat is orange ... the cat is so cute! Cat. Cat. This is a cat."

Effective use would look like, "The cat is orange. Cat". (While pointing to the cat.)

Over-complicated: It's easy for us to chatter away without thought for how advanced our own adult speech patterns are. It can be difficult for toddlers to pinpoint certain information or words within many. In instances where we are focusing on a toddler's speech development and communicating with them directly, less is more.

Speaking too quickly: Similarly to complicated language, firing words at a rapid pace can make them harder to process and gives a toddler less time to attempt and mimic.

Too many questions: A popular approach to language development is questioning a child; for example, "What colour is this?", "How about this one?", "Can you show me where the blue ball is?" While some questions are absolutely fine, too many, especially in quick succession, can become overwhelming.

Stating facts can be more effective, essentially offering a child a chance to hear, process and, in turn, mimic what you say. Too many questions will feel more like you are testing their knowledge, as opposed to offering an opportunity for them to speak. If they are unsure or frustrated, they are more likely to throw the blue ball at your head as opposed to having a guess at its colour!

Adding pressure: Forcing a child to say a word can lead to them backing away from an attempt, either due to a typical power struggle or a lack of faith in themselves. The same goes for a lack of patience; if their attempts are met with, "NO! Not dink, it's drink!" they will be less inclined to try next time.

Offering rewards: "Say 'drink' and you can have your drink" may seem like a motivational tactic, but if they cannot physically pronounce the "dr" sound yet, you will either have a very thirsty toddler on your hands or you will have just offered up a scenario where your words aren't very meaningful. Either way, when it comes to a natural skill that a child will benefit from practising, rewards don't need putting in place … and certainly no consequences either.

Screen usage: Passive screen time, which is where a child is engaged only observationally in the content on screen, can be detrimental to the development of language. This is because there is no opportunity to react verbally, mimic words, answer or ask questions. This can not only dampen a child's willingness to converse but also the actual need to.

Some content is better than others. If the presenter or character on screen appears to make eye contact with the viewer while asking questions, before pausing to "hear" an answer, using a warm, friendly tone, this is hugely preferable! However, even the most high-quality screen time does not knock real-life interaction off the top spot when it comes to effective ways to help speech develop. Ultimately, screen time is pre-recorded, leaving no room for initiative, real-time reactions, relevant comments or back-and-forth communication in its truest sense.

Lack of interaction: A lack of real-time interaction with trusted people will have a negative impact on a child's communication skills. It can also hinder the development of self-esteem, sense of belonging, and an understanding of the world around them.

Nanny Amies' Top Tip: If you are particularly lacking in energy and not up for a chat, offering your child eye contact and a smile are still important markers for communication. Throw in a hug and an "I love you", and you have definitely helped their communication skills develop.

Stuttering

You can be great at all this, and yet, sometimes things just don't go quite as planned. This was evident to me within one family home, where the parents had an incredibly sensible approach and predictable routines, but the children displayed behaviours that neither of them ever expected.

It became clear to us all that the toddler had a prominent stutter. This presented itself as long pauses between words, or the beginning of a word being repeated several times before the full pronunciation came through. They would also mispronounce certain sounds too; for example: "I, I, I, I … w w w w want … m my, at". (Instead of "I want my cat".)

It was as if the first few syllables were huge hurdles to jump, but once over them, the rest of the sentence flowed with relative ease, minus the odd missing sound. Sadly, this led to much frustration on the toddler's part because it was difficult to understand them at times.

The toddler had met all their previous milestones, didn't really have screen time and spent quality time with their parents – and with me – and interacted with peers too. Not to mention the fact that their older sibling was very chatty. So most, if not all, boxes were being ticked in terms of their exposure to language.

The parents had hoped it was "just a phase" (perhaps the most commonly used term when talking about toddlers), but as the months crept on, the stutter and mispronunciation appeared to have settled in for the long term.

> **Nanny Amies' Top Tip:** Typically speaking, "phases" are short-lived changes in a child's behaviours or habits which last a month, or two, max. Once a phase has passed, behaviour or habits then return back to the child's "normal". Anything that outlives a short timeframe may be due to reinforcement from environmental factors or requires extra support.

The parents weren't keen to let too much time pass, so they booked in weekly trips to a speech therapist. From both a professional and personal level, I really enjoyed the sessions. I loved to see the therapist at work, incorporating specific words, strategies and therapy as the toddler simply enjoyed "playing". To the toddler, the therapist's room was something of a treasure trove, yet it was clear to see that each toy had been specially handpicked to ensure that just the right level of communication could be had while interacting with them.

So, I observed, took notes and printed out speech therapy to-do lists, sharing them with my bosses and the nursery where the toddler had begun attending a couple of mornings per week, just to ensure that we were all singing from the same hymn sheet.

The toddler in my care loved soaking up new experiences and was clearly very bright. I felt proud of them while they unknowingly worked hard in each session. Yet progress was slow. Slow to the point where the therapist recommended that we take the toddler to a hearing specialist. It was discovered they had a severe case of glue ear, which required surgery. It escapes me how we had all missed this previously.

I'll never forget how when they came out of surgery, the toddler asked repeatedly, "W w w w what's ... a a a at sound?" (What's that sound?) when a car drove past, a dog barked in the distance or a bird sang in the trees, and it was as if they were hearing it for the first time. They had been experiencing life almost on mute. Within a month of surgery, their speech had made an incredible turn-around. This was a classic case of no matter how effective the approaches were, nature had mapped out the ability of this toddler ... for a short time at least.

> **Nanny Amies' Top Tip:** There are many common speech "mistakes" that toddlers make such as dropping syllables, swapping sounds and missing sounds from words, for example. These things do not automatically mean the toddler has a speech impediment. If you have any concerns, discuss them with your doctor.

How can we help?

There are lots of ways you can help! Here is a mini guide to improving your toddler's speech – let's call it a table of stutter dos and don'ts.

Do	Do not
Be patient	Show frustration (though it's understandable to feel it at times)
Wait for the child to finish a sentence	Critique the child's speech
Make eye contact	Ignore the child or limit time with them
Smile and listen	Tell the child to hurry up
Repeat the child's sentence back for them to hear	Tell the child to try again
Speak clearly (the child may lip read too)	Cut the child off or finish their sentence
Let the child know you are trying to understand	Tell the child that you cannot understand them

Create a code: Make a list of the sounds or words that your child mispronounces (without them knowing). While this may sound like a lot of effort, if your child mispronounces a few sounds per sentence, it can be difficult to understand what they are trying to say. Having access to this list will be like creating a code for you to refer back to, which will reduce frustration. For example:

Zak's pronunciation	Correct pronunciation
Lake, lack, leep	Snake, snack, sleep
Dink	Drink
Yeg, yots, yong	"l" leg, lots, long
Babbit	Rabbit

Repeat it back: When you hear your toddler say a word incorrectly, say the correct pronunciation to act as a model for them to hear, process and copy. For example:

Toddler: "I like my babbit."

Parent: "Yes, you do like your rabbit!"

Encourage listening ears: Help your child to listen, process and make sense of all the sounds available to them by taking note of what you hear. For example, "Wow, I can hear the birds singing", while looking up at the trees or, "Ooh, I can hear the phone ringing", as someone calls you.

Being able to make sense of the familiar sounds children hear around them is great practice for processing the words spoken to them. You can extend this during play by pretending their play telephone is ringing and mimicking a conversation with them.

Use facial expressions: Use facial expressions and gestures to back up your communication and help your toddler understand the emotions behind some of our communication. This can happen naturally and in a staged manner too. For example:

Drop a toy during play, raise your hands to your face and say, "Oh dear, I dropped the toy!"

Open your arms wide in an attempt to initiate a hug, while smiling and say, "I love you".

Furrow your brow and look scared as you read a worrying part of a story.

Use correct labels: It's so tempting to speak at the same level as your toddler and refer to all their favourite things using the sweet little words they do. However, this can delay their progress. For example, a toddler will go through a stage of referring to things as the sounds they make, so it's a "woof woof" for dog. Our job is to model the correct label and offer them multiple chances to hear the correct pronunciation.

Encourage turn-taking: Try to create a few purposeful moments in a day where you get down to your toddler's level to talk with them. Make eye contact, perhaps some physical touch, and say a very clear, simple sentence. Then remain in their line of sight, pause for a moment and wait for them to offer some form of communication back.

Even if you do not fully understand what they say, this is the beginning of a flowing, back-and-forth conversation, which all adds up once they become more fluent. You can expand this by using objects as directed below.

Model speech: While holding a toy or object of interest, try these three stages of modelling speech for a toddler.

1 First, model an appropriate word, sound or short sentence. For example, "The car goes beep, beep!" as you wheel it on the floor.
2 Second, remain silent for a moment to give the toddler a chance to process what they heard.
3 Third, repeat the same word, sound or sentence while offering your toddler the toy or object.

This allows toddlers to observe both visually and audibly. Multi-layered learning via play offers them a wonderful leg-up at most skills.

Use descriptive narration: Tell your child simple stories that narrate their play, mealtimes or outings. This models appropriate language use for them to mimic and also offers them a chance to connect to and understand their surroundings. For example:

- "Let's cross the road here, so we can get to the park."
- "You are building a BIG, tall tower. Wow!"
- "I've got some carrot on my fork, you have potato."

Using tone and enthusiasm (when you can muster it) will enhance certain bits of information and engage your child.

Create the need to converse: You can create opportunities for your little one to speak, ask for help or use problem-solving language that has benefits far beyond their language development. It might be that you place a favoured toy within a box so that your child will need to draw your attention to this issue and also ask for help. If they become frustrated, calmly model how to get help or problem-solve. For example, "Oh dear (hands to face), teddy is stuck in the box ... let's see what happens when I lift the lid up. There you are, teddy! Were you hiding?"

When things like this are done with a smile during play, your child begins to understand how to deal with adversity and things not going their way. I have to say, it's wonderful to see them put this into practice too!

Use signs: You can introduce signs alongside simple words to offer up a layer of visual information for little ones to process. You can do this using baby sign language, Makaton (see page 272) or making up your own simple gestures.

One simple example of this is waving. We learn from a young age that waving typically means goodbye, and we say "goodbye" as we wave. So, if you wave silently to a child, they may say "goodbye" as they process what that sign means.

You can do this with a range of things such as "drink", "eat" and "more", and it can really help to remove frustration for young children trying to express their needs effectively. This may lead to fewer tantrums and further development of cognitive thinking, which helps a child to learn, remember, focus, comprehend and communicate.

Use positional language: Use positional and factual language to represent an object's size, position and any other information that will help your toddler to better navigate their surroundings. For example, "The teddy is behind the pillow" or "The ball is bigger than the car".

Offer choices: During play, offer your toddler two clear choices to help encourage word formation. For example, while holding two cars, one in each hand, invite them to make a choice such as, "Would you like the blue car or the red car?", then hold out the relevant choice.

They might only respond with a gesture at first or reach out to take their preference, but when they do, reinforce their choice. "The blue one? Nice choice", as you hand it to them. Over time, they will attempt to back up their choices with verbal cues as well.

Books and music: There are endless resources available to you that can help promote language and communication, but perhaps the easiest (and one of my favourites) are good, old-fashioned books! Reading the same book each day helps children to remember, predict, process and attempt to mimic the language within.

Songs and nursery rhymes are wonderful for language development too, as the melodies add another layer of information that helps support children to remember and attempt the words and actions for themselves.

Be positive: Be animated when you chat to your toddler. Try to make learning how to speak fun and low pressure. Even if you have any concerns about your toddler's language development, I promise that your child will make more progress if they feel like they are playing or just getting to spend time with you.

A word a week: If you feel your toddler needs a bit of extra support with their speech, perhaps focus on one word or sound per week. Starting small and working up means less pressure on you and your child. Emphasize the sound or word they are struggling with while keeping the experience no-pressure.

Anyone for a strawberry? Back when I was a live-in nanny, one of my little charges displayed typical speech "mistakes". Like so many do, my charge struggled with sounds such as "st", "sh" or "sp". These sounds are longer than many, therefore harder to produce, which results in many toddlers swapping it for sounds which are easier to produce like "p", for example. So "stop" may become "pop".

Strawberries were a favoured food, so whenever my charge saw them, they'd gesture toward the delicious fruit while saying, "Plonk, plonk". You see, the word strawberry is tricky, starting with a long "s" sound and also having three syllables. Toddlers will naturally reduce the number of syllables within a word or double up on an easy one to enable them to mimic the flow of a word.

I must admit, I found hearing the toddler say "plonk plonk" adorable, but I knew deep down we needed to try to move past it. So, I made it my mission to teach them the word strawberry. Out came the basket of play fruit. We had strawberries for breakfast, lunch and dinner. We drew strawberries, sourced some strawberry stickers, you name it ... I may as well have danced around in a giant strawberry costume with all the attention I was paying this one word!

The toddler's older siblings got involved and one dinner, a few days into my mission, we were all sat around the table. When it came to portioning out some fruit, I held a strawberry over the toddler's bowl and tried a new tactic.

Me: "Straw ... " while keeping a hold of the strawberry.
The siblings watched quietly.
Toddler: "Staw ..."
Excellent! Progress at last! The siblings clapped.
Me: "Berry ... "
Toddler: "Bey ... "
Fabulous! The siblings cheered.
Me: "Strawberry ... " I finally placed the fruit in their bowl.
Toddler: [with the biggest grin] "Plonk, plonk".

They threw back their head giggling. The siblings (and me) laughed too!

They'd been having me on! Most likely holding out and waiting for me to dress up as that giant strawberry. Out-foxed by a two-year-old child in the name of attention and connection. While it did begin as a natural speech difficulty, they must have loved the focus I was applying to them and their favourite fruit, so I really couldn't blame them for dragging it out and making it a fun game. However, I learned from this and avoided sensationalizing specific words in the future.

Baby talk vs child-directed speech

Some people will be reading this wondering why we need to rush a toddler out of their cute mispronunciations – what's the harm? Baby talk is cute, right? Let's take a look at the different ways parents and children talk to throw some light on this topic.

I've posted videos online of how I converse with toddlers, and many have been quick to say I sound patronizing or like I'm dumbing things down for them. Using the same language as your toddler or simplifying phrases is known as "child-directed speech" or "parentese". It really splits adults down the middle in terms of how they feel about it. Are we "dumbing down" or helping a toddler to converse? How do we get the balance right?

Let's look at some adult-directed speech and compare it to how a toddler or baby might talk.

Adult-directed speech	Child-directed speech	Baby talk
Formal	Fun	Silly
Complex	Simple	Incorrect
Fast-paced	Slower-paced	Quick-paced
Monotonal	Melodic	High-pitched
Direct	Offers support	Reinforces speech difficulties

Examples of adult-directed speech	Examples of child-directed speech	Examples of baby talk
"The dog is really big and fluffy. His fur is so thick and needs brushing. I'll do it later. He's very happy to see you; I can tell because he's wagging his tail."	"The dog is wagging their tail, hello dog", with a wave gesture.	"Ooh, such a wovely doggy woggy! He's sooooo SWEET! I could just muah, muah, muah!"
"NO! There's no more snacks today, you've eaten lots of snacks already. You have to wait until dinner time now."	"It's not snack time, we'll have dinner first."	"You'd like a snacky snack? Ooh, I know they are yummy scrummy but you can't fit anymore in your ickle belly welly!"
"If you don't brush your teeth, the plaque will stick to them and make holes in your teeth. They'll hurt a lot and you will cry. Brush your teeth."	"Time to brush teeth, you can sit here or stand on the step."	"Let's brush those ickle teethies! They are yucky yucky, so we must scrub, scrub, scrub!"

The baby talk may sound fun and innocent, which of course it is in small bouts. It's just worth considering the long-term impacts of referring to objects, animals and toys as made-up or incorrect words and phrases. Adult-directed speech can leave toddlers missing out on chances to process important information due to the speed and complexity with which it is offered to them.

You'll speak to your child however you feel most comfortable and that's important, especially when it comes to helping them develop this vitally important life skill.

Nanny Amies' Top Tip: What might sound like nonsense or baby talk from your toddler, if in response to your interaction, is still communication. Mirroring the appropriate pronunciation for them to hear in these instances is still important.

When should I get my toddler help?

If you feel that your toddler needs some extra support, seek advice. I'd rather hear, "You're worrying over nothing", than wish I'd acted sooner. However, in a bid to help you make this choice wisely, I would consider seeking help when your toddler is two years old and a few of the following are true.

- You struggle to understand any of your child's communication. It's common for non-family members not to understand a toddler at this age – the key here is if you understand or not.
- Your child says very few words.
- Your child cannot yet put two or more words together.
- Your child struggles to follow simple instructions or to answer simple questions with words or gestures such as "Where's the ball?"
- Your toddler is continuously avoiding eye contact or not responding to your spoken words.
- Your toddler has developed a stutter or has begun to rhythmically repeat certain words.
- Your child is struggling to articulate certain sounds past the typical toddler speech "mistakes".
- A lack of communication skills is negatively impacting socializing.
- You don't witness age-appropriate developmental progress in your child's speech and language skills.
- You have consistently implemented strategies or advice and seen no progress.

Ultimately, home is the best place for children to learn how to talk. Even an expert speech therapist would tell you that there is only so much they can do in a quick weekly session. Working alongside a trusted parent or carer allows toddlers to enjoy meaningful engagement where they are comfortable and relaxed, which means their brain can focus on the task at hand. The home environment also offers up daily opportunities for consistency.

> **Nanny Amies' Top Tip:** Sometimes toddlers can repeat the same sentence or phrase as a normal part of their development. This is usually down to them practising their newfound skill and feeling part of a conversation. When your toddler is stuck in a loop, acknowledge them and redirect them to another topic. For example, "Yes, the teddy is pink. Ooh, I love that book ... ".

How you communicate with your toddler now impacts how you speak to one another throughout their childhood. Like the saying goes, listen to the little stuff now and they'll be more inclined to share the big stuff with you later. I know that after I moved out and moved city, my mum still appreciates seeing my name pop up on her phone as I ring for a quick chat. And I love it too.

CHAPTER 13

ILLNESS AND TRAUMA

"Caller, what's your emergency?"

READ ME FIRST!

Before we get into this chapter, and if you read no more than the next few words, please take this advice:

Attend a paediatric first aid course.

First aid shouldn't only be something that professional childcare providers attend. I truly believe that anyone who spends time with children, especially parents, should know the basics – that means *all* parents.

I am going to cover the basics of first aid here too, but learning how to do it in a class can really help to cement your response in an emergency. We are also going to look at illness and how I cope with it as a childcare provider.

You should also know that there is a reason I have chosen to leave this topic for the final chapter. I hope that, by now, you will feel like you've got to know me a little better before I go on to describe what was one of the worst days of my life, and certainly of my career.

This was a day I found so traumatic that in the weeks and months afterwards, I had to dig incredibly deep to remain in the field of nannying. Still now, a decade on, something can trigger a memory and I'm right back in a beautiful family home, holding a tiny tot in my arms thinking the worst had happened. While I have never underestimated the privilege of caring for someone's child, when you experience severe illnesses or emergency scenarios with them, it alters anything you think you thought you knew about childcare. I would never forgive myself if I were not able to hand a child back over to their parents at the end of a shift. Apologies in advance if you find this difficult to read because I know I am going to find parts of it difficult to write.

My worst nightmare

This day started as any other had, to the sounds of my 18-month-old charge rustling around in their cot as they began to stir. They woke happy, we dressed for the day, ate breakfast and attended a music class.

After music class, still in good spirits, we walked through a beautiful park and, as my little charge was cooing and waving at the ducks, I felt very lucky to be their nanny.

We arrived home shortly afterwards and went up to their room for a nappy change. As I lifted their legs to slide the fresh nappy under their bottom, I saw their eyes roll to the back of their head. In that same spilt second, their legs stiffened and slammed back down onto the changing mat as their arms shot above their head. They began to convulse violently. My brain could hardly process what I was seeing.

A conversation I had had with one of their parents six months ago on my first day on the job suddenly hit me like a truck: "When the baby was eight months old, they had a minor febrile convulsion. Very out of the blue and they've been entirely fine ever since, so it was likely a one-off."

Not worried in the slightest, I replied, "Okay, thanks for the heads-up. Fingers crossed we won't see another one".

The parent walked toward a drawer, pointed at a box and confidently said, "You won't need it, but if ever they have another, and it lasts more than five minutes, pop this tube in their bottom and squeeze out the contents. It will help to stop the convulsions".

I picked the toddler up to take them with me to the bathroom to find the medication. It wasn't five minutes, but surely I couldn't wait that long?

I started to make my way down the stairs as I shouted for the housekeeper. After descending to a lower level of the house, I stopped to try to open the medication in case I needed it. I laid the toddler down on their side in a recovery position across my knee. Thank you first aid classes!

And then, my little charge began foaming at the mouth.

Terrified, I popped the medication out the wrapper. I was faced with a terrible decision – do I wait and hope the convulsions stop soon or just use it now? Gosh, I couldn't think straight for the sound of my pulse in my ears and the pounding of my heartbeat.

I realized that, as well as a foaming mouth and the continuous volatile convulsions, my charge's lips had turned completely blue and their skin was pale. Whether it had been three minutes or four, I couldn't fight the urge to hold off with the medication a second longer. Rightly or wrongly, I made the decision to squirt the tiny tube of medication into their bottom.

Because I was now seated and holding the little one in the recovery position with one hand, I could reach the phone in my pocket, and I dialled 999.

In my naivety (and in all honesty, panic), I had assumed that the medication was some form of adrenaline. At that point I had no memory of ever covering convulsions in my first aid courses, but my brain conjured up an image of me administering it and my charge just springing back to life. This is when the world seemed to close in around me because, instead of my hopeful image becoming reality, the toddler looked worse than ever.

As I was on the phone trying to explain the scenario, the little one stopped convulsing and went floppy, before simultaneously vomiting their dinner and emptying their bowels. In that moment I genuinely thought they were dying.

So there, on the landing of that beautiful family home, covered in vomit and diarrhoea, holding this precious, floppy, lifeless toddler across my lap, in my mind my life was over too.

At this moment, the housekeeper finally made it upstairs and, upon seeing the horrendous scene, immediately threw herself on the floor, shouting, "Please god, don't let it be true! Please don't take our baby!"

In my guilt-ridden, utterly heartbroken state, while the housekeeper prayed, I leaned down over the toddler's tiny body, my ear to their mouth, looking toward their chest in the hope of seeing them breathe. My first aid training told me to think about rescue breaths. I turned the toddler on their back, readying myself to pinch their tiny nose, while keeping their chin pushed back to stretch out their airways, when suddenly, they gasped. I cannot tell you the relief I felt in that moment.

The community first responder arrived in minutes and stayed with us while we waited for the ambulance to arrive. This gave me the chance to ring my boss and explain what had happened, still trying to hold on to a modicum of professionalism while holding back the sobs.

My bosses turned up at the same time as the ambulance, and one parent picked up the toddler, placing their limp body almost in a burping position over their shoulder. As they walked down the stairs, the toddler projectile vomited again.

As we all reached the front door, a car horn sounded as it drove by. The toddler lifted their head, just long enough to say a very meek, "Beep beep!", before flopping back down onto their parent's supportive shoulder.

The relief I felt in hearing that gorgeous "Beep beep" will stay with me forever. I waved them off, closed the door and immediately collapsed into a heap of tears.

I later learned that the medication had been an intense dose of diazepam (a type of muscle relaxant) which helped deal with the convulsions and then lulled them into a deep, relaxed state. It had done its job.

Have I done mine and convinced you to book that first aid course?

Convulsions and seizures

It is thought that around 1 in 25 children will experience a seizure, fit or convulsion. It can happen when a child's temperature suddenly peaks, like a short-circuit in the brain, causing the child to convulse. Despite my harrowing first experience with febrile convulsions, they are not usually serious or life-threatening, but you must, of course, seek medical intervention should your child ever have one.

While they are truly horrible to witness, generally speaking, children do not remember or fully realize what has occurred, suffering no adverse or long-lasting effects either. Typically lasting for two or three minutes, febrile convulsions are something they tend to grow out of without the need for long-term medical support.

Once a child has had a convulsion, it makes sense to be prepared for another. We got another prescription of diazepam and I put one in their nappy bag too. I simply would not consider going anywhere without one.

When the toddler had another convulsion on a long-haul flight, I was incredibly grateful for the medical pouch packed in their flight bag. Always be prepared.

So many bugs doing the rounds

Thankfully, not every situation is life-threatening. Most of the time, it is the everyday bugs and illnesses we need to deal with. Toddlers seem to catch everything. Whether it be a common cold, a tummy bug or a case of chicken pox, illness is no walk in the park and can have a domino effect on daily routines, sleep and behaviours. It is quite common for an entire family unit to be floored, emotionally and physically, by illness.

> **Nanny Amies' Top Tip:** While we can't avoid all bugs, ensuring your toddler's nutritional intake is sufficient can certainly help them ward off and/or recover more quickly. Offer your child immune-boosting foods (vitamin C-packed options) alongside a multivitamin for children.

Back in my first ever nannying role, despite all my previous years as a nursery nurse, I remember being shocked at how regularly the children in my care would actually be poorly. Noses seemed to stream constantly, nappies would require hazard waste warnings and I was a regular at the local pharmacy for the treatments required. And guess who else is getting ill every five minutes? Yep, us adults too!

Once a child begins attending nursery or any place where they come into close contact with other youngsters, you can pretty much guarantee you'll experience most of the common childhood illnesses before their first term is through. Being prepared is important. Of course, we cannot predict all eventualities, but having a small medicine supply ready to go means that you can attend to your child effectively sooner rather than later, and you are ready for any night-time needs.

Nanny Amies' Top Tip: Wash hands! Every time we enter the home, I always wash (or wipe clean) little hands. I also do this before snacks and mealtimes. I will also, at some point, discuss germs with my toddlers, and how they can spread from our hands to our tummies, making us unwell.

Medicine cupboard

Some households I've worked in had a fully stocked medicine cupboard, whereas others have used Nanna's old biscuit tin to store various medications in – the presentation really does not matter, it's just important to have the essentials ready. I always keep the following in stock.

- Age-appropriate paracetamol/acetaminophen (e.g. Tylenol)
- Age-appropriate ibuprofen
- Age-appropriate antihistamine
- Baby-strength eucalyptus oil and vapour rubs
- Thermometer
- Medication syringes (as opposed to the measuring spoons)
- Well-stocked first aid kit, including dressings and antiseptic spray/wipes

It's also important to ensure that these things are kept out of reach of little hands and monitored in terms of their shelf life.

Nanny Amies' Top Tip: Try to educate yourself on signs and symptoms of serious illnesses – for example, meningitis. Reading up on these things while your head is clear and your child is healthy is preferable to going on the internet at midnight in a panic while they are fighting a fever.

You never know when symptoms of an illness may pounce and, because of this, I would also pack a medicine bag for flights and long travel days.

My child won't take medicine

It's incredibly common for youngsters to avoid, or refuse, medication, even in sweet tasting liquid form. This can be due to a combination of factors and often it's a couple at once. Here are some examples.

- While feeling unwell, the child has no appetite for anything.
- While feeling unwell, the child is likely irritable and doesn't want any fuss.
- The child is genuinely cautious toward the taste.
- The child has a negative association with medicines due to a prior experience.
- Refusing medication feels empowering, especially if parental reactions are heightened.

To be honest, there seems to be a new parenting hack that pops up every day that suggests novel ways in which you can "trick" a youngster into taking medicine. Here is how I help a toddler who is refusing medication but desperately needs it to help lower a fast-rising temperature, reoccurring illnesses or other symptoms.

1 Approach giving medicine confidently, as if it's any other normal part of the daily routine. Keep a check on your body language and facial expressions to ensure your demeanour doesn't send the wrong message.
2 Use positive statements such as, "This will help you feel better", as opposed to "Can Laura give you some medicine?" If a child's need for medication is not optional, I will avoid making it sound so.

3 I won't linger. While encouraging body autonomy is an important aspect of raising children, they cannot yet fully grasp how medication helps them, so if they are ill, this is where we need to get in, get it done and get back out again.

4 I will offer the child a choice where possible. For example, "Would you like to sit here and do it or over there?" A toddler feeling utterly powerless is far from ideal, so a quick choice can help them take age-appropriate control of the situation.

5 I will validate the child's feelings, while reassuring them, "I can see you don't like it; we'll get it done quickly and then have a lovely hug".

6 If the child becomes upset, I avoid trying to stop the tears. Tears are an expression of the emotion they are experiencing and, when received calmly, can be a healthy way to show how they feel.

7 If they are refusing any medication they need, I will first prep the medication and then sit down, placing the toddler sideways across my lap so I can pop their legs between mine and hold them still by gently clamping my knees together. I will then place their arm closest to me under my non-dominant arm, while holding their other arm down with my non-dominant hand. This leaves my dominant hand free for administering the medication.

8 If giving liquid medicine, I aim the syringe into the child's cheek area, toward the back of their mouth. This means they are less likely to spit it out. I will also split the dose in half if I feel this will make it easier for them to accept.

9 I ensure that I have a drink to hand to help the child wash it down afterwards.

10 Finally, even if the child has screamed the house down, I will calmly tell them how well they did and hug it out before quickly moving on.

If you offer lots of attention toward their refusal, it will become a bigger deal than it needs to be. Allowing them to work through their feelings and understand that they go on to feel better afterwards is more effective.

> **Nanny Amies' Top Tip:** If your toddler struggles with taking medication, I recommend working on it during times of good health by playing. Let them give medicine to their toys, for example (see below).

Thinking outside the (medicine) box

A great way to help your toddler become more confident around medical procedures and inoculations is to introduce an toy medical syringe to bath time (using it as a water squirter is great fun). Having fun can help to shift any negative association they have. You could even offer them some drinking water in it, after you've had a try first of course!

Consider playing doctors and nurses as part of a role-play activity. There are some wonderful outfits and kits (with mini stethoscopes, etc.) on the market, and I'm yet to meet a toddler who doesn't enjoy pretending to be a medic or the patient. To your toddler, this will just be a fun thing to do with their beloved parent, but they will gain a lot of confidence from it. It also offers you the chance to use formal terminology such as, "Hello, how are you feeling today?" or "Let me check your temperature".

Involve favourite teddies, siblings and other adults to allow your toddler the chance to see others behave and respond in a way that offers a calm response. Helping them to understand the process, to practise and then go through the motions offers them opportunities to realize getting medical care isn't so scary. If your child then has to have medical care in the future, hopefully they will feel more able to cope.

There are some excellent books out there about going to the doctor or hospital. I have a wonderful collection of books that I use to help children learn about topics that are scary to them, books that make things seem more normal and welcoming. So, do look out for some books to help you too.

Nanny Amies' Top Tip: Do monthly temperature checks on your toddler when they are in good health to help you get an idea of what their natural, baseline temperature is. While normal body temperature is in the region of 37°C/98.6°F, this varies slightly from child to child, so these monthly readings will come in handy for times of suspected ill health.

Dealing with emotional trauma

It's a tricky thing to be a professional live-in nanny while dealing with anxiety about illness and residual trauma left over from a harrowing experience. My home was also my place of work, so while you can close your bedroom door once all the children are in bed, you are still very much on duty should the need arise. And this is especially true of a parent who is dealing with a childhood long-term illness or the memory of a traumatic incident like the one I experienced (see page 241).

In my case, I felt tremendous pressure to keep checking on the toddler through the night, while fearing my actions wouldn't be enough should we find ourselves in another emergency situation. Essentially, I tortured myself week-in, week-out for some time. So, how do you deal with these feelings if something has happened to your child in your care? This is how I managed.

Through reading and research, I began to focus on the facts instead of my feelings. I learned to view the experience from a completely different perspective. I thought the worse had happened, but it didn't. My blossoming charge was the same "wave at the ducks as we pass" toddler that they were before. They were happy, healthy and still a joy to care for, so enough was enough.

The following things helped me process my emotions and deal with any anxiety that cropped up. I hope it helps you to deal with any health worries or trauma you might be experiencing.

1 **Acknowledge your feelings:** Without acknowledgement you cannot begin to process and move through your feelings. If your child is ill, of course you will worry. But it is important to know that worrying is a sign of caring and not of guaranteed impending doom.

2 **Talk it over with someone:** I talked about the terrifying incident with someone I trusted, who sat on neutral ground in terms of not knowing my precious charge. I could be 100 per cent honest, without having to worry about their feelings getting hurt. That was a game-changer and really helped me.

3 **Reflect on how lucky we were:** I was grateful that the febrile convulsion happened when I was with the child, as opposed to during the night, when they were alone. That was a positive I really began to lean on.

4 **Confront fears by fully assessing the facts:** For example, initially, I worried every day that the child would have another convulsion, but factually, that had only happened once in six months. Therefore, the odds were stacked in our favour.

5 **Avoid too much internet research:** It's only the scariest accounts and blogs which seem to sit at the surface of an internet search and that does not make for relaxing bedtime reading. If you need advice, talk to a doctor or health visitor, or visit only trusted medical websites. In the UK, the NHS website has logical and reliable advice. You can call 111 for NHS medical support, if needed.

6 **Attend regular first aid courses:** If it's been a while since you went on a course or you haven't found time yet, book it today. You will feel more relaxed for it.

7 **Acknowledge the good times:** A natural negativity bias means we so easily focus on the negatives. Notice and enjoy having strong, happy and resilient children.

Learning how to cope with negative emotions is hugely beneficial. Although, it could never replace the peace that may have resided before an incident, it adds to that emotional armour and resilience I'm forever banging on about if you are able to find a way to process it and move forward. That's not to say you won't ever feel dread or worry, but you'll hopefully be able to cope with it when you do.

> **Nanny Amies' Top Tip:** Teach your toddlers how to call for help. While the chances are very slim, if the day ever comes when you are the one needing help, it's incredible if your child knows how to use a phone to get help.

Atishoo atishoo, we all fall down

There's a reason why the common cold is called "common" – it is by far the most widespread illness I've had to deal with.

> **Nanny Amies' Top Tip:** To limit the spread of infection, teach your toddler to sneeze or cough into their elbow. Do this by modelling the behaviour both naturally when you sneeze in real time and during play with pretend sneezes. Add an "Excuse me" for politeness.

While every child will handle a cold differently and respond to the virus with a variety of symptoms, typically speaking we can expect high temperatures, runny noses, coughs, sneezing, headaches and almost-guaranteed increased irritability!

A bunged-up, congested nose can make sleep (as well as breathing in and out!) a real challenge. If a toddler's sleep becomes disturbed, everything is that bit tougher. Sadly, there aren't any cold remedies which will eradicate all symptoms, but there are certainly things we can do to help a toddler feel more comfortable and help us to feel a little less helpless.

1 Gently raise a toddler's mattress at the head end. I roll a towel up and place it underneath the mattress, well out of reach. With children under the age of 18 months, I will not add pillows inside the cot. Raising the toddler's head slightly will encourage mucus congestion to drain through the nasal passages.

2 I offer plenty of drinks to help keep the child hydrated. You could offer a new straw or water bottle to help them accept ample amounts. Warm (not hot) drinks can be soothing. Do not be tempted to give your toddler a cough sweet to ease a sore throat or cough. They are extreme choking hazards.

3 I swear by eucalyptus essential oils. They are a wonderful way to naturally open up the nasal passages. Add a few drops to an essential oil diffuser, placed safely out of reach. You could also put a few drops on a muslin and place it close to the bed, but make sure it is out of reach as the oil really stings if you get it in your eyes, and yes, I'm speaking from experience.

4 Room humidifiers can be beneficial as they add moisture to air which can help to keep airways from drying out. They can be useful at night, while your little one sleeps, to reduce coughing.

5 Vapour rubs act in a similar way to eucalyptus oils but can be rubbed directly onto skin, helping to loosen mucus and open up the airways. Check for age guidelines – only specific brands are suitable for younger toddlers.

6 A steamy bathroom can help to thin congestion, so do continue to bathe them before bedtime if they are well enough.

7 Whenever possible I try to stick to most of our usual daily routine, as trying to keep a general rhythm to the day can help overall mood and behaviours. We do, of course, miss toddler groups and meeting others to avoid spreading germs. Getting outside for some fresh air is certainly helpful too, but if you can't face getting outside, try to keep your rooms airy.

8 Perhaps obvious, but a good dose of TLC is essential. Understanding that your toddler feels unwell and supporting them through however we can will be a welcome remedy, indeed.

Nanny Amies' Top Tip: During play time (perhaps when playing doctors and nurses, see above), have your toddler practise blowing their nose. Initially, learn how to blow air out of the nose by holding a clean tissue in front of their mouth and have them blow air to move the tissue. Then try again with the nose. You can do this first, to show them.

Tracking medication

One toddler I cared for seemed to catch every respiratory infection going. We often had nights when they would cough, struggling to sleep. The parents and I often worked as a team to help the patient get back off to sleep. The most important thing I found in homes where multiple adults would care for a poorly child was to track what medication had been administered and when. This was essential to making sure we didn't offer an overdose. Even if it is just you, when you are also tired or ill, keeping track can be tricky.

There are phone apps that offer a medication tracker, but personally, I find the easiest way is to keep a simple chart, written down on paper, next to the supply of medicine. It's quick, easy and impossible to miss that way.

Day	Time	What	Amount
Monday	7pm	Paracetamol	5ml
	11pm	Ibuprofen	5ml
Tuesday	3am	Paracetamol	5ml
	7am	Ibuprofen	5ml

When to seek help

One of the best things you can count on in terms of assessing your little one's health is your gut instinct. You know your child better than anyone, so you can usually spot times when they are feeling unwell or just aren't themselves.

It's time to reach out for medical help if your little one:

- Has a high temperature of 38°C (100°F) or above, which is not responding to over-the-counter medication
- Has a high temperature with cold extremities (hands and feet)
- Has an extreme temperature, high or low
- Is feverish, hot to touch and/or shivering
- Is unusually lethargic, floppy or listless
- Is inconsolable, crying constantly and uncharacteristically
- Has unusually dry or clean nappies
- Has no appetite and isn't eating as they normally would
- Is wheezing, breathing rapidly or has blue lips

- Is obviously struggling to draw breath
- Has pale, blotchy or ashen skin
- Is difficult to wake or seems disorientated in some way

CALL THE EMERGENCY SERVICES

Do not hesitate to call an ambulance if your toddler:

- Stops breathing
- Will not wake up
- Has a rash which does not fade when you roll a glass over it
- Has a febrile convulsion for the first time
- Has a severe allergic reaction to something
- Suffers a serious injury

Illness is, unfortunately, part of life. As a species we are so incredibly lucky to have a huge variety of interventions available to us via medication, research, knowledge, natural remedies and medical professionals. However, we also have a huge sense of love and protection toward our nearest and dearest which makes dealing with illness very challenging.

I remember being quite young and asking my mum, "Does a mummy rabbit feel sad if a kestrel catches one of her baby rabbits? She has so many babies, would she know that one was missing?" And ever since, it's struck me that with our intelligence and huge capacity to feel, we pay the price in heartache, worry and grief. Worry is the price we pay for love, and when all is considered, it's a small price to pay to enable us to grow close to one another and truly appreciate those dear to us.

On a very soppy final note, teaching children how to love, to be loved and to appreciate family and friends (with or without a bunged-up nose) is a beautiful gift and surely what life is truly all about.

APPENDIX

Consequences

There is a consequence to every action we take, some good, some bad, and understanding this can help toddlers to shape their awareness of others, their self-control and behaviour. We can use "consequences" as a parenting intervention to help children reflect on their own actions. These do not need to be big and scary, and many happen naturally without the need for much input from ourselves.

There are three main types of consequences: natural, logical and positive. Using each one appropriately will help your child connect to their behaviours and the impact they can have within their environment.

Natural: A natural consequence allows children to experience the reality of their decisions or actions without the need for much intervention from us.

Logical: A logical consequence is very important to encourage children to make good decisions and establish self-control. This involves offering up a consequence that is relevant to the behaviour itself. Using illogical consequences does not give the toddler a chance to learn. For example, if at 10am, Tim hits Aaron, and Tim is told there's no ice cream after lunch as a punishment, the time and consequence are not relevant to the action, which limits Tim's learning for next time.

Positive: Positive consequences are my favourite, but they do take a lot of presence of mind and effort to deliver. Here, we draw attention to the good behaviour we want to see more of via connection, descriptive praise and positivity.

Consequence	Behaviour	How to respond	Why
Natural	Refuses to put coat on when cold outside.	In these instances, I take the coat with us, either popping it in my bag, under the pushchair or I have the toddler carry it in a rucksack, for example. Once we've been out for a few minutes, I may comment on the weather and attempt to put it on for them. If they refuse, I will offer a choice; for example, "We can wear our coat and stay at the park or we will head home".	Often, young children do not fully understand why they need their coat. They are warm inside and enjoy their freedom, so the thought of a coat doesn't sit well with them. Allowing them a few moments to feel the temperature drop helps them to appreciate why the coat is necessary. Refraining from a back-and-forth debate lessens the attention on the refusal. (By the way, colds are not caught from being outside in the cold for a short time. Colds are caught when in close proximity to someone with a virus. So, be careful not to say, "You'll catch a cold", as this isn't strictly true.)

Consequence	Behaviour	How to respond	Why
Logical	Drawing on the walls, after being told not to.	Very calmly approach the toddler, get down to their level and use a simple phrase such as, "We draw on the paper; we'll try again later". Calmly put the crayons out of reach. The crayons can be returned later the same day, with you saying, "Colours can stay out when we draw on the paper".	When we offer an immediate consequence, which is directly linked to the behaviour, children are able to experience the emotion attached in real time. For example, being disappointed that the colours have to be put away will help them to remember not to draw on the walls next time. Delivering a logical consequence calmly is essential to children taking on board the message behind them. When our volume and anger levels rise, we risk modelling challenging behaviours which can actually negate the consequence.
Positive	Sitting, reading calmly.	Sit beside the toddler, place a hand on their arm and make eye contact, then offer a sentence to help them connect to the moment; for example, "I love seeing you read your books! Which is your favourite?"	It's common for the opposite of this to be true. Usually, if a toddler is playing calmly, they are left to it (understandably). However, if they become loud or aggressive, for example, they then receive our full attention. This can work against us.

Consequence	Behaviour	How to respond	Why
		This obviously doesn't need to happen every time they are engaged in reading or play. We don't want to continuously distract them from their play, and of course, you won't always have the time for this. But note the good stuff when you can!	Noting their efforts, showing love and affection, and just being present for them during times of calm, allows toddlers a boost in self-esteem, awareness of their capability and a chance to take pride in their own actions. When this balance weighs heavily in the opposite direction, behaviours may decline.

Temperament traits

Our natural temperament impacts how we respond to the world around us. Psychologists have identified nine traits, listed in the following chart. There is no "right or wrong" trait to have. Looking at where a child sits in each trait can help us to determine how much of their behaviour is part of their natural make-up and how much may have been formed due to environmental factors. It can also help us to understand how a toddler is most likely to react to their experiences, essentially putting us one step ahead.

Trait	High in	Low in
Physicality	Constantly moving, fidgeting or seeming restless. In some instances, the need for sitting still may cause anguish. For example, once they have eaten all that they desire, they are keen to get out of their high chair and move around.	Can sit still for longer periods and appear generally calm. In some instances, they may even seem difficult to motivate. For example, once they finish their meal, they may be happy to sit back in their high chair and observe those around them.
Adaptability	Easily switches from one activity to another, adapting quickly to change or new experiences while appearing calm and relaxed. For example, if they are playing with a toy and you tell them it's bath time, they will be more inclined to stop play and head toward the bath.	Needs time to adjust to a change of plan or current activity. Can become frustrated more easily and may rebel against change. For example, if they are playing with a toy and you tell them it's bath time, they may cry and refuse to stop playing.
Intensity	Displays very strong, emotional reactions to triggers. May be particularly loud and even seem confrontational at times. For example, if they cannot have a desired object, they may scream and/or throw things, escalating their behaviour on a regular basis, while also finding it hard to move on from the trigger.	Seems easy-going or even quiet at times. For example, if they cannot have a desired object, they may cry for a short time before recovering and moving on to a different object or activity.

Trait	High in	Low in
Mood	Appears happy, upbeat and optimistic. May show signs of being able to cope with disappointment fairly easily. For example, they may use positive narration to describe a play scene and comment happily on day-to-day routines.	Appear to be more subdued and can lean more toward pessimism. This doesn't mean they are unhappy. For example, they may play quietly or pick out the negatives. Some may seem to have lots to complain about.
Sensitivity	Reacts strongly to environmental cues such as sounds and lights, etc. Pain and emotional stress are expressed strongly. For example, they may become very upset when you wash their hair or if they drop a toy on their toe.	Less affected by environmental cues and more likely to keep playing after falling over, for example. For example, they may continue to play with bath toys as you wash their hair or seem unfazed by small/minor injuries.
Rhythmicity	Enjoys, seeks or even requires predictable meal and sleep schedules. Behaviour will be impacted by a lack of sleep and/or well-timed food. For example, if you head out for the day and lunch is offered later than usual, their behaviour may become very challenging.	Free-flowing in relation to when sleep and meals are had. Behaviour is predictable, irrespective of time or hunger levels. For example, could experience a late bedtime and behaviour will remain the same the following day.
Distractibility	Particularly short attention span, flits from one thing to another. May need lots of encouragement to see a task through. For example, they may pull a toy out of a basket and discard it soon after for another one.	Can focus on the task at hand for relatively long periods and can block out noises and distractions. For example, they may choose a toy from a basket, sit down with it and thoroughly engage with it before deciding to choose another.

Trait	High in	Low in
Persistence	Will try hard to reach desires, overcome challenges and generally be very strong-willed. They will remain focused until they get their perceived needs met and can display anguish when things aren't going as they hope. For example, they may ask for the TV to be put on every few minutes until a parent gives in or until they are significantly redirected to something else.	More likely to move to a new toy rather than stay on target and problem-solve. Asks for help frequently or gives in. Isn't overly motivated by goals or desires. For example, they may ask for the TV to be put on and, if the parent says no, they may find it relatively easy to accept and find another activity.
Approachability	Willing, open-minded, investigative and shows little hesitation toward new places, activities and people. For example, when you introduce a potty to the bathroom, they may happily sit on it and investigate its purpose.	Shows hesitation or may back away from things. May appear fearful or anxious of new situations. For example, when they begin their potty-training journey, they may be hesitant or fearful of the potty and the new regime.

While the traits above cover nature, how the world around us responds to us – nurture – shapes behaviours, habits and opinions. Knowing a child is high in intensity doesn't mean we should throw our hands in the air after they've hit a sibling and say, "Oh well, little Timmy is high in intensity, what can we do?" Therefore, I've chosen some traits that I deal with commonly to show how we can use this information to our benefit (see page 264). There are infinite approaches and ideas once you begin to think outside of the box.

Trait	What	Why
High in physicality	Encourage movement whenever possible, as opposed to restricting it. For example, go outside to do some star jumps or bunny hops before sitting down to eat. Have movement breaks on long car journeys. Offer props within the home such as a collapsible tunnel or balance board to help the toddler engage in gross motor movements. Create assault courses using cushions, toys and floor tape to help them explore the space around them. Give them daily opportunities to move around outdoors freely.	Understanding that children high in this trait often have a physical urge to move regularly can help you prevent them from having a build-up of energy which can then be displayed via outbursts, hyperactivity or restlessness. It's really common for adults to ask children to sit still, calm down or stop causing a scene, however, if children have pent-up energy, that can be almost impossible for them. A classic case of prevention being better than cure here.
High in intensity	Try to be as low in intensity as you can, especially during times of your child's outbursts. Limit your volume, word count and anger in a bidto lessen stress levels. Where possible, give them space and time to work through the emotion without negotiation or increased attention. If you are struggling to remain calm and it's safe to do so, take a breather in a separate room. See the SCREAM acronym, below.	It's natural for parents to want to change their child's mind or feelings to either make them happy or to stop them from crying, etc. If your child has naturally strong reactions to things, it's important that they learn how to cope with those feelings. Intense behaviours can easily become a firm part of their repertoire if they result in intense reactions from parents.

Trait	What	Why
High in sensitivity	When a toddler shows an aversion toward a sensory activity which needs doing, such as hair-washing, for example, try to tread a fine line between validation and redirection, while getting the job done. Remain calm and confident, taking the lead, while offering a choice. "I understand you don't want your hair washing, we'll do it really quickly." "I can wash your hair with the shower head or with the jug. You choose." Sometimes children may like to practise washing your hair, their dolls, or teddies' hair, etc. Leaning on fun can work well.	If you avoid certain activities altogether, children miss out on opportunities to become desensitized. However, to a highly sensitive child, discomfort can feel very real; hence, striking a balance between validation and moving past an upsetting scenario is a great way to help them to develop resilience. Doing this will be harder during trigger times; for example, close to bedtime. Instead, think about doing hair-washing at another time, before true tiredness or hunger creeps in.
High in distractibility	Acknowledge that your child will only play with a toy for a few moments and think of ways to stretch their focus. For example, pick up a toy they have discarded and draw them back in with an interested tone and comment, such as, "Wow, this car goes so fast! Watch!" Play games which help children to build up their concentration levels, such as hide and seek.	All young children have a certain level of distractibility. Attention span and focus are something we build on with age. However, when they are particularly high in this trait, they need support to practise moments of concentration for them to stay engaged; for example, sit down with them to do a puzzle together. It can be much easier to offer screen time to children who are high in this trait, but sadly, that will only decrease their ability to focus on real-world toys and activities.

Trait	What	Why
High in persistence	Hold your boundaries in place, firmly and predictably. Offer simple choices and avoid lengthy negotiations.	It's important that children get a chance to be in control of some decisions, but when it comes to essential tasks such as bedtime, healthy eating habits and safety, for example, we mustn't let their persistent nature take charge. Offering two specific choices can help a child to determine that their preference isn't possible at that time but they can have some control in that moment. This, alongside choosing your battles, where possible, can release a lot of tension within family homes.
Low in approachability	If you are about to embark on a new milestone, or visit somewhere new, confidently offer your child a brief heads-up. For example, "We will see the dentist after lunch. Shall we take Ted or Bunny?" Don't avoid the things that need doing or speaking about them, but validate any fears or worries they may have instead. Routine maps (see page 267) can help your toddler see what's coming next. Offer calm support and role modelling to help them in the moment.	Knowledge is power, so the more a child understands something and gets to experience it, the easier it will be for them to process what will happen. Essentially, practice makes progress and, while it's much easier to shy away from the things they don't enjoy, if the tasks are essential, that won't help them in the long run.

EXTRA RESOURCES

Unfortunately, I couldn't fit all I wanted to say within the chapters of this book. So, here are some resources that may offer you a further helping hand throughout your journey of raising a toddler. As my consultancy is UK-based, my personal go-to resources tend to be UK-centric. However, for US readers, I have added US-based resources too. While I haven't used these resources personally, I very much hope that they can help. If you are outside of the UK or US, please carefully consider the resources that are local to you.

First, here's my website, where I have lots of advice, webinars, fairy experiences and different services if you want to check them out further: lauranannyamies.co.uk

Tantrums

My book recommendation: *No More Tantrums*, Big Steps series, Campbell Books. This is a lovely resource to look through with a toddler to help them understand emotions.

Visual routine map: Using a visual routine map (a series of photographs or illustrations showing daily tasks) helps a child to see what is happening next, offering another layer of predictability to the day-to-day activities. The maps can be very simple, and I often make my own, but you can also buy them online. Each image represents a part of the daily routine and allows children to absorb information via visual aid alongside verbal instruction. If you take each picture down after that part of the routine is complete, it can further reinforce a daily chain of events (not essential though).

On my social media: My TikTok "Tantrum taming" series: I have an in-depth series on TikTok @nannyamies, which talks parents through many aspects of tantrums, including how to deal with them and how to prevent them effectively without appeasement. For those stuck in tantrum hell, I hope you find it very helpful.

Aggression

My book recommendation: *Sometimes I am angry*, Little Big Feelings, Campbell Books. This is another great book. Reading this together can help a little one begin to understand why feeling frustrated is normal but that aggression isn't okay.

Do and do not cards: Imagine the old-school posters you'd see at the swimming pool that have various pictures displaying safe or dangerous actions – some with big green ticks against them, others with big red crosses through them. You can also get these for toddlers to highlight behaviours that are acceptable and those that aren't. You can find these online (search "Behaviour cards") or make your own.

On my social media: Across my social media platforms, I have lots of posts and videos addressing aggression which are at least worth a peek. For example, my aggression highlight on Instagram and aggression playlist on TikTok.

Potty training

My book recommendation: *No more potty*, Big Steps, Campbell Books. This is another great book for your collection!

My go-to websites: Eric.org.uk. Eric is a UK-based charity dedicated to helping families improve bowel and bladder health. It has a helpful potty-training section. Its free helpline is 0808 801 0343. Also, check out nhs.uk to find straightforward advice and links to external help. And finally, healthychildren.org is a US website with some resources on potty training too.

On my social media: My step-by-step "Potty-training" series on TikTok @nannyamies details how to prepare, approach and tackle potty training confidently. There's also a stumbling blocks section which helps parents to overcome any challenges they may face along the way.

I also have lots of free potty-training tips in my TikTok potty-training playlist and Instagram potty-training highlight.

Social skills

If you are looking for new social groups and places to explore for your toddler, your local council website is a great place to start in the UK. Outside the UK, look for local groups advertised. Also look on café noticeboards, in libraries, in local newspapers and on social media. My local page recently posted "Our Five Top Favourite Walks" and, despite me living in my hometown for the majority if my life, I'd only heard of three of them! Toddler groups can help you create opportunities for your toddler to socialize with peers and children of a similar age. I know that attending these groups can feel a little daunting; however, many are in the same boat. Places of worship, town halls, stores, community centres and nursery schools often advertise local toddler groups. You might like to try a few until you find one you both enjoy,

Neurodiversity

Any playgroup, soft play, park or event should be entirely inclusive and open to any family hoping to attend. I have included these websites because parents have confided in me that it can be nice to meet with families who have experienced similar journeys to their own.

Children's health: nhs.uk/conditions and actionfor children.org.uk in the UK, and kidshealth.org in the US.

Autism: autism.org.uk in the UK and nationalautism association.org/resources/signs-of-autism/ in the US.

ADHD: adhduk.co.uk in the UK and chadd.org in the US.

Online safety

In the UK, The National Society for the Prevention of Cruelty to Children (NSPCC) has a page on their website dedicated to children's online safety: nspcc.org.uk/keeping-children-safe/online-safety

In the US, America's Cyber Defense Agency (CISA) has advice on how to keep your child safe online: cisa.gov/news-events/news/keeping-children-safe-online

Screen time

In the UK, have a look at the NHS's page which covers play ideas for babies and toddlers: nhs.uk/conditions/baby/babys-development/play-and-learning/baby-and-toddler-play-ideas. The National Childbirth Trust (NCT) also has some ideas on how you can manage screen time effectively: nct.org.uk/baby-toddler

In the US, check out the Mayo Clinic website, which has a really interesting article on screen time:

mayoclinichealthsystem.org/hometown-health/speaking-of-health/children-and-screen-time

On my social media: I have an in-depth screen time series called "Using screen time effectively" on TikTok which delves into the good the bad and the ugly parts of screen usage for children, offering practical tips, helpful approaches and lots of ideas on how to encourage play and get outside more too.

Sleep

The Lullaby Trust website has a huge amount of information relevant to sleep and sleep safety: lullabytrust.org.uk

In the UK, see the NHS website for tips on helping your little one to sleep: nhs.uk/conditions. In the US, you can find useful information on the American Academy of Pediatrics website: aap.org/en/patient-care/safe-sleep/

My big book recommendation: There are hundreds of books on the market which can become a much-loved part of the bedtime routine and offer fun stories about bedtimes and sleeping. I love *I'm Not Sleepy* by Campbell Books.

Dummies

In the UK, The National Childbirth Trust (NCT) has information on dummies: nct.org.uk as well as The Lullaby Trust: lullabytrust.org.uk. In the US, Baby Center answers your top questions about dummies (pacifiers): babycenter.com/toddler/behavior/pacifiers-and-your-toddler_12254#

On my social media: I have various posts and videos on my @nannyamies social media platforms on how you can reduce dummy usage and wean a child off entirely, if you so choose. For example, my Dummy Fairy Highlight on Instagram.

Eating habits

My book recommendation: *Which Food Will You Choose?*, Claire Potter and Ailie Busby, Featherstone. In this lovely book, a family go on the hunt for foods of different colours.

Other resources: If you feel that your child's food intake is restrictive and past the point of developmental eating habits, first speak with your doctor and also take a look at the Avoidant/Restrictive Food Intake Disorder (ARFID) website. This is a non-profit organization that aims to spread awareness, information and support: arfidawarenessuk.org

In the UK, the NHS has a web page on the topic of eating habits: www.nhs.uk. In the US, the Communicable Disease Center (CDC) has an article on picky eaters and what to do: cdc.gov/nutrition/infantandtoddlernutrition/foods-and-drinks/picky-eaters.html

Speech and language

Speak with your doctor and/or health visitor if you have any concerns about your child's language skills. Also, check out the NHS website for information on helping your little one's speech to develop: nhs.uk/conditions. In the US, have a look at this article on different development milestones in a child's speech and language journey: www.nidcd.nih.gov/health/speech-and-language

Many families also find Makaton – a language program that uses signs, symbols and speech – an incredibly useful tool to help boost communication skills: makaton.org

WHEN TO CALL 999 (OR 911)

Take a look today at the NHS website for details of when you should dial 999 in the UK: nhs.uk/nhs-services/urgent-and-emergency-care-services/when-to-call-999/

Take a look at the 911 website for guidance of when to call 911 in the US: www.911.gov/calling-911/frequently-asked-questions/

If your child does appear to be seriously ill, follow your gut and dial 999.

Illness and trauma

In the UK, to read about childhood illnesses and symptoms, visit nhs.uk/conditions. You can also dial 111 in the UK to get support with your concerns about your little one's health. You can also look at 111 online: 111.nhs.uk

First aid courses: There are lots of organizations that deliver first aid courses, both in person and remotely. I have attended St John's Ambulance courses and found them to be really helpful: www.sja.org.uk. In the US, there are similar courses run by the Red Cross: redcross.org

Support for parents

If you need support for something you are going through or you are dealing with past trauma, there are many resources to help you.

- The NSPCC offers support for UK-based parents and is a good place to start: nspcc.org.uk
- This is also a good international place to visit: parents.com/parenting/

- Very Well Family has some good resources: verywellfamily. com/toddlers-overview-4581805
- Parents Helping Parents have a helpline to call if you're struggling: parentshelpingparents.org/stressline

Don't be afraid to reach out to professionals, friends and family if you are struggling with any aspect of parenting. If it was easy, there wouldn't be a need for books like the one you have just read!

ABOUT ME

Laura Amies (AKA Nanny Amies) here to say hello and explain a little about how I found myself writing a book that anyone who spends time with toddlers should read.

From the age of 16 when I became a trained children and baby shoe-fitter, right up to the present day aged 41, I have dedicated my career to helping parents and I have worked closely with young children. Over the years, I have used both my hands-on experience and study in child psychology, sleep health and children's mental health (to name a few) to help many different family's lives run a bit more smoothly.

I have supported hundreds of families during their potty-training journeys, times of disturbed sleep, phases of selective eating, stressful tantrums and all that lies in between. Since appearing in Channel 5's *Toddlers Behaving (Very) Badly*, where I travelled to various family homes around the UK in a bid to help parents approach their toddlers' challenging behaviours, I've become a recognized source of effective, no-nonsense and heartfelt advice for parents worldwide.

Having featured in *Hello* magazine and been invited to discuss topical childcare themes on programmes such as Jeremy Vine, I felt it was high time to consolidate my advice into this book. Helping parents is all I've ever wanted to do, so I have used this guide to create my most effective advice to date, advice that will not only help you to survive the toddler years, but hopefully enjoy them, too.

Laura x

ACKNOWLEDGEMENTS

It's much trickier to get the true sentiment of a heartfelt thank you across via the written word compared to looking someone in the eye and telling them how truly grateful you are ... unless, I hope, it's written within the pages of your first ever book. A book that is in print due to a few people who had faith that it was indeed worth printing.

Therefore, my first thank you must go to Oscar Janson-Smith, who not only gave me the time of day (which I had found to be almost impossible within the land of literary agents), but also had an open mind toward the potential I held. Oscar doesn't know this, but when he agreed to represent me, I cried. Tears of happiness but also of relief that I no longer had to convince someone I was worth a shot.

Thank you to Watkins Publishing and the entire team who have supported and encouraged me throughout. It turns out that, while I know a great deal about child behaviour and can certainly tell a good tale, I know (well, knew) nothing about how to write a book, and I don't mind telling you that the team at Watkins must have had to dig pretty deep to get my ever increasing word count down to something readable.

I must also thank you, the reader, for choosing to read this book. Knowing you have chosen to read it truly means more than any words I could write here on this page.

Finally, thank you to all of the children who have been unequivocally themselves in my care, for teaching me how to be a better childcare provider and ... for keeping me on my toes throughout!

INDEX

A

adaptability 43, 261
age factors 99, 129, 189
aggressive behaviour 39–59,
  104–6, 120, 268
anxiety 120–1, 137, 160–1, 175,
  213, 217–19
apologies 53–4
appetite 52, 180, 188, 190–2, 217,
  247, 255
approachability 263, 266
attention deficit hyperactivity
  disorder (ADHD) 102, 270
autism 102, 270
Avoidant/Restrictive Food
  Intake Disorder (ARFID)
  193, 272

B

baking 108–9
biting 40, 47–9, 53, 54, 59
blackout blinds 146
body language 25, 53
bond-building activities 108–10
boundaries 8–16, 9–10, 23–4, 32,
  36, 44–5, 89–90, 106, 127, 138,
  188, 210, 266
brain 20, 115–16, 120, 124, 153,
  203, 213–15
breathing techniques 214
bribes 25–6

C

circadian rhythms 136–7, 139
clothing, spare 83
co-sleeping 145
colds/flu 252–5
collections 109
confidence 60–1, 82, 211
connection 74, 89–90
consequences 54, 257–60
consistency 74, 103–4, 126
convulsions/seizures 241–
  4, 250–1
cortisol 120, 124, 135, 138–9, 142
countdowns 90–1
crying 160, 163, 201–2, 248

D

days out 80–93, 192
decision-making 211
desensitization
  techniques 198–9
detachment 21, 22
developmental leaps 152–3
disappointment 211
distractibility 262, 265
diurnality 135–6, 154
"doing nothing" 31
dopamine 89, 118, 121, 184
dummy dependency 156–77, 271
dummy fairies 173–4
dysregulation

child 21, 24, 103, 205
  parental 23–4

E
eating habits 136, 178–99,
  272
  child-led 181–2
  and food preparation
    186, 196
  new foods 188–9, 197, 198
  over-eating 194–5
  picky/fussy eaters 190–4,
    195–9, 272
egocentrism 41, 55, 58, 96
egos, boosting 110
emergency services 242–3,
  256, 273
emotional development 32,
  42, 160, 200–19
  and aggressive behaviours
    41–3, 45, 47–50, 50
  and tantrums 19–20,
    22–6, 31–8
emotional trauma 250–2
emotional validation 112
environmental factors 2–4,
  12, 44–5, 129, 192
expectations, realistic 50
experiences 3, 4, 13, 116, 192
eyesight 81, 120

F
facial expressions 53, 218, 221,
  223, 231
fear 22, 26, 67, 77, 153,
  204, 217–19
"fight or flight" mode 24–5, 31,
  34, 40, 203, 212
first aid 83, 240, 252
food allergies/intolerances 193
food aversion 193
food diaries 193

food shopping lists 186–7
free time boxes 125
frontal lobe 20
fun, having 196

G
game-playing 51
gratitude 14
grounding techniques
  203, 212–13

H
habits 130, 165–6
  see also eating habits
"high five" technique 214
house rules 106
hugs 31
hunger 179–81, 183, 191
hyper-focus 103

I
illness 191–2, 240–56, 273
  serious 241–4, 246, 255–6
impulse control 41, 51, 96
individual factors 3, 4, 12–13
infections 245–6, 252–5
intensity 43, 261, 264
involving toddlers 90, 189–90

K
kindness 112

L
learning challenges 103

M
mealtimes 83, 164
medication 246–50, 254–5
melatonin 12, 119, 135, 137, 146
meltdowns 103, 104
memory boxes 109–10
meningitis 246

modelling 31, 63, 111–12, 119, 188, 205–6, 232
mood 262
motor skills 40–1, 81
movement 90, 115, 264
music 88–9, 213, 234

N
name-calling 100
nappy explosions 87–9
nature vs nurture debate 2–4
needs, children's 115–16, 221
neurodiversity 63, 102–4, 118, 152, 162, 224, 270
'Nooo!' 75–8

O
online play 116
online safety 270
outnumbered, being 91–3
oxytocin 31, 82, 89

P
parental aggression 45
parental breaks 117, 126–8
parental dysregulation 23–4
parental support 273–4
parenting styles 2–18, 130–1
  authoritarian 5–6, 18, 24
  authoritative 5–8, 18
  gentle 7–8, 181
  logical 8–9, 14–17
  neglectful 5–6, 11, 18
  permissive 5–8, 10–11, 18, 24, 34, 181
parents, as "safe places" 59
patience 206
persistence 263, 266
physical factors 3, 4, 12
physical wellbeing 43–4
physicality 261, 264

picnics 91–2, 197
play 197–8
  associative 97
  by age group 95–8
  cooperative 94, 97–8
  difficulties with 100–4
  imaginative 163
  independent 128–32
  online 116
  parallel 95
  and social skills 94–100
  solitary 95
play dates 98–100, 194–5
portion sizes 192
positivity 73, 89–90, 234
poster-making 109
potty training 60–79, 153, 268–9
  and the 3 Cs 60–1
  accidents 61, 68–72, 74
  adult-led 73
  child-led 67
  cleaning from front to back 78
  combined approach 70
  and elimination communication 67–8
  equipment 64–5
  Laura's approach to 72–9
  low pressure approach to 73
  and "Nooo!" 75–8
  preparation for 60, 63–6, 74
  routines 69, 73
  signs of readiness 62–3
  snag list 78–9
  three day 68
  timed 68–9
  when to begin 61–3
power struggles 192
praise, descriptive 50–1
pressure 73, 188, 226
proactive behaviour 108

pronunciation 103, 224–5,
227–8, 230–1, 236–7
public transport 70–2

Q
quality time 51, 216
questions, asking 25, 112, 225–6

R
rashes 193, 256
reactive behaviour 107
redirection 51
reflection 206
rescuing behaviours 211
resilience 82, 160, 210–16, 219
rewards 177, 226
rhythmicity 137, 262
routines 49–50, 69, 73, 111, 125,
130, 135, 146–7, 188

S
"safe places", parents as 59
"saying what you see"
approach 53, 64
screen time 85, 113–33,
226–7, 270–1
the bad 118–19
bedtime use 122–4
and brain
development 115–16
content 120, 132–3
the good 116–18, 133
and screen addiction
120, 121–2
too much 124–6
the ugly 119–21
screen-free zones/days 126
scripts 102
sedentary lifestyles 119, 192
self-esteem 13–14, 16, 18, 74,
90, 100, 107, 110, 196–7
sensitivity 43, 262, 265

sensory overload 103
sharing 55–7, 96, 111–12
siblings 104–10
signs 233
singing 88–9, 213
sleep 124, 134–55, 164, 170–1, 271
non-REM 144, 171
REM (rapid eye movement)
144, 171
sleep associations 144–5
sleep clocks 151
sleep cycles 143–5
sleep deprivation 119, 134–5, 155
sleep disturbances 139–42,
152–3
sleep environment 146
sleep pressure 138–9, 142, 147
sleep regressions/
progressions 152–3
sleep routines 135
sleep training 145–52
snacks 83, 99, 180–4, 185
social interaction, need for 116
social skills 94–112, 269
space, giving 31
spatial awareness 82
speech and language 32, 90,
103, 110–11, 132, 220–39, 272
adult-directed speech 236–7
baby talk 236–7
child-directed speech 236–7
complex 26
and dummy dependency 156,
163, 166–8
and eating habits 195
expressive language 223
factors which impede 224–7
help with 238–9
positional language 233
and potty training 73
receptive language 222
stimming 103, 104

stirring method 151–2
story-telling 197, 232
stress hormones 24, 115, 120
    see also cortisol
stuttering 227–36
sucking reflex 158
sunlight, and vitamin D 82
superiority complexes 9–10

T
tantrums 19–38, 138, 164,
    184, 203, 267–8
    acceptance stage 20, 21
    bargaining stage 21
    causes of 20–31
    escalation stage 21
    fuel for 24–6, 32
    moving on from 36
    staying calm during 35–6
    tamers 31–5
    triggers 20, 22–4
teamwork 73
temperament traits 42–3,
    128, 260–6
temperature checks 250, 255
threats 26, 99
three Rs 111
thumb-sucking 156, 175–7
time issues 31–2, 99, 111
tiredness 83, 139, 191
touch 31
toys 52, 55–7, 111–12, 129–30
    open-ended 130
    rotation 125
trauma 240–56, 273–4
triggers, and aggression 49,
    51–2, 58
turn-taking 231–2

U
unresponsiveness 49

V
validation 36, 96, 112, 248
vegetables 186, 190
visual routine maps 266, 267–8
volume 25

W
wake windows 124, 142–3, 146
weaning 179–80
"Which five things?"
    technique 213
whispering 32

WATKINS
1893

The story of Watkins began in 1893, when scholar of esotericism John Watkins founded our bookshop, inspired by the lament of his friend and teacher Madame Blavatsky that there was nowhere in London to buy books on mysticism, occultism or metaphysics. That moment marked the birth of Watkins, soon to become the publisher of many of the leading lights of spiritual literature, including Carl Jung, Rudolf Steiner, Alice Bailey and Chögyam Trungpa.

Today, the passion at Watkins Publishing for vigorous questioning is still resolute. Our stimulating and groundbreaking list ranges from ancient traditions and complementary medicine to the latest ideas about personal development, holistic wellbeing and consciousness exploration. We remain at the cutting edge, committed to publishing books that change lives.

DISCOVER MORE AT:
www.watkinspublishing.com

Read our blog

Watch and listen to
our authors in action

Sign up to
our mailing list

We celebrate conscious, passionate, wise and happy living.
Be part of that community by visiting

f /watkinspublishing   **X** @watkinswisdom
▶ /watkinsbooks   **O** @watkinswisdom